ANAMIKA PUBLISHERS & DISTRIBUTORS (P) LTD.
4697/3, 21A, Ansari Road, Daryaganj, New Delhi 110 002
Phones: 011-2328 1655, 011-43708938
E-mail: anamikapublishers@yahoo.co.in

First Published 2017

ISBN 978-81-7975-719-2

PRINTED IN INDIA

Published by Anamika Publishers & Distributors (P) Ltd., 4697/3, 21A, Ansari Road, Daryaganj, New Delhi 110 002. Typeset by Shivani Computers, Delhi 110093 and Printed at Vikas Computer & Printers, Tronica City, Ghaziabad

Order of Kabirpanth During Modern India

Purnendu Ranjan

Order of Kabirpanth During Modern India

Contents

Acknowledgement

This book is entirely based on the extensive field-work based research conducted in between 2013 and 2016 roughly. I am truly indebted to the University Grants Commission, New Delhi for awarding me this Major Research Project, without which it was inconceivable to conduct a nationwide field-work as has been attempted by us. I am equally grateful and thankful to millions of the Kabirpanthis living across 18 provinces of India, who have developed hundreds of ashrams/maths to spread Kabir's teachings; many of their Mahants/leaders have been helpful in sharing with me available information with them, both in oral and written forms. In addition, a number of libraries such as NMML, Teen Murti; National Archives, New Delhi, National Library, Kolkata; Central Library, JNU, New Delhi; and Joshi Library, Punjab University, Chandigarh have been mines of resources for my study. I owe my gratitude to the cooperative staffs of all these institutions.

I am immensely grateful to a number of my colleagues; namely Suresh Kumar, Dr. Gurmel Singh, Dr. Harmeet Sethi, Associate Professors of the Departments of Physics, Punjabi and History respectively, who have been supportive to me all through these years. I must also thank Miss Ramanpreeet Kaur and Amandeep Kaur of

Psychology and English Department respectively for sparing their precious time in proof-reading some of the chapters of this book. From non-academic world, Sri R.R. Jowel, the Additional Chief Secretary of the Haryana Government, late Sri Sadanand, Retd. IAS, Sri Bharat Bhushan, Rtd IAS, Harnam Singh Heera, Rtd. Deputy Director (Education, Haryana), Hukum Chand Khundiya, and Rajiv Parmar of Chandigarh, who have been of real help to me in more than one ways. I cannot help mentioning the name of Swagat, my 12-year old son, who have been helping me in getting hundreds of pages printed and xeroxed during the course of the finalization of the books. Last but not the least, I must also register my heartfelt thanks for the kind consideration of Prof. Binu Dogra, the Principal of our College, who have been quite considerate in offering an unstinted support to complete the book.

Introduction

The study of the Kabirpanth in Modern India becomes pertinent in view of the births of two prominent architects of the modern India in the Kabirpanthi families–Mahatma Gandhi and Baba Sahib Bhimrao Ambedkar, coming from two different regions of India, Gujarat and Madhya Pradesh–the first from mother's side, and the second from both of his parents's sides. Kabirpanth's legacy thus acquires a distinct national dimension once we factor in the role of the Kabirpanth ideologies in shaping the paramount personalities both these national figures have come to hold in our social life and polity. Yet, this fact has not been given due consideration in the existing studies on Gandhi and Ambedkar. On the surface, allegiance of both these builders of modern India to the Kabirpanth may appear far-fetched and superfluous proposition, yet when we hear the high premium both of them had attached to Kabir's teachings and his influence on their life, we perforce realize the academician-cum-scholars's neglect in acknowledging such influences on them.

However, the same fact, to me, has been a motivating factor to sustain my protracted interest into a historical study of the Kabirpanth in a rather objective and systematic way. In my last book, *Kabirpanth Till the End of the Medieval India,*[1] I have tried to present an objective history of the panth as having unfolded in course of its expansion, initially in an ideological form and then gradually taking on an organizational character, presumably by the turn of the eighteenth century. These tendencies were evident in its internal feuds and consequent alienations among diverse groups of disciples in several parts of then pre-modern India.

Before we broach on the influence of Kabirpanth on Gandhi's life, it would be startling to find that the harbinger of the movement for the depressed classes during the early phase of the emerging modern India, Jyotiba Phule (1827-1890), had equally deep impact of Kabir and the panth during the mid-nineteenth century. One of the scholars, M.B. Shaha, who have studied Jyotiba, writes,"He was primarily influenced by two books–one by Ashvaghosh's *Bajrasuchi* and another by *Bijak* of Kabir, which was provided to him by Gyangiviri Baba, a Kabirpanthi ; '*Vipramati,*' a word used in the Bijak (*sic*), had a special attraction for him."[2] We must also bear in mind Jyotiba Phule as having been the third teacher of Ambedkar as he himself declared so, and described below, in one of his lectures in 1954.

In the following years, Mahatma Gandhi who showed equal if not more commitment and interest in the upliftment of the depressed classes, to whom he had rechristened as *Harijan* (recently an outlawed term declared by the apex court of India), had inherited Kabir and Kabirpanth tradition, in his blood through her mother, Putlibae and his maternal uncles. The fact of his Kabirpanth legacy became an open secret when he, in course of his tours called *Harijan Basti Yatra,*[3] publicly declared in a mammoth *sabha* he was addressing at the Kabir-Chaura Kabir Math in Benares in August 1934. He also expressed his immense contentment he had relished at Kabir Chaura, the plaçe where Kabir himself had once lived, and to whom he as well as his mother had always been worshipping.

David Arnold, in his scholarly book '*Gandhi, Profiles in Power*', hints at Putlibai's Kabirpanth association in these words:

> "Putlibai came from the small Pranami sect, whose eighteenth-century founder had sought, like Kabir, Guru Nanak and the leaders of a number of other religious reform movements across India, since the middle ages–to unite Hindu and Muslim belief and practices." [4]

We must also keep in mind that the Pranami sect has just been a sub-sect of the Kabirpanth as commonly acknowledged by most of the liberal Kabirpanthis as well as scholars.

Margret Chatterjee, another scholar on Gandhi, in her *Gandhi and the Challenge of Religious Diversity, Religious Pluralism Revisited*, pointedly remarks:

> "Among the thinkers who pioneered a form of *sadhana* or a path leading to self-transformation (the word may not be inappropriate here) which was ambiguous as between Hindu and Muslim belief, it is probably Kabir who is the most important figure in the formation of Gandhi's religious thought."[5]

Besides these pointers, we have also found Gandhi's own admission to the fact of Kabir's high place in his life and philosophy. In a hand written letter, addressed to Motidas of Baroda, Gujarat, he declares that he has been a worshipper (*pujari*) of Kabir.[6]

Gandhi's letter written in Gujrati

With respect to Bhimrao Ambedkar's inheritance of the Kabirpanth, we have clinching evidences both from his own speeches as well as related references in some scholarly biographical works and commentaries on him. While attributing his life-achievements to Kabir, being one of the three grand personalities who had inspired him, Ambedkar, on occasions, himself spelt out to what extent he had owed to Kabir and his inheritance to the panth. To quote him from one of his lectures having delivered at Purandare Stadium, Mumbai on 28 Oct., 1954:

> I have three masters as everyone else has. I am not an ascetic nor a renouncer. But I have masters. My first and best master was Buddha. When I was a 12-13 years old, my father was a devotee of Kabeer....My second master was Kabeer. My father was a devotee of Kabeer faith. Through him I was greatly influenced by the life and philosophy of Kabeer. According to me, Kabeer truly grasped the essence of the Buddha's philosophy. I never called anyone great. I did not call Gandhi Mahatma because as Kabeer said, 'It is difficult to be human being, how much more so to be Mahatma.' How, one who has not been a man, can become a Mahatma? My third master was Jyotiba Phule.[7]

Almost one and half years ago, while addressing a mammoth gathering of educated women in the women's conference at Rawali Camp, Mumbai on 13 July 1953, Ambedkar ruminated as follows:

> ....Second thing about religion. Man must not seek self alone but in some measure others also. Religion is needed for this only. My doing all this is meant for you only. I have been taught this by religion....Be

> deligent as per Kabeer's couplets to the effect, 'Do some deed: eat and let others eat.'.... There have been many who have worked in the cause of the abolition of caste and untouchability. Of these, who can be mentioned, Ramanuja, Kabir and others stand out prominently, can you appeal to the acts of these reformers and exhort the Hindus to follow them? [8]

Apart from his speeches, we do have some scholarly biographical works on Ambedkar that too shows how he and his parents were profoundly indebted to the Kabirpanth. To cite some of these works, Dhananjay Keer, an authoritative biographer of Ambedkar, comes to our mind first:

> His father Ramji Sakpal was the instructor in the military school. He had fourteen children. He became a follower of Kabir Panth and was an admirer of Jatibao Phoole, who pioneered major reforms among the lower classes in Maharashtra from the later part of the nineteenth century.

Ambedkar's mother, Bhimabae, belonging to Thana district of then Bombay state, also belonged to Kabir cult. [9]

Christophe Jaffrelot, a French scholar,[10] and Ananya Vajpeyi, including many others, refer to the bravery of the Mahar regiment, a specially recruited regiment by the Britishers to ensure victory over Maratha *sardars* during second Anglo-Maratha war in 1818. Later on, Ambedkar's father himself, being a member of the Mahar regiment, had retired in the following year when the British government had discontinued to recruit Mahars in 1893. Restriction on Mahars conscription had left adverse impact on the former. The impact can be felt in Ambedkar's decision to take part in one of the commemorative rallies organized to showcase the past bravery of his community in Pune in 1927. Many of these soldiers enrolled in the English army, according to these scholars, were, in fact, Kabirpanth followers, belonging to Mahar community, and had been nursing fierce grudges against the Maratha maurauders.

Ananya Vajpeyi, in this seminal book, '*Righteous Republic*' goes a step further in her enquiry as to why Ambedkar did not convert *en masse* into the Kabirpanth, instead of Buddhism alongwith about half-million of then Dalits, despite former being his family religion. To quote her:

> There could be several answers to this question; one is that many Mahars were already Kabirpanthis. Another is that the Kabirpanth was a religion-or rather a minor sect-associated mainly with Untouchables, Hindu as well as Muslim. Ambedkar, however sought a creed that was not in any way confined to lower caste and outcaste groups–a major world religion, in other words, not a small sectarian identity that caste Hindus would denigrate just as much as they denigrated other Untouchable belief and practices.
>
> The third reason is that though Guru Ramanand, a Brahmin who accepted the unlettered, Untouchable Muslim weaver Kabir as his student, according to some legends, Kabir....he no longer held any value as a true symbol of opposition to organized caste-based Hinduism, in Ambedkar's view. Ambedkar himself might have looked upto Kabir and followed

> the true import of his iconoclastic poetry, but he did not trust his followers to be able to keep Kabir apart from mainstream Hinduism....Ambedkar did not seem interested in converting anyone to the Kabirpanth. [11]

Having noted several other instances of the antagonism between Maratha marauders and predominantly a peace-loving Kabirpanth followers, we have now solid ground to believe the oral tradition as we had come to know in Cuttack, Orissa, that entire property and Math buildings of the Jagodasi Kabir Math situated in the Chauliaganj area[12] was ransacked and subsequently captured by the latter, forcing Orissa's one of the earliest Kabir Math to close its establishment forever and shifted to a safe place, Bidupur, district Vaishali in present Bihar during the mid-eighteenth century.

Primary Sources

Among the sources which enable us to delineate the spread of Kabirpanth, the lists of sub-branches preserved at some of the *Acharya-Gaddis*[13]are equally valuable. These lists are mostly hand-written. When such a list is not available the current Acharya or concerned Mahants dictate the names of the Maths affiliated to their branch.

Field work has however, proved to be of tremendous value for this research work. I could attempt to understand the process of interaction between the followers of the panth and the mainstream Hindus and Muslims, on the basis of disciples' memory. I also noted that the growth of Kabirpanth had passed through different phases. My description of the pattern and the process involved in the expansion of Kabirpanth is entirely based on the responses of these disciples. They also recalled how caste and inter-and intra-family relationships played a significant role in its growth. The internal differences and resulting feuds within the panth also came to my knowledge through these interviews.

Oral tradition in Kabirpanth is evidently important and its reliability can be judged from the manner in which the disciples recounted the events. It seems as if the information has been passed down from one generation to another. Further, we verified this information from different groups of the people spread over many villages. I, however, have accepted only those oral traditions which could be verified from more than one source.

Apart from the field materials, information on Kabirpanth have been obtained from the writings of the British officials who conducted surveys in north Bihar in the nineteenth century. For instance, Francis Buchanan's survey[14] contains copious information on several aspects of north Indian society including the general condition of Kabirpanth and its followers in north-eastern district of Bihar in the then Bengal province in the early decades of the nineteenth century. Buchanan's survey is a first-hand account which helps us to reconstruct the history of Kabirpanth during this period. Buchanan noted that almost 100 Maths were active in Purnea district alone, which gives us an idea of the extent of the spread of the panth, and that, in an area which was almost 100 kms away from any of the Acharya *Gaddis*, the terminology which acquired currency for the chief centre of then diversifying branches of the panth. He observed that these Maths were of 'recent origin'[15] thereby underlining the fact that Kabirpanth had presumably begun to expand its base in the region towards the end of the eighteenth century.

Some of the primary sources directly relate to the traditions of the Kabirpanth. In the following decade, the description of the Kabirpanth occurs in the ethnographic work of Horace Hayman Wilson,[16] a medical practitioner, written in the early nineteenth century. Considering Kabirpanth as a Hindu religious sect, Wilson, having emerged an eminent Orientalist, dilated on its social composition, organizational form, and myths and rituals. He has, in fact, based his account on some devotional texts, his personal interview and a few religious scriptures of the panth.

The scholars on Kabir initially used to prepare lists of works attributed to Kabir and several seemed to have been unable to push their acquaintance with Kabir any further than this during the nineteenth century. For example, the first historian of Hindi literature, Garcin de Tassy, between 1837 and 1847 composed his famous work[17] in which he devotes fourteen pages to Kabir. De Tassy seems to have relied largely on H.H. Wilson, who, in 1832, had written considerably on Kabir and the Kabirpanth.[18] In 1883, Sivasingh in his *Saroj*, the first attempt in Hindi at a history of Hindi literature, and in 1888, George Grierson,[19] in his *Modern Vernacular Literature of Hindustan*, both presented lists of Kabir works and offered some brief information on their author. It would appear that in academic circles knowledge of Kabir and his works was very sketchy at the end of the 19th century. Even his date seems shrouded in uncertainly and the most that Grierson would venture to say was that Kabir would have lived around 1400.

The census reports, prepared by the colonial government from the late nineteenth century, do tell us much about the Hindu sects. The unrealistically small number of Kabirpanthis, given in the first census of the then Bengal province,[20] however, does not seem to be accurate in view of Buchanan's description of Purnea district in the early nineteenth century. This miscalculation seems to have stemmed from the fact that the census officials[21] considered Kabirpanthis to those followers alone, who entered 'Kabirpanth' in verbatim, as their 'religion' in the given column of the enumeration form, provided to them for the purposes of survey by the census department. It seems that most of the Hindu followers among Kabirpanthis entered 'Hindu' as their religion in the prescribed form, instead of the name of the sect to which some of them entered as their religion. Yet in the first census of the British India conducted in 1872, census officials described Kabirpanth in most of the provinces, as a sect which did not admit of caste differentiation.

In the following census of the Bengal province in particular, which then included major part of present day Assam, undivided Bengal, Bihar, Jharkhand, parts of eastern Uttar Pradesh as well as Orissa, however, census department decided to stop collecting statistics on sects such as the Kabirpanth. The official reason then stated by them had been, as mentioned in the report, the progressive political insignificance of these sects in view of the colonial rule after 1872. Interestingly, the religious groups of the Muslims found enumeration in the following censuses onwards. However in other parts of the British India, they continued to enumerate the Kabirpanthis too, probably because the Britishers perceived them relatively more significant than Bengal province. The statistical survey of W.W. Hunter,[22] conducted in 1874 also contain some information on the Kabirpanth, although he primarily relied for the data on the first census.

Probably owing to the wide diffusion of the Kabirpanth and the popularity of aphorisms and proverbs attributed to him, Kabir continued to attract the attention of the scholars. The first real critical study was that of George Herbert Westcott, *Kabir and the Kabir Panth*, published in 1907.[23] This study is based mainly on the *Bijak*, the *Guru Granth Sahib* and the literature of the panth. Westcott was the first to take note of the problem of establishing the authenticity of texts and his comment in this regard is interesting: "At any rate we have no right to assume that the teaching of Kabir was identical with that given at the present time by the Mahants of the Panth that bears his name."[24] Westcott was a Bishop and also a fellow of the Allahabad University. His Christian bias is reflected in his estimation of Kabirpanth. He has largely relied on his own observation to describe the history of two of the Kabir Maths in north India. He also checked Wilson's description of the panth. However, his account is largely based on his own ten years' study of the religious scriptures of the panth, supplemented by his personal observation of the Kabir-Chaura and the Dharmdasi branches respectively at Kashi in the then United

Provinces and Kawardha in the Central Provinces. He concluded that the religious practices of Kabirpanth were 'influenced by Christianity.'[25]

Some Indian scholars also provide us with the then contemporary condition about Kabirpanth during the late nineteenth century. Among them, Pramatha Nath Bose and J.N. Bhattacharya are foremost. Pramatha Nath Bose,[26] in his history of the socio-religious groups active in late nineteenth century Bengal and United Province, noted that Kabirpanth had a sizeable following, mostly belonging to the low castes. He noticed that the Kabirpanthis were not Hindus as they had broken away from the parent religion, just as the Buddhist and the Sikhs had done it much before them. J.N. Bhattacharya[27] also noted that the Kabirpanthis believed in monotheism, which distinguished them from the other Hindus.

In 1920, Ayodhya Singh Upadhyay 'Hariaudh', working under the guidance of Shyamsundar Das, published a text with some general information on Kabir's thought.[28] Later on Shyamsundar Das himself brought to light two remarkable manuscripts which he published in 1928.[29] One of these manuscripts carried the date 1504 and the other 1824. It was certainly an important finding. Shyamsundar Das recorded his estimation in these words: "After looking over these two copies, it is evident to me that we took all the works now attributed to Kabir, we would find a good nine-tenths of them in these two."[30] A sober look at the abundant variants amongst manuscripts and traditions eventually came to light, which led scholars to a more critical view of the material published by

Shyamsundar Das in 1928. However, his *Kabir Granthavli* remained the standard text for the next thirty years and is still regarded by some scholars as the most reliable. Shyamsundar Das uncovered the real textual problem of studies on Kabir but, apart from publishing manuscripts, he engaged in no notable textual criticism.

The non-Hindi world in the main came to know more of Kabir after Rabindranath Tagore in 1914 published a verse translation in English of a selection of readings compiled by a fellow Bengali scholar, Kshiti Mohan Sen.[31] The name of Tagore, coupled with a preface by the English religious writer, Evelyn Underhill, gave this small work considerable prestige, but to William J. Dwyer, its unscholarly nature soon brought this work under criticism. For example, one of the earliest editors and translators of the *Bijak*, Ahmad Shah writes:

> This translation is supposed to be based on the Hindi text (in Bengali characters) with a Bengali translation by Kshiti Mohan Sen, who has gathered from many sources a large collection of poems and hymns to which the name of Kabir is attached.[32]

Shah actually himself made a careful examination of this translation and found that it was based not on the Hindi text, but upon the Bengali translation which is far from accurate. Kshiti Mohan Sen's collection is in four volumes and contains 341 poems. The one hundred poems translated by Tagore are taken from the first three volumes, which contain only 264. Of these hundred, there are, according to Ahmad Shah, only five, which in a mutilated form, can be safely attributed to Kabir.

Kshiti Mohan Sen himself, in his famous research

based book on *Medieval Mysticism* does mention the names of important centres of the Kabirpanth, a valuable information on contemporary condition of the latter. To quote him:

> Besides the two principal ones, there are other sects of Kabir. Of these the sect led by Bhaggu is to be found at Dhanauti in Tirhut (Bihar) and the Math of the sect led by Jaggu is in Cuttack (Orissa). The Jnani sect has its head-quarters at Majhni near Sasaram (Bihar), while the Taksari sect is in Baroda. Nityanand, Kamalanand and Chaturbhuj were ordered by Kabir to go for sadhana to the Dravir country which was the native place of the Bhakti cult. It is not known whether they left any sect behind them.[33]

He also felt the need to clarify the close relation between Guru Nanak and Kabir in the same book. We can note his findings in the following:

> In 1469, Baba Nanak was born in the village of Talbandi (sic) near Lahore. According to some bhaktas, Nanak was then a young man when he met the old Kabir. On seeing him Kabir is said to have remarked that he had no misgivings about the future; for he was seeing an able man before his leaving the world. This incident may or may not be true but Nanak was possibly much influenced by Kabir's ideas. The central theme of many of his sayings agrees with the doctrine of Kabir a number of whose songs have been included in the Granth Sahib. Nanak's sayings are in Hindi with an admixture of Punjabi.[34]

Kabir has been an important figure in the Sikh tradition. He is regarded by several scholars as well as Kabirpanth's sikh followers as having been Guru Nanak's spiritual mentor. When the fifth Sikh guru, Arjandev was compiling the Adi Granth, completed in 1604, he included verses attributed at that time to Kabir. These have been preserved more or less unchanged, to what constitutes the oldest and most authentic tradition of Kabir's verses. Many scholars estimate that roughly around the time the Adi Granth was compiled, the *Bijak* also must have been compiled or composed. While describing different versions of the *Bijak*, Frank Ernest Keay writes–"This is the probable account of the *Bijak*. The compiler may have been Bhagwan Das, and the compilation perhaps was not made till somewhere about 1600."[35] The most striking feature of the *Bijak* is that while Kabir is claimed as its author, it shows little evidence that he would have been primarily an exponent of bhakti and for this reason the author, in all likelihood, might have been a Kabirpanth follower. The centuries that followed must have seen a flourishing of the spurious Kabir literature much of which is still popular in the panth.

Ahmad Shah was one of the converted Christians, as the name itself suggests, from the Muslim community and a renowned scholar of the time. He had previously translated Bijak in Hindi after compiling it from several reliable collections in 1912. In 1915, he completed its English rendition, and got it published with the support of the financial grant from the then colonial government of the United Provinces. He points out:

> After going through all these printed editions as well as some of the available manuscripts, particularly one which I saw in Chunar with Pundit Bhan Partap Tiwari, I tried my best to present the public with a text as accurate as possible in my Hindi Text published in 1911.[36]

Ahmad Shah further points out that the oldest printed edition of the *Bijak* was dated back to 1868, and was printed at Benares. The second printed edition of the *Bijak*, according to him, was printed in Calcutta in 1890, edited by Prem Chand, of the Baptist Mission of Monghyr, Bihar. Its third edition was printed by the Newal Kishore Press, Lucknow, in 1898. He clarified that it was a complete *Bijak* with commentary by Raja Vishwa Nath Singh of Rewah. The fourth edition was issued at Allahabad in 1905. It is called the *Bijak*, with commentary of Puran Dass of Burhanpur. The last printed edition which he had seen was one that was from Bombay printed in 1906. This was then called the Raja of Rewah's edition, similar to that of the Newal Kishore Press, Lucknow, but it has a life of Kabir in verse and at the end *Sayar Pad Bijak* and a genealogy and history of the *Bhagel Bansha*, and *Mul Ramaini*. It has some fresh *sakhis* and contains an imaginary picture of Kabir and also a likeness of the Raja of *Bhagel Bansha*. Ahmad Shah commented that this edition contained many mistakes and in some places the text was spoiled, but it has preserved the original beauty of the language.

Besides offering us a detailed account of the literary development within the Kabirpanth, Ahmad Shah also comments on the raging debates on the origin of the

Kabir and Kabirpanth. He points out:

> In modern India organised attempts, such as that of the Brahma Samaj, to correct the abuses in Hinduism tend to be branded as disguised Christianity. It may be noted that an interesting, if unconvincing, attempt to connect the Kabir Panth with the teaching of the Jesuits has been made by Pt. Walji Bhai of the Irish Presbyterian Church. It seems probable that a similar tendency caused Kabir in his own day to be called a Moslem; while the Moslems on the whole welcome his efforts, as a help in combating the idol worship of India, and acknowledged him as a Pir for his self-denial and pious life.[37]

Based on his own research, Ahmad Shah further apprises of the main Principals or Commandments of the Kabirpanthis then guiding them as follows, which still, to me somehow, constitute core of the Kabirpanth doctrines:

1. To believe in One Avagat, Atit, Brahm, Satya Purush. His bhakti should be practised.
2. Satya Purush and Kabir Sahib are one. Satya Purush manifests himself in Kabir.
3. Faith in the Guru and in his teaching.
4. True Sadhus should be served.
5. Show mercy and love towards all Jivas.
6. To abstain from all kinds of meats.
7. To abstain from all kinds of intoxicating things.
8. To abstain from adultery.
9. No visible object in this world should be worshipped.
10. Anything offered to images should not be eaten.

Everything you get to eat, offer it first to the true God, then eat it.

11. Do not tell lies.
12. Do not steal.
13. Do not gamble.
14. Mark your body in 12 places (Tilak).
15. Use clean clothes.
16. Wear Tulsi necklace.
17. Repeat Satya Nam.
18. Practise bhakti of Satya Purush and preach him,
19. Do not believe in charms, amulets and other superstitious things (Jantr, Mantr and Tantras).
20. The way of salvation cannot be found in any other books but in Swansan Ved.
21. Besides Satya Kabir and his Hans, no one will be able to save.
22. Without True Guru no one will get salvation.
23. Apart from bhakti of Satya Purush all other bhaktis will drown in the world and will not save any one.
24. Tirath, Barat, etc., are all bands of Yama and people are tied with them.
25. Nine kinds of bhakti and four kinds of Muktis are banned only.
26. Those who worship Nirgun or Surgun they are always bound down.
27. Hindu, Moslem and any other sect can join Kabir's religion.
28. Heaven and hell and other Loks have no existence except for the ignorant.
29. Without the knowledge of Sar Shabad no one can attain salvation.

30. Abuse, deceit and jealousy are enemies of salvation.
31. Humility is a great virtue.
32. The way of salvation is very narrow.
33. Whatever troubles you have to face do not ask help from another god, but from God.
34. Whoever accepts Sat Gum should serve him with all his heart and power.
35. Kabir is bodiless. His body never suffers.
36. Give thanks for the gift of Sat Guru.
37. The fear of God is the sign of salvation.
38. Without true love of God the practice of bhakti is fruitless.
39. Blessed are those who renounce the covetousness of this body and remain in devotion.
40. Without thinking of others' good no one can attain salvation.
41. To speak moderately is a great virtue.
42. To read Sat Guru's words is a great virtue,
43. Kabir Sahib has established his religion through a certain family: only that should be honoured. (It has been the core belief of the Dharamdasi *vansh Gaddi* branch presently centred at Damakhera, Chhattisgarh and also has been the main *beta noire* vehemently opposed by all other branches of the Kabirpanth for centuries, leading to repeated splits within the community, emphasis mine.)
44. Do not curse any one.
45. One should know the Supreme Spirit.
46. Proud persons cannot know the Supreme Spirit.
47. To follow the Guru's instructions is great worship.

48. So long as one thinks much of his body and nourishes it, he cannot know God.
49. The ignorant and unwise and without understanding will never know how to attain salvation,
50. So long as one is proud of his body and considers it a real thing, he will never be able to be called bodiless while having body. [38]

Frank Ernest Keay's Study,[39] originally written as a doctoral thesis submitted with the London University, is even more useful for us, as he described the origin of Dhanauti and Bidupur Maths, which have been two main headquarters of the Kabirpanth branches popularly called Bhagtahi/Bhagodasi and Jagodasi/Jagudasi centred respectively in present Bihar, yet not mentioned in details in previous English works. And despite these critical doubts on authenticity, F.E. Keay's work was published three years after Shyamsundar Das *Kabir-Granthavali* without noticing apparently his knowledge of its existence. This, to Charlotte Vaudeville, exemplifies a kind of divorce between the old school of British scholars-cum-missionaries and the new 'native' scholarship.'[40]

Among the notable Kabir scholars of the period Hazari Prasad Dvivedi, one of the towering personalities of Hindi literature, is worth consideration. He published *Kabir*, a critical study of various aspects of Kabir's thought in 1942, with revised and enlarged editions coming later. Like F.E. Keay before him, he made some attempt to disengage Kabir's thought from the mass of Kabirpanthi teachings which had overgrown it, but his work suffered from the serious defect of overlooking the importance of authenticity of texts. Hazari Prasad Dvivedi seems to have relied almost entirely on the compilations of poems made by Kshiti Mohan Sen, and this disregard for textual scholarship is still found in the 1971 edition of his book.[41] However, some of Hazari Prasad Dvivedi's insights into Kabir's life and thought are of great value and highly commendable by Hindi scholars. Yet a number of Kabir followers find Dvivedi's some explications of Kabir's *sabad* untenable and erroneous.

One feature of the development of interest in Kabir has been the extraordinary popularity of the *Bijak* which has gone through thirty-two editions in the last hundred years and continues to appear in popular editions.[42] In 1972, Shukdev Singh had prepared what is the first critical edition of *Bijak*. Renowned scholars like Charlotte Vaudeville are of the opinion that the importance of the *Bijak* should not be overlooked and that it may, in the long run, prove to be closer to the original Kabir than any other text.[43]

Among other texts on Kabir commonly accepted in academic circles has been the *bhagat* Kabir section of the *Guru Granth Sahib*, published by Ramkumar Varma. He also published a study of Kabir mysticism entitled *Kabir Ka Rahasyavad*.[44] This is one of many valuable studies done on Kabir's thought and allied subjects of which the forerunner was P.D. Barthwal's *Nirguna School of Hindi Poetry*.[45] During 1940s and 50s, some followed study of the background of Kabir's religions, but textual criticism remained the neglected aspect in Indian academic circles.

The most important event in modern studies on Kabir undoubtedly was the publication by Parasnath Tiwari of Allahabad University of his textual work on Kabir to which he gave the title of *Kabir Granthavali* in 1961.[46] He applied the criteria of the science of textual criticism to all the available manuscripts and printed texts, purporting to have Kabir as their author. He eventually arrived at a sizeable body of verse which he claims to be the closest could come in the then present state of research into Kabir's original verses. However, even this achievement has not met with unquestioning approval from all scholars. For example, Sarnamsingh Sharma,[47] has offered a very stringent criticism of Tiwari's work as less scholarly. Charlotte Vaudeville, too, while admitting the value of Tiwari's work and basing her own English version of Kabir largely on it, had pointed out flaws in it.[48] For all this, it has to be admitted that Tiwari's *Kabir Granthavali* was the only attempt at claiming Kabir's authorship and hence it took precedence as Kabir's thought.

Parashuram Chaturvedi's study of the *sant* tradition in North India[49] deals with Kabirpanth in details. He relied mainly on the religious scriptures of the panth and the then unpublished research of Kedarnath Dvivedi on Kabirpanth. Dvivedi had been one of his students. We have a detailed account in these two studies of the Premier Maths then existing in several parts of the north India except post-independent Punjab. Kedarnath Dvivedi[50] had, however, conducted extensive field-work to delineate the spread of Kabirpanth. In his work, oral tradition has been given primacy over religious texts. The antiquity of a Math is judged on the basis of the

Guru-pranali.

In the last 50 years or so, there has been a spurt in the study of Kabirpanth on the basis of oral traditions. Baidyanath Sarasvati's paper[51] on the socio-religious aspects of the panth, Mohd. Sahabuddin's unpublished Ph.D. thesis on Kabirpanth[52] and R.L. Khandelwal[53] study of the social composition of Kabirpanth in north India are some prominent examples. The scholarly unpublished work of late Kathleen Marie Erndl,[54] written as a thesis for master course in the Department of the Oriental Studies, University of Arizona, USA in 1977. In her research on Kabir and Kabirpanth, she had discussed Kabir against the background of the *Sant* tradition, as well as in terms of his life and original contributions to Indian religion. She also, describes both of its major branches, in terms of its continuity and transformation of Kabir's teachings and its relation to mainstream Hinduism. (I am thankful to authorities of the library of University. Arizona USA, who had no objection in getting her thesis published as a chapter in my book.) While I was completing my first book on Kabirpanth published in 2008, I was not aware of her book, yet I had also applied the theories of structure, anti-structure, communities of Victor Turner,[55] in examining the myths and rituals prevailing among diverse groups of these followers, some of the concepts, which I have recently found, she had already used in her present thesis. Her work is originally titled, *Formation of a Counter Formation, Kabir and the Kabir Panth in the Context of North Indian Religion* submitted and approved under the supervision of renowned scholar, Richard M. Eaton. I reproduce her thesis *ad verbatim* as a micro-study of Kabirpanth in this book, alongwith my own micro-level study.

The studies of David N. Lorenzen[56] specifically on religious developments within Kabirpanth in north India deserve special mention. He has supplemented his field observations with available printed materials primarily at the library of the Kabir Chaura Math, Banares, which itself owes a lot to the scholar for its re-ordering and cataloguing. He has also written extensively on aspects of the panth's social constituencies, ideological moorings, political involvement of Sadhus and Mahants, extant religious scriptures and above all on the historical evidences that could be made use for histriographical perspective. The depth of his scholarly interest in the Kabirpanth can be measured by the sheer fact that he published his latest work on Kabirpanth in the light of Marco della Tomba in 2012.

Apart from these works, two scholars have focused exclusively on the myths of the panth. David Scott[57] has collected some of these myths and has attempted to situate them in the socio-religious milieu prevailing at the time of Kabir. Uma Thukral's book[58] and articles on Kabirpanthi myths and traditions have also been valuable to us.

At the turn of the 21st century, we have some insightful works on Kabir and Kabirpanth. The most prominent among them, in my view, have been those written respectively by Purushottam Aggrawal, Vinay Dharwadker and David N. Lorenzen.

Vinay Dharwadker's *Kabir, The Weaver's Songs* (2003), has in fact been a magnificent translation of Kabir's hundred poems collected by him from various written and oral sources, he also devotes 96 pages of the book on the historical context of the widespread popularity of these songs within India and beyond. Apart from his brilliant exposition and translation of the mystic Kabir's *sabad*, this work also delineates the disparate traditions associated with the poetry within Kabir panth and Sikh panth as well. He further goes on to underline the same standpoint which I have demonstarted in my recent book (2016) that Kabirpanth as an ideological formation was well laid down and widely spread during Kabir's life time. To quote him–"A few stories in Kabir's poems as well as other sources circulated before the middle of the seventeenth century imply that the poet's audacity may have had repercussions in his lifetime."[59] However his description of the extent of the Kabirpanth falls short of my findings in that he confines its expansion 'from Bihar and Orissa to Rajasthan and Gujarat'[51] whereas this book describes its expansion from Meghalaya, Sikkim, Bhutan in the north east to Jammu and Kashmir, Punjab, Himachal Pradesh, from Andhra Pradesh and Karnataka in the South to Maharashtra in the western India.

Purushottam Agrawal's *Akath Kahani Prem Ki*, published in 2009, although a great piece of literary work on Kabir, makes some unqualified claim where he writes that Dharam Das created Kabirpanth in the early seventeenth century, by negating the evolutionary character of the panth.[60] However, his description of Kabir's birth, descent and interpretation of near contemporary writings on Kabir is *par excellence*.

David N. Lorenzen's persistent interst in the Kabirpanth has continued till date. His writings on Kabir and Kabirpanth has in his own words primarily veered around "social dimensions of the beliefs and practices that they have advocated and more specifically on the dissent they have expressed against the more dominant socio-religious ideology of the Varnashram dharma."[61] However his recent translation of the notes of Marco dell Tomba has been a testimony to the fact that his interest in Kabirpanth has touched upon several other dimensions of the panth. Mention could, however, be made of the Italian Capuchin missionary, Padre Marco della Tomba, who spent nearly twenty years in or around the town of Bettiah in northern Bihar in the middle of the eighteenth century. He recollected his contacts with a sect he called Cabiristi, presumably some branch of the Kabirpanth and actually translated that Kabir was the preceptor of Alexander, the Great. It was possibly the difficulty of distilling history out of such fantasies that drove the English scholar, Wilson, to doubt whether Kabir ever existed.

Secondary Sources

Some of the anthropological and sociological works have helped me to deal with the sociological and symbolic order of the panth. Historical works of various regions have facilitated me to locate the growth of Kabirpanth in the prevailing socio-religious conditions of the respective regions from the nineteenth century onwards. Historical works on the political inclination of religious organizations in the modern period have been of great help in understanding the political involvement of the Kabirpanthis, which I have described in details in my previous book (2008).[62]

I present the above fragmentary sketch of the studies of Kabir over a long period, in order to give some idea of the ups and downs in the dwindling interest of scholars pertaining to his thought. It does not give a full picture of the development of interest in Kabir or of his discovery process in Europe or his rediscovery in India. Some interesting figures in this process have been omitted mainly because their work had no lasting effect.

Most of these works have relied on oral evidence, primarily due to the absence of written records related to the panth. Lack of written documents has perhaps dissuaded scholars from studying Kabirpanth in the historical perspective. At best, some of these studies have attempted to present its history on basis of the traditional belief about the formation of its main branches. There is no attempt on their part to describe the spread of the sub-branches of a particular region in a chronological sequence. There is neither much discussion of the organizational form nor the manner of functioning of the panth in the existing historiography.

However, these works offer an overview on the early history of Kabirpanth as preserved in popular memory. These make it clear that Kabirpanth has drawn its following predominantly from the intermediate and lower castes wherever it has spread its influence. They also mention that there exists considerable similarity in the myths, rituals, organizational network, the status of the Mahant, and even the pattern of internal feuds in Kabirpanth all over north India have emerged quite clear in these studies.

Conducting the project, we have been able to gather field data from at least 19 provinces of India in which

Kabirpanth has moderate to widespread existence; namely, Andhra Pradesh, Assam, Bihar, Chhattisgarh, Gujarat, Haryana, Himachal Pradesh, Jammu & Kashmir, Karnataka, Madhya Pradesh, Meghalaya, Maharashtra, Odissa, Punjab, Rajasthan, Sikkim, Uttar Pradesh, Uttarakhand, West Bengal. Field-works in all these provinces have added to the existing knowledge about various aspects of the Kabirpanth history; viz origin, pattern and process of its expansion as well as specific elements of regional and national character as enshrined in the panth. For instance, we have come to know for the first time that Kabirpanth has sizeable presence in the present provinces of Haryana, Himachal Pradesh, Punjab and Jammu region of Jammu and Kashmir,[63] the main constituents of northern states of India. Our study demonstrates that the Kabirpanth, in some form or the other has continued to exist in some of these regions, at least since turn of the sixteenth century. Our findings also tend to suggest that the present Sikh religion probably had close relationship with the tradition of Kabir during their early stage.

Apart from field studies, we also visited some national and state libraries, archives and *waqf* boards of Shia and Sunni Muslims.[64] Among the libraries that we consulted, most important have been the National Library, Kolkata; NMML, New Delhi; Central Library, JNU, New Delhi, and A.C. Joshi Library, Punjab University, Chandigarh; A.N. Sinha Institute Library, Patna among some others.[65]

Visit to these libraries has familiarized me with a number of primary and secondary sources pertaining to the Kabirpanth. Primary sources on the condition of the

Kabirpanth during the colonial period available in the libraries have been the ethnographic works of scholars and census reports of the 19-and-20th centuries.

Among the archives, we could check just two of these– West Bengal State Archives, College Avenue, Calcutta and National Archives, New Delhi.[66] But we could not find a valuable material relating to the Kabirpanth in the archives except a few travel-related documents of the migrating disciples of Kabir during early 20th century.

Yet my visit to the *Sunni Waqf* Board Office, Lucknow, Uttar Pradesh has been of immense value. The Chairperson as well as the sub-ordinate officials of the Board had been kind enough to share with me some revenue documents relating to the Kabir Mazar of Magahar, district Sant Kabir Nagar, Uttar Pradesh.

Based on these findings, I have chapterized the history of the Kabirpanth in accordance with its gradual unfolding in time and space during the emergent modern India, a pattern which I had not initially proposed in the original research format. Even as scholars on Kabirpanth were aware of its presence in parts of several states, but our field works add further to our understanding of their probable origin and expansion in the each of these present Indian provinces. In almost all these states, we had to conduct more than one round of field trips to get required information about the panth's history.

The findings of the project have enabled me to present these at national and international fora. A few of these papers are already accepted for publication and soon to be published. I had presented a paper on the history of the Kabirpanth in Punjab region in the 2013

Session of the Indian History Congress, which is already published in a journal.[67] Another paper on the diasporas of the Kabirpanth globally was presented in an International conference organized at Mansfield College, Oxford University, Oxford, UK, in between 6-7 April 2014.[68] The paper is also published in an international journal of history.[69]

Religious sects have been one of the most neglected themes in religious studies in India. My emphasis throughout the work has been on these aspects of Kabirpanth. There have been some of the gaps in the existing historiography on the panth that I have attempted to fill up. Ultimately, it is the construction of the community identity of the Kabirpanth that has been at the centre of my study, even though I have never specifically raised the question of identity formation. Thus, my entire efforts to reconstruct its history have finally turned out to be the history of institutional growth of the Kabirpanth in India and abroad. My work attempts to trace the history of the Kabirpanth at the national level. I have tried to describe its growth in a chronological sequence as indicated in the available sources. Despite the paucity of written evidence, I have tried to understand the evolution of a religious order in the historical perspective.

References

1. Purnendu Ranjan, *Kabirpanth Till the End of Medieval India*, Gyankosh Publishers, Chandigarh, 2016.
2. M.B. Shaha, *Bhartiya Samaj Ke Kranti Janak, Mahatma Jyotiba Phule*, Hindi, Radhakrishna Publishers, New Delhi, p. 60.
3. *Aaj*, a Hindi daily newspaper, Banares, 3 August, 1934.
4. David Arnold, *Gandhi, Profiles in Power*, Routledge, New York,

2014 (2001), p. 31.

5. Margaret Chatterjee, *Gandhi and the Challenge of Religious Diversity, Religious Pluralism Revisited,* Promilla & Co., New Delhi, 2005, pp.116-118.
6. Uday, my project fellow had procured this hand-written letter of Gandhi from the collection of the Jamnagar Kabir Ashram, Gujarat.
7. C. D. Naik, *Thoughts and Philosophy of Dr. B. R. Ambedkar*, Sarup & Sons, New Delhi, 2003, pp. 129-130.
8. *Ibid.*, p.130.
9. Dhananjay Keer, *Dr. Ambedkar: Life and Mission*, Popular Prakashan, Bombay, 1962 (1954), pp. 9-10.
10. Christophe Jaffrelot, *Dr. Ambedkar and Untouchability, Analysing and Fighting Caste*, Hrst and Company, London, 2000.
11. Ananya Vajpeyi, *Righteous Republic, The Political Foundation of Modern India*, Harvard University Press, Cambridge, 2012, pp. 26-27.
12. The site where samadhis of the Jagodasi Acharyas lay buried is presently outside the temple complex of the Samadhi Mandir, having idols of Kali, Krishna and Hanuman in the sanctum sanctorum, said to have been erected after demolition of the Kabir Math in the mid-eighteenth century.
13. Acharya Gaddis are the seats of the Chief Mahant called Acharya Mahant for each separate branch of the Kabirpanth. Their number has presumably gone up in course of the splits the panth has undergone over the years.
14. Francis Buchanan, *History, Antiquities, Topography and Statistics of Eastern India*, (ed. by M. Martin), Vol. IV, Cosmos Publication, Delhi,1976 (1838).
15. *Ibid.*, p. 304.
16. H. H. Wilson, *Religious Sects of the Hindus* (ed. by Ernst R. Rost), Indological Book House, Varanasi,1972 (1877).
17. Garcin de Tassy, *Historia de la literature hindoui et hindoustanie*, Vol. II, Paris, cited in William J. Dwyer, *Bhakti in Kabir*, Associated Book Agency, Patna,1981, p. 3.
18. H.H. Wilson, *op. cit.*, pp. 64-65
19. George Grierson, *Modern Vernacular Literature of Hindustan*,

Asiatic Society, Calcutta,1889 and Shiv Singh Sengar, *Shiv Singh Saroj*, Naval Kishor Press, Lucknow, 1926 (1883).

20. *Census of British India, Report on the Census of Bengal,1872,* Vol., Microfiche, Central Library, JNU, New Delhi.
21. *Census of British India,* Report on the Census of Bengal, 1882, Vol. I, Microfilm, NMML, New Delhi, p. 91.
22. W. W. Hunter, *Statistical Account of Bengal,* Vol. XIII & XV, Concept Publication, Delhi, 1976 (1877).
23. G.H. Westcott, *Kabir and the Kabir Panth,* Sushil Gupta, Calcutta,1907.
24. *Ibid.*, p.VII.
25. *Ibid.*, p. 58.
26. Pramatha Nath Bose, *A History of Hindu Civilisation During British Rule; Socio-Religious Conditions, Social Condition, Industrial Condition*, Asian Publication Services, New Delhi, 1975 (1894).
27. J.N. Bhattacharya, *Hindu Castes and Sect: An Exposition of the Origin of the Hindu Caste System and the Bearing of the Sects Towards Each Others and Towards Other Religious Systems,* Editions Indians, Calcutta, 1968 (1886), pp. 216-218.
28. Ayodhya Singh Upadhyay 'Hariaudh', (ed.), *Kabir Vachanavali,* Nagari Pracharani Sabha, Varanasi, 1964 (1946).
29. Shyamsundar Das, (ed.), *Kabir Granthavali,* Nagari Pracharani Sabha, Varanasi 1959 (1930).
30. *Ibid.*, p.1.
31. Rabindranath Tagore, *Songs of Kabir,* (trans.), Samuel Weiser, York Beach, Maine, 1995 (1915).
32. Ahmad Shah, *The Bijak of Kabir*, Author, Hamirpur,1917.
33. Kshiti Mohan Sen, *Medieval Mysticism of India,* Lizac & Co., London,1929, p. 108.
34. *Ibid.*, p.102.
35. Frank Ernest Keay, *Kabir and His Followers*, Association Press, Calcutta,1931.
36. Ahmad Shah, *op. cit,* p.17.
37. *Ibid.*, p.40.
38. *Ibid.*, pp. 44-45.
39. F.E. Keay, *op. cit.*, p. 105.

40. Charlotte Vaudeville, *A Weaver Named Kabir: Selected Verses, with a Detailed Biographical and Historical Introduction*, Oxford University Press, Delhi,1993.
41. Hazari Prasad Dvivedi, *Kabir: Kabir Ke Vyaktitva, Sahitya aur Darshanik Vicharon ki Alochana*, Hindi, Rajkamal Prakashan, 1990 (1941).
42. *Bijak* has undergone a number of editions and still on; the latest version I was provided by late Ramrup Goswami, the prominent Bhagatahi Mahant, published by him in 2012.
43. Charlotte Vaudeville, *op. cit.*, p.7.
44. Ramkumar Varma, *Kabir Ka Rahasyavad,* Hindi Sahitya Bhawan, Allahabad, 1948.
45. Pitambar Dutta Barthwal,*Traditions of Indian Mysticism Based upon Nirguna School of Hindi Poetry,* Heritage, New Delhi,1978 (1930)
46. Parasnath Tiwari, (ed.), *Kabir Granthavali,* Hindi, Hindi Parishad, Prayag Vishwvidyalay, Allahabad,1961.
47. Sarnamsingh Sharma, *Kabir: Vyatitv, Krititv Evam Siddhant,* Hindi, Bhartiya Shodh Sansthan, Jaipur, 1969, pp.124-128
48. Charlotte Vaudeville, *op. cit.*, p.17.
49. Parashuram Chaturvedi, *Uttari Bharat Ki Sant Parampara*, Hindi, Bharti Bhandar, Allahabad, 1950, Kedarnath Dvivedi was one of his Ph.D. scholars.
50. Kedarnath Dvivedi, *Kabir aur Kabirpanth*, Hindi, Sahitya Sammelan, Allahabad,1965.
51. Baidyanath Sarasvati, 'Notes on Kabir: A non-literate Intellectual,' In S.C. Malik (ed.), *Dissent, Protest and Reform in Indian Civilization*, IIAS, Simla,1977, pp.167-187.
52. Mohd. Sahabuddin, *History of Kabirpanth*, Unpublished thesis, History Department, Aligarh Muslim University, Aligarh, 1975
53. R.L. Khandelwal, 'Kabirpanth and Its Social Contents,'In S.P. Sen (ed.), *Social Contents of Indian Religious Reform Movements in the Nineteenth Twentieth Centuries*, Institute of Historical Studies, Calcutta,1978, pp.75-83.
54. Kathleen Marie Erndl, *Formation of a Counter Formation, Kabir and the Kabir Panth in the Context of North Indian Religion, unpublished, uploaded on Google, 2018.*

55. Victor, W. Turner, *The Ritual Process:Structure and Anti-Structure,* Routledge, New York, 2017 (1969)
56. David N.Lorenzen has worked extensively on the Kabirpanth's socio-religious moorings and their impact on the movement. Although his primary interest in the last few decades has shifted from this panth to the aspects of the dominant religious traditions in India, yet he does not miss an opportunity to write on Kabir related themes emerging in the scholarly world. He appears to be correct when he considers Kabir as his *alter ego*. His insightful writings on Kabir and Kabirpanth can be seen in the bibliography as well as in my references in the chapters of this book.
57. David, C. Scott, *Kabir's Mythology, The Religious Perceptions, Doctrines, and Practices of a Medieval Indian Sant,* Bhartiya Vidya Prakashan, Delhi, 1985.
58. Uma Thukral, *Kabirpanth: Sahitya, Darshan, Evam Sadhana,* Hindi Book Centre, New Delhi,1998.
59. Vinay Dharwadker, *Kabir, The Weaver's Songs,* Penguin Books, Gurgaon, 2003.
60. Purushottam Agrawal, *Akath Kahani Prem Ki, Kabir Ki Kavita aur Unka Samay,* Hindi, Rajkamal, 2009.
61. David N. Lorenzen, *Marco della Tomba,The Scourge of the Mission, Marco della Tomba in Hindustan,* (trans. and ed. by David N. Lorenzen),Yoda Press, 2010.
62. Purnendu Ranjan, *History of Kabirpanth, A Regional Process,* Anamika Publications, New Delhi, 2008.
63. In this province, we could not conduct field work in some of the places in the Kashmir valley where a small number of migrant Kabirpanthis are said to have been living.
64. I had personally visited libraries of the both the Boards situated in Lucknow, but I could not spend adequate time in the Shia Waqf Board, although there is all the probability that it has some documents relating to the landed grants given to the resourceful Daligang Kabir Math, Lucknow by the predecessors of Wazid Ali shah, the Nawab of Oudh.
65. A.C. Joshi Library, PU, Chandigarh had a hard copy of a volume of the 1882 census, which proved very handy for me, although its physical condition was pathetic.

66. Most of these archives did not have relevant documents for my purposes, yet West Bengal Archives have a few files which relate to the Kabirpanth diaspora beginning during the colonial period.
67. Purnendu Ranjan, 'Kabirpanth in Medieval Punjab', *Central Indian Journal of History and Archaeology Research*,
68. I had presented a research paper titled 'Diaspora in Kabirpanth in an international seminar organized at Mansfield College, Oxford University, Oxford, April, 2016.
69. Purnendu Ranjan, 'Diaspora in the Carribean Countries', *CIJHAR*, Vol. v, April-June, Patna, 2016, pp. 57-61.

Kabirpanth in the Nineteenth Century

Kabirpanth, fortunately for its followers and readers, found a number of ethnographers, scholars-cum-missionaries and British administrators, apart from its own eminent scholarly personalities, who have left their accounts on the then prevailing condition of the panth. Based on these accounts, we can establish that while Kabirpanth continued to expand its geographical horizon in hitherto unpenetrated areas of the British India, its splitting tendency too intensified in this century. In regions like Panjab, it also psersumably had to confront proselytizing acts both of the Sikhs and the Arya Samajis, leading to reduction in the numerical strength of the Kabir followers as noted in the next century. Due to continued splits, the headquarters of the Dharmdasi branch once again shifted to Damakhera, whereas, Kabir-Chaura and Bhagodasi branches found patrons in some royal families of their localities, adding to their material resources. Towards the end of the century, Kabirpanth had acquired not just an all-India character in terms of its geographical presence all over the country but also an international presence.

We have found some revenue judgement papers of 1840s, written in *Persian*,[1] which testifies the resourceful 'Zamindari' character the Dhanauti Math had acquired by this century. Besides it, the initial centres of the Bhagatahi branch at Chetia-Barharwa had also taken on the similar characters of a petty zamindar. I have found a bundle of about 50 pages of such judgement papers from the Dhanauti Math written in *Persian* language, then official language of the imperial revenue courts. One of the earliest passed judgments pertains to a dispute of 1804, in which the then *sadar amin ala* (Chief Magistrate), Mr. William of district Saran, had passed an order in favour of Shivpal Gosain in 1852. The details of judgement, as mentioned, refer to Laheji Math, and direct Dariya Bhagat, Jairam Bhagat and Ganpal Bhagat to refund the money in instalments to the then Mahant. Gunpal Goswami is shown as the 13th Mahant of the Dhanauti Math whereas Gopal Gosain was the 15th Mahant of the Chatiya-Barharawa Math.[2]

The intervention of the colonial agencies in the Kabirpanth's criminal disputes was also seen in the Central Provinces during the early nineteenth century at least twice as described in the *Nad Vansh Ka Itihas.* The first intervention of the British *thana* police was noted in the arrest of Sewa Das and his 13 companions on the false charge of theft levelled by Haqnam in Raipur in 1813, and the second in the criminal court of Raipur in1816, when a European judge named Agni Laut (sic) was reported to have delivered his verdict in favour of Sewa Das.[3]

In the midst of unfavourable developments some centres of Kabir continued to emerge in the southern part of then Bihar during the early part of the nineteenth century. One of these was at Pavapuri in Nalanda district of Bihar, which was incidently one of the ancient most religious centres of the Jainism in India. It has been famous for being the *nirwan sthal* of Mahavir.

The founder of Pavapuri Kabir Math was Kunjal Das, whose life is shrouded in obscurity. Kunjal Das was one of the natives of this village born in a Rajput family.[4] It is, however, said that he was another eminent disciple of the Kabir-Chaura and had been closely associated with Kabir-Bag Math of Gaya. Then local Zamindar of village Pava had donated about 100 *bighas* of land to Kunjal Baba as the prevailing tradition goes in the region. He is also accredited to have written another *Panchgranthi*; but to some, it was originally the *Panchgranthi* of Ram Rahas Das, which got a few lines just added by Kunjal Das. Whatever be the fact, Kunjal Das has presently acquired a legendary name as Kunjal Baba in the surrounding villages of Pavapuri. In addition, Kabir-Chaura's sub-branches began to be founded at some other places in its vicinity.

Apart from Pavapuri, another Kabir centre was formed at village Bahadurpur of Nalanda district during the same period. It's founder was Narayani Das[5] who had obliged a Muslim zamindar of Rajgir. The zamindar is said to have donated a land tracts of 100 *bighas* to the sadhu.

Another sub-branch of the Bahadurpur Math was opened at Sikandarpur[6] which also developed its 'zamindari', as a money-lending institution within the area of its influence during the British rule.

A Kabir-Chaura sub-branch was opened at Samanpur in the west Champaran area, where a number of the Bhagatahi Maths had been in operation for about three centuries. Samanpur Math has been one of the oldest and the richest centre of the Kabir Chaura in that part of Bihar. Tradition has it that two later disciples of Lal Das had been instrumental in its formation.[7]

The dissident group led by Sewa Das did not see any reason to stay any more at Singhori, Chhattisgarh and they all had left Singhori ashram forever in favour of a wandering life of a sadhu in 1813. Finally they decided to establish their own Math on persistent requests of resourceful disciples of Nadiya in 1814. It is, in all probability, the earliest split of the Dharmdasi *Vansh gaddi* resulting from differences on the longstanding issue as to who should head a Kabirpanth Math; a *virakta* or a house-holder.[8] The group of Kabirpanth followers who had been advocates of a *virakta* was then led by one Sewa Das. He had a long life of 102 years (1734-1836).

The accounts of Dhyan Das in the manuscript clarifies that village Nadiya as well as a large number of villages in the then Chhattisgarh region had come under the influence of Sewa Das before a Math was inaugurated there. Mangaturam and his two sons, Raghudas and Bhora Das of Nadiya had been inviting and imploring Sewa Das to open a Kabir centre of devotion, where Sewa Das finally founded the Math. However, he had been getting the similar request for opening a centre from a number of adjacent villages such as Ameri, Dharmatari, Fingesar, Rohasi, Bhawanipur, Baloda etc. spread across the present Chhattisgarh.

The Nadiya Math was founded at the donated land of Mangatu Das, whose original name was Halwa Thakur. He was also of Kasaundhan *bania* caste; and professionally a *malguzar* of the Khujii *pargana*. Dhyan

Das's account, as described in this published book, apprises us that Mangatu Das had surrendered his entire paternal property of 261 acres of land, 50 cows, 10 buffaloes, 24 oxen, 10 he-buffaloes used in ploughing, 2 horses, 25 pieces of bronze utensils and many other items then existing in his possession.[9]

Dhyan Das further stresses the fact that the foundation of the Nadiya Math also initiated a tradition of the *Nad Vanshi* sub-sect of the Dharmdasi branch, which would usually have a *virakta* sadhu as the head of its Math. Sewa Das left for heavenly abode in 1836. He is credited to have composed three religious scriptures-*Paati vandana, Bachan Bahar* and *Nij Anubhuti Sudha* – the texts which were then preserved in manuscript form at the Nadiya Math.

Dhyan Sahib breathed his last in 1831. Born in 1759 (1816 vs) in a village name Kheragram near Bandhogarh, he had met Sewa Sahib at the age of 11. He died at the Kabir Ashram, Pahandangram, a part of then Raipur district. Therefore his *Samadhi* was built in the ashram of the same village.[10] We do have some accounts of Haqnam's arrogance and rough dealing with Sewa Das and the Math founded by him at Nadiya. Haqnam was the then head Mahant at the Singhori Math, the headquarters of the Dharmdasi branch. This split, too, veered around the issue of legitimate succession to the *gaddi* of head Mahant.

While Kabirpanth centers continued to increase in number simultaneous with splits in certain branches, British colonial agencies also began to take note, among many others, of the presence of the Kabirpanth activities in their accounts so that the colonial government might acquire adequate knowledge of indigenous society and culture.

Existing colonial documents on the Kabirpanth suggests that one of the earliest detailed descriptions of Kabirpanth as a Hindu *nirgun* sect can be seen in the imperial survey conducted by Francis Buchanan in various districts of colonial Bengal between 1809 and 1812. His survey[11] incidentally forms part of one of the earliest surveys conducted by the colonial government in the eastern India. That way, his description of the religions and its practitioners in the Bengal province can indisputably be taken by us as a representative account of the colonial government on the matter. Buchanan described the life, beliefs and practices of both lay and *virakta* followers of the panth. He provided us with an objective description of the number of Kabirpanth Maths then existing in some towns and villages which he visited. He went on to describe the specific castes of the founders of some of Maths and factional groups then observed in the sect; such as *Bakataha* and *Sat kavirs* in the then Purnea district of present Bihar. *Bakataha* or *Bhaktahis* in all probability referred to the disciples of the *Bhagodasi* or *Bhagwandasi* branch of the panth, as F.E. Keay also referred to the *Bhakatahis* seen active in Bihar in the 1930s.[12]

We can have a first-hand account of Francis Buchanan in the old Purnea district forming part of the narratives during the first decade of the nineteenth century as follows:

Ramananda had a pupil, who assumed the name of

> Ram-Kavir and who had a pupil named Dharmadas, who denied the corporeal nature of god, and established a new way to heaven, called after his preceptor's name Kavir Panthi, a name well fitted to give fine employment for etymologists in discussing the mysteries of the ancient Kabiri. Dharmadas had a pupil called Baktaha, who discovered another way to heaven. Those who follow both ways are called Kavirs; but the disciples of Dharmadas are called Sat Kavir, and the followers of Baktaha are distinguished by his name. There are in this district a few followers of these Kavirs who live in Akharas like other Ramayits. The chief of the Sat Kavirs in the district is a Mahanta, by birth a Brahman, but he has deserted the world, and lives at Purniya. He has under him several Sudras.... The Kaviri use the *Amarmal*, which gives an account of controversy between Dharmadas and the other Ramayits.[13]

While surveying the district Gorakhpur, Buchanan does not fail to describe the Kabir tomb situated at Magahar, which I consider as a nineteenth century account of Kabir Mazar. To quote his words:

> The adherents of the Kavirpanth (sic) are far from numerous, although a tomb, where that personage was buried, is still shown at Magahar, is a good deal frequented. I found no person more intelligent than Bibekdas of Patna, to give me a better account of doctrines of this sect, which is here reckoned by the Brahmanas a damnable heresy (*Nastik*). I shall therefore here confine myself to the history given by

the keeper of the tomb. A certain Muhammedan weaver of Benares had married a girl in the vicinity, and was bringing her home, when she, being dry, went aside to the tank called Chandatal, near that city, to quench her thrist. She found there a beautiful child floating on a leaf of the Nelumbium (Kamal), which miraculously bore the infant on the suface of water. Although the child was apparently new born, it could speak on proper occasions, and refused to drink water or milk from his nurse's hand; but directed, that there should be brought to him a two year's old cow, which of course had never bred; but he sucked her whenever he required nourishment. As the child thus showed an aversion to the faith in Muhammed, a Brahman was employed to give it a name, and it directed, that this should be Kavir. Some years afterwards the weaver wished to have the child but Kavir declined this ceremony, and became anxious to receive *Upadesa* from the Pandits; but they declined entrusting him with this secret, as he consorted with the Muhammedans. Kavir had therefore recourse to stratagem, and one night laid himself privately at the door of a cell, where a holy man dwelt. Towards morning the saint, having occasion to come out, stumbled over Kavir, who, as usual among the natives on such occasions, called out, "father, father," (*Baap re Bap*); but the good man, not knowing the impurity of Kavir, answered, "do not call on your father, but say Rama Rama." Kavir seized on these words, and insisted that they were an *Upadesa* , and in fact the whole instruction usually given by the Hindu sages to the low tribes consists of the name of some god, which they wish to pray. Kavir then became celebrated for his learning and sanctity, and went to Jagannath, where *Raja* Indradyumna had been in vain attempting to rear the celebrated temples; but the sea had repeatedly swept away the buildings. Kavir having blessed the work, it has remained untouched ever since, and a monument has been there erected to his memory. He then visited several remarkable places, until he came to Magahar 540 years ago (A.D.1274), and there he apparently died. His disciples were partly Moslems, partly Hindus; but the former seized his corpse, and buried it according to their rites, at which the Hindus were enraged, wishing to have had it burned. While the disciples were in eager dispute about this important point, Kavir, who was in fact at Brindaban, and had only shaken off his old body, sent them word, that if they would open his grave, they might save themselves the trouble of disputing about his body. This was accordingly done, and nothing could be found, except a delicious fragrance... When Kavir went to Brindaban, he appointed 12 disciples, each of whom formed a Panth or route to heaven, but most people adhere to that of Dharmadas, a Kasongdhan Baniya. This is the account given by the Muhhamedan, who calls himself a follower of Kavir; but says, that he also adheres to the prophet, and Koran.. Kavir, besides his celebrity as a divine, has acquired reputation as a poet, and is said not only to have celebrated the battles and loves of demigods and heroes, which will always be considered the most interesting themes of poetical effusion; but has

> chosen subjects more suited to the taste of some of our modern composers, such as frogs, weavers and their wives, and the like. He differs indeed from our worthies, and does not treat these subjects seriously, but imitates the blindness of old Homer in making sport of such characters.[14]

We can then see Buchanan's account of the Kabirpanth in the then old district of Patna in the following:

> The Kavirs in this district have some followers, and their Gurus take the name of Vairagi, whether they have originally been Brahmans or Sudras. Several women have taken this order, among whom is Bibekdas, born in the west in the family of a Kanojiya Brahman. Shc is reckoned the most intelligent person of the sect in Patna, and gives me the following information. She reads in the vulgar language, and is not at all affected in her manners. She does not even wear a veil, and visited me without hesitation. The Kavir do not give any secret form of prayer, but in its place instruct their followers in their doctrine; nor do they worship images. They reject the fire worship (hom), all sacrifices. They pray to none of the Hindu gods; but apply to Kavir alone, and conceive that he is omnipresent, and the same with Parabrahma, and that all souls are a part of the divine essence. She considers the Purans, & c. as of no authority. The proper name of their convents is Sthan, and the chief of Sthan is properly called Sadhu, although, in the country, the convent is usually called Akhara, and the chief Mahanta. The Vairagis male and female never marry, and they have no Purohits.

When they die they may be either buried or thrown into the river. Some married man act as Gurus, but my informant considers this as quite irregular, although some of them are alleged to be descended of Dharmadas, but these reside in Bundelkhanda. I suspect that these married men are of Baktaha sect, for whom Bibekdas seems to profess a great abhorrence. The Kavirs have in fact divided into 12 Panthas, all on very bad terms with each other, but I have not learned the circumstances which have given rise to their schisms. The flocks of Kavirs apply to Purohits, and these pray for their employers to any gods that they please; but they are not allowed to eat or kill anything that has life, nor to offer sacrifices. Although these Kavirs seem to differ as much as the Buddhists from the commonly received opinions, and are perhaps a remnant of that ancient sect, or at least have adopted many of its tenets, they are admitted to be orthodox (*astik*), and are usually said to be sect of Vishnu; and this do not deny, because Kavir, the master of Dharmadas, was a pupil of Ramananda. Dharmdas appears to have been a weaver, and perhaps originally a Muhammedan, from which sect he has probably borrowed several of his ideas. The hatred between the Ramanandis and Kavirs is very bitter, nor do I know that the former and the Dasnami Sannyasis look on each other with a more pure ecclesiastic bitterness. The Ramanandis deny that Dharmadas was a pupil of Kavir, and, sect of the Kavir is evidently quite modern, it seems to have been in order to show that Dharmadas could not have been a pupil of Kavir, that they have

> invented the fable of Ramananda, the master of Kavir, having been contemporary with Alexander, the Great.[14]

Buchanan further points out that the Kabir *Mazar* as developed by the turn of nineteenth century had come to have two establishments; the recently developed one in the charge of the Hindu Mahants and the other, the original tomb, in the Muslim care-takers. To quote him once again:

> At Magahar is a tomb of Kavir, whom Abul Fazil calls the Unitarian, and it is difficult to say whether he was a Mohammedan or a pagan, as I shall afterwards have occasion to explain. The present buildings were erected by Nawab Fedi Khan, who about 200 years ago, was Superintendent (*Chuklahdar*) of Gorukhpoor (sic). They are in a very good repair, but are not large, and are totally destitute of elegance. The place where Kavir was buried is under the charge of a Muhammedan disciple, whose ancestors have held the office ever since the funeral; while the monuments of the first Hindu Mahants, which contains his ashes and unburnt bones is under charge of his successor. Both are objects of worship, each person taking the offerings that are made at the place, of which he was charge. About 5000 assemble annually at the fair (mela) and there are many occasional visits.[15]

In his account on the Kavir panthis of then Shahabad district, he goes on to share with us the exact number of Kabirpanthi gurus living in the Bhojpur Kingdom, major part of the district. To quote him- "1/16 of the Hindu follow the new routes to heaven: the Kavir Panth has 10 Gurus,who occupy Mathiyas, some of them married,some single; while there are 20 persons,that adhere to the docrine of the Siva Narayan."[16] It is noteworthy that Buchanan had applied the measure of 16 *annas* as a unit and one *anna* then comprised of the Kabirpanthis.

The significant point that requires emphasis is slightly more complex. Buchanan's description of the sectarians dimensions in Gangetic Bihar and eastern Uttar Pradesh took two distinct forms. On the one hand, Buchanan conceived of three main divisions of Hindu religion: Shiva-Shakta, Vaishnava and *panthi* (the more recent "routes to heaven" espoused by Kabir, Nanak and the like). On the other hand, within these large divisions were religious communities organized around the institutional ties of Gurus, which usually took monastic form. Dasnami sanyasis represented the main shaiva monastic group; Ramanandis (often referred to as Ramawats) the main Vaishnava monastic group. The main panthi community that emerges in Buchanan's accounts was the Nanakpanth, associated with the teaching of Guru Nanak, which was particularly influential in south Bihar, then emerging as the golden mines of raw materials to be exploited by the British colonial rulers.

About adecade later, H.H. Wilson,[17] a European orientalist writing his articles on the conditions of the Hindu religion and sects, originally for the *Asiatic Researches* during 1828 and 1832, described the Kabirpanth as a Hindu sect among many others. He was a Boden Professor of Sanskrit, in the University of

Oxford, previously an Assistant Surgeon in the service of EIC, chiefly at Calcutta and Benares. More famous as the translator of the *Meghdutta*, he returned to England in 1832 and died there in 1860. In India, he had spent almost 19 years in various services of the East India Company. He is also known as worthy successor of Sir William Jones and H. T. Colebrooke. Quite interestingly, Wilson also found Kabirpanth's beliefs and practices different from the Brahmanical Hindu tradition. He however considered Kabirpanth, including many other *Vaishnava* sects, as a part of such a diverse Hindu tradition. According to him:

> ....it is no part of their faith, however to worship any Hindu deity, or to observe any of the rites or ceremonials of the Hindus, whether orthodox or schismatical, such of their members as are living in the world conform outwardly to all the usages of their tribe and caste, and some of them even pretend to worship the usual divinities, although this is considered as going rather farther than is justifiable. Those who have however abandoned the fetters of society, abstain from all the ordinary practices, and address their homage, chiefly in chanting Hymns, exclusively to the invisible Kabir.[18]

To him, Kabir was, in all probability, a generic rather than an individual denomination! It implied that Kabir, the *Satguru* of the lakhs of panth followers and the most prominent inspirer of a number of religious traditions in India was not a historical figure. Yet, as he found, Kabir's followers 'are included amongst the Vaishnava sect', which is still attested by many followers whom I have till date interviewed. To quote him:

> As to Kabir's being a Mohammedan, I shall allude to the improbability, I may say impossibility, of this in the text; nor is Col. Malcolm more accurate when he calls him a celebrated Sufi.....Indeed I think it not all improbable that no such person as Kabir ever existed, and that his name is a mere cover to the innovations of some freethinker amongst the Hindus; perhaps some one of those considered as his principal disciples: his names are very suspicious, and Jnani, the sage, or kabir, the greatest, are generic rather than individual denominations....nothing more than the Takhallus, or assumed names...[19]

He also attempted to study their political inclinations in particular, their relationship with the then dominant *sagun* sectarian group known as *Ramavats* or *Ramanandis*. In this respect, he observed that 'the *Ramavats* especially' maintain a 'friendly intercourse and political alliance' with the Kabirpanthis.

Explaining the spread of these followers largely in North India alone, he attributed it to 'the doctrine of outward conformity and the absence of visible objects of worship' preventing this sect from spreading 'very generally throughout India.' He found the concentration of these followers in upper and central India except in Bengal. He further pointed out that unlike several Hindu sects, "their [Kabirpanthi] mendicants also never solicit alms, and in this capacity even they are less obnoxious than the many religious vagrants, whom the rank soil of Hindu superstition and the enervating operation of an Indian climate so plentifully engender."[20]

It is necessary to bear in mind that Wilson too finds faint resemblance of Kabirpanth with certain groups of Christianity where he compares their practices to the 'quaker' but very cautiously, as an actual successor of William Jones and Colebrooke, the forefront orientalists of the time. To quote him, where he explains, that the "*quaker*-like spirit of the sect, their abhorrence of all violence, their regard for truth and the inobtrusiveness of their opinions render them very inoffensive members of the state."[21]

He further noted that the Kabirpanth was then divided into twelve branches excluding some important branches of the present states of Gujarat and Maharashtra. He described the divisions of the Kabirpanth as then prevalent as follows:[22] Surat Gopal Das; Bhago Das, the author of *Bijak*: his successor resides at Dhanauti; Narayan Das and 4. Churaman Das, sons of Dharam Das at Bandho near Jabbalpur (sic), *Vansh* Dori; 5. Jaggo Das, the *Gaddi* at Cuttack; 6. Jivan Das, the founder of Satnami Sect, 7. Kamal of Bombay 8. Taksali of Baroda 9. Jnani of Majjhani near Sahasram; 10. Sahib Das of Cuttack, known as Mulpanthis 11. Nityanand, 12. Kamalnad, settled somewhere in Deccan.

He goes on to apprise us of the distinctive attire and common practices of the Kabirpanth devotees then noted by him. We can have thus an idea of the Kabirpanthis of the early nineteenth century in his words:

> ...such of their members as are living in the world conform outwardly to all the usages of their tribe and caste, and some of them even pretend to worship the usual divinities, although this is considered as going rather farther than is justifiable. Those who

> have however abandoned the fetters of society, abstain from all the ordinary practices and address their homage, chiefly in chanting Hymns, exclusively to the invisible Kabir: they use no peculiar mode of dress and some of them go nearly naked, without objecting however to clothe themselves in order to appear dressed, where clothing is considered decent or respectful-the Mahants wear a small scull cap: the frontal marks, if worn, are usually those of the vaishanava sects, or they make a streak with Sandal, or Gopichandan along the ridge of the nose: a necklace and rosary of Tulasi are also worn by them, but all these outward signs are considered of no importance, and the inward man is the only essential point to be attended to.[23]

Wilson appears to be the earliest scholar who attempts at offering us the numerical strength of the Kabirpanth followers particularly in a specific gathering taking place during the early decades of the above century. He writes that:

> Chet Singh also attempted to form some estimate of the numbers of the sect, and if we may credit the result, they must be very considerable indeed, as at a grand meeting or mela, which he instituted near Benares, no fewer than 35000 Kabir Panthis of the Monastic and Mendiacant class are said to have been collected".[24]

Towards the end of the nineteenth century, we have works of two different types: a voluminous compendium on *Modern Hinduism* by W.J. Wilkins[25] and the other data and details provided by the first and second censuses of British colonial administrators. Wilkins devotes roughly five pages of his work to the description of Kabirpanth. The Kabirpanth, to him, was being "regarded as belonging to the *vaishnavas* though the members need not worship the Hindu deities; and where they do so it is more out of compliance to the wishes of others than from any good they expect from themselves."[26]

Further, the first census of British India, which was directly conducted by the British government in 1872, too, did not seem to follow the so-called pan-Indian project when it came to categorizing the Kabirpanth as a sect which did not recognize caste. However, we do have numerical data on the Kabirpanthis of several other regions of colonial India at least till the censuses of the early 20th century. If one takes into consideration the census data, Kabirpanth, by the late nineteenth century, had begun to emerge somewhat as a separate religion with its specific feature of a casteless religious community as was earlier observed in case of the Sikh religion in the Punjab. Some of these followers thus began to demonstrate that the Kabirpanth was different from the Great traditions of Hinduism and Islam. Moreover, such a process was not specific to a particular sect but seen among different religious traditions all over India.

According to the first census report,[27] the Kabirpanth had a number of followers who entered 'Kabirpanth' as their separate religion in the prescribed census enumeration form given to them at the time of collecting requisite information for the purpose. In Tirhut division alone, the total number of Kabirpanthis[28] having entered it as their caste was 418. From the second decennial census of the Bengal province, however, the data on the Kabirpanthis became unavailable for the simple reason of their insignificant political role in the total schema of British rule – the reason as stated by the census officials in the same report. To quote the census report itself:

> The fact is that any such details for Bengal would be perfectly worthless, whether regarded from a statistical, a religious or a political point of view. The figure would have been inaccurate because hardly any Hindu in Bengal know to what sect they belong, and in practice it was found that the information was entirely omitted in millions of cases. Secondly the political or social importance whatever attaches in these provinces to these sectarian details, for it is seldom that, as in other parts of India, jarring sects break the peace of cities or rival preachers galvanise the countryside, and when it has been stated that Bengal Hindus are broadly divided into Saivism and Vaishnavism, all that is needed has been said.[29]

The early censuses of the British India also talk of the acceptance of Kabir as their liberator for most of the weaver castes such as *Julahas, Meghs and Batwals* particularly in the Panjab region. The report found that Julahas in the region were synonymous to *Bona, Bona-Kabir, Kabir-bansi, Kabirpanthi.*[30] There have been a number of groups of Kabir disciples particularly in parts of present Panjab, Haryana and Himachal Pradesh, which still call themselves Kabir-Banshi Kabirpanthi. In the census reports of Panjab in 1881, Kabirpanth was, however, considered as one of the old religious sects. The old sect in the census was just one of the groups of the six main heads of the Hindu religion, the same categorization which characterized, unlike the Bengal Province, all the succeeding Censuses in Punjab till 1941.

According to Sir Denzil Ibbetson, the main architect of the first systematic census of Punjab in 1881, these six main heads of sects were: i. Old Sects ii. Reformers, iii. Sects essentially of low castes, iv. Miscellaneous Sects, v. Sects analogous to other religions and vi. Unspecified.[31] Descriptions of these religious groups including Kabirapnth from 1881 onwards in these reports throw valuable light on many developments then obtaining in the religious sphere.

He also found it apt to point out the comparative strength of Kabirpanthis in the region. In this context, he wrote that 'the sect of Kabirpanthis is probably better known in the Gangetic Valley than in the Punjab'. He further informs us about the geographical distribution of these followers in this region.

H.A. Ross[32] had however found most of the Hindu Julaha caste identifying themselves as a Kabirbanshi in his ethnographic glossary. Ross had reported that these Julahas related their descent from the lineage of Kamali, the alleged daughter of Kabir. It also implied thereby that Kabir to them, had been a married saint, had a son and a daughter. Following Kabir they never felt to abandon family life, as Kamal and Kamali too had led a family life. They have been followers of Kabir, not because they have been initiated into the Kabirpanth by a guru, but for their lineage as the descendants of Kabir's son and daughter. Although Kadar Nath

Dvivedi[33] considers them as a separate branch of the Kabirpanth, but, to me, it would not be fair to categorize them into a distinct branch.

Describing the groups of the Kabir followers particularly among Julahas in the old Panjab region, Ibbetson provides us following details on them in 1881:

> The Kabirpanthis are the followers of Kabir Bhagat, *Chela* (disciple) of Ramanand, founder of the Ramanandi sect of the Bairagis. Kabir is said to have been born at Benares and adopted by a Musalman Julaha during the reign of Sikandar Shah Lodi (1488-1512 A.D.). The story goes that Kabir wished to be Ramanand's chela but he refused to adopt him as he was a Muhammadan. So one day Kabir lay down on the road by which Ramanand went to bathe in the Ganges every morning, and by chance Ramanand touched him with his foot. He exclaimed "Ram, Ram," so Kabir took the word *Ram* as his Guru mantra and assumed the *mala* or beads and *tilak* or forehead mark of a *Bairagi*. At first Ramanand was opposed to him, but after some discussion he accepted him as his chela. His doctrine and precepts are very popular and are embodied in the *Sukh Nidhan Granth,* the *Bijak* and other poems.[34]
>
> Kabir used to earn his livelihood by weaving blankets which he sold for 7 takkas a piece. One day Falsehood (*Jhuth*) appeared to him in human guise and urged him to demand 12 takkas instead of 7: he did so but only received 9, so he said,
>
> *Sache Kahan to mariye—Jhuthe jagat Patiawe,*
> *Sat take Ka Bhura,— Mera nau take bik Jawe.* (" If I speak the truth, I shall suffer, since the world is

> content with lies, so I spoke false and sold my blanket for 9 *takkas*.")
>
> Since then falsehood has been rife in the world. Starch owes its origin to a sparrow having let its droppings fall on Kabir's cloth, as he was weaving. Every weaver invokes Kabir or Luqman on beginning work.

Ibbetson also saw particular need to describe the strong-hold of Kabirpanth among Julahas, a weaver community, which had identified themselves with Kabir. To quote:

> As a Kabirpanthi or the follower of Kabir's teaching, the Julaha calls himself Kabirbansi or a descendant of Kabir, just as the Chhimba prefers to be called Namdevi (descendant of Namdeo). They will never take a false oath in the names of these supposed ancestors and even when in the right, seldom venture to swear by them. Both castes are offended at the ordinary names of Julaha and Darzi, i.e., Chhimba)......
>
> The Julahas, like the darzis, are recruited from various castes, but especially from the Dhanak and Chamar below, whereas the tailors are recruited from the castes above them.
>
> Many of the Julahas in the Punjab return their caste as Kabirbansi and many of those who return their sect as Kabirbansi or Kabirpanthis, are probably little more than ordinary weavers who have no idea of distinguishing themselves from other Hindu weavers in matters of doctrine.[35]
>
> The Kabirbansi are found in Ambala and Kangra, and

> apparently this word has become a true tribal name and now includes Musalman Julahas. It is derived from the great Bhagat Kabir of Benares who was himself a Julaha, and whose teaching most of the Hindu Julahas profess to follow.[36]
> On the other hand the Hindu Julahas of these Phulkian States are divided into sectarian groups, such as the Ramdasis and Kabirpanthis.[37]

H.A. Ross further draws our attention to the dominant character of the Kabirpanthis in that:

> It is noticeable, too, that Kabir instead of impressing on his disciples, like most Hindu leaders, the necessity of absolute adherence to the Guru, was fond of stimulating enquiry and encouraging criticisms of his own utterances."Kabir Panthis of Rankhandi[38]

We also have some information on the then prevailing rituals among these followers in this census of 1881.

> It is however very doubtful if the view that Kabir was probably a Muhammadan Sufi can be accepted with confidence and Dr. G. A. Grierson would regard the sect founded by Kabir as one of the Bhakti-sects. A common feature of many of those sects is the *Mahaprasada* or sacramental meal. On the evening of the appointed day, the worshippers assemble and the mahant or leading Mahant, reads a brief address, and then allows a short interval for prayer and meditation. All who feel themselves unworthy to proceed further then withdraw to a distance. Those that remain approach the senior celebrant in turn and placing their hands together receive into the palm of

the right hand, which is uppermost, small consecrated water and two other articles of consecrated food. They then approach another celebrant, who pours into the palm of the right hand a few drops of water, which they drink. This food and water are regarded as Kabir's special gift, and it is said that all who receive it worthily will have eternal life. Part of the sacramental food is 'reserved' and is carefully kept from pollution for administration to the sick. It is possible that this rite was borrowed from the Jesuit missionaries at Agra, the rite is now likely to be a survival of historical influences.

The Kabirpanthi sadhus or faqirs in this Province wear generally clothes dyed with brickdust colour (geru); and both they and the laity abstain from flesh and spirits. The present followers of Kabir hold an intermediate position between idolatry and monotheism, but the mission of Kabir himself is generally looked on as one directed against idolatry; and at Kauwardeh, near Ballabgarh, in the Delhi district, there is a community of Kabirpanthis descended from an Aggarwal *Bania* of Puri, who used to travel with 52 cart-loads of Shivs and Saligrams behind him, but who was convinced by Kabir of the error of his ways. The sect of Kabirpanthis is probably better known in the south east of the province; but considerable numbers are also returned from Sialkot and Gurdaspur, and it is said that the Meghs and Batwals, so common in those districts, are very generally Kabirpanthis. The sect is also very largely recruited from the Chamar (leather worker and Julaha (weaver) castes, and it is open to men of all classes to

> become Kabirpanthis. The Kabirpanthi will almost always describe himself as a Hindu, but a certain number have returned the name as that of an independent religion and some as a sect of the Sikhs.[39]

About the Dharmdasi branch, Ibbetson outlined that 'An offshoot of the sect is the Dharm Dasias, founded by a wealthy merchant of Benares who turned sadhu. The Dharm Dasias, however appear to differ in no way from the Kabirpanthis in doctrine, and they are very rarely found in the Punjab.[40]

Ibbetson had also noted a distinct caste of *Kabirwah*, a Rajput clan (agricultural) in then district of Multan. [41]

It was the Punjab where the most popular and voluminous text of the Dharmdasi branch titled *Kabir-Mansur* was first published in 1881.[42] It was written by Parmanand, a native of village Doda, near Ferozpur and Muktasar of then Panjab, as he himself introduced in the first edition of the voluminous scripture. Madhavacharya, the translator of the original Urdu text, points out the opposition of radical Sikhs to Parmanand's *Kabir Mansur* and said to have compelled the author to publish revised version of the book in *samvat* 1885 (1942). However the increasing readership of the book led to the publication of its third revised version in April 1927.

We find further tabulation of Kabirpanthis among many other groups showing their percentage in the total population of the Hindus in the British India in the Census Report. In Table IV of Vol. II, which should be read with the tables preceding it, the proportion borne by the professors of any one religion to the total population is shown for each province and for the total

Empire. From this it will be observed that every 10,000 of the entire population in India consists of the following religious elements- [43]

Hindoos	7,402	*Satnamis	16
Mahammedans	1,974	*Kabirpanthis	14
Aboriginals	253	*Nat worshippers	6
Buddhists	135	*Nat worshippers	5
Christians	73	*Jews	5
Sikhs	73	Parsees	3
Jains	48	Unspecified	2

It will be seen from these figures that the Hindoos (sic) form virtually three fourths of the entire population. The remaining one fourth of the population is thus distributed—Eight tenths are Mahammedans, one tenth aboriginals and of the remaining one tenth the Buddhists form nearly one half; of the remaining one twentieth the Christains and Sikhs in equal numbers comprise six tenths, the Jains constitute two tenths, the Satnamis and Kabirpanthis three twentieths, and the Parsees, Jews, Brahmos, and unspecified making up the remainder.[44]

We have the most elaborate details on the social, numerical and religious life of the Kabirpanthis then living in the Central Provinces of the British India. The numerical strength of these followers in each divisions of the Provinces can be seen in the report of the Census of 1881.[45] It enumerates the total number of male and female Kabirpanthis in the Central Provinces as 347994 and 171691 respectively. Table IV contains their number obtained in each division of the Provinces. Nagpur division had a total of 4599 male and 3210 female devotees, Jubbalpore (sic) 5656 and 4178, Nurbadda (sic) or Hoshangabad 2392 and 1684 and Chhattisgarh had 63758 and 50007 having highest number among all the divisions.[46]

The Kabirpanthis were also only recorded in the Central Provinces, though they undoubtedly were to be found in small numbers in other parts of India. They were 50,000 less in numbers than the Satnamis, who, according to Mr. Bath, "are, in a way, branches sprung from the sect of Kabir".[47]

Regarding the religious doctrines of the Kabirpanthis, he gives the following information:

> The most perfect representative of the reforming movement was Kabir, or, as his disciples, who revere in him as an incarnation of the deity, also surname him, Juanim, the one who has knowledge, the seer. So little is known of a positive kind Juanim, the one who has knowledge, the seer, in regard to this remarkable man that some have gone so far as to doubt his existence. The most probable hypothesis is that he was born at Benares, and was of the weaver caste. That he was a Vairagin of the sect of Ramananda, perhaps as tradition surmises, an immediate disciple of that master, and that he taught at the beginning of 15th century, the legend making him live 300 years, from 1149 to 1449. Kabir has left no writings, but his sect possesses pretty numerous collections in Hindee (sic). The composition of which is, with more or less reason, ascribed to his first disciples, in which are preserved a great number of the sayings of the master, forming at times pieces to some exent, in verse as well as in dialogues, reproducing controversies which are in part,certainly

imaginary and in which he is the interlocutor. In these teachings of his, Kabir sets himself against the whole body of Hindu superstitions. He rejects and ridicules the Shastras and the Puranas; he severely chastises the arrogance and hypocrisy of the Brahmins; he rejects every malevolent distinction of caste, religion and sect. All who love God and do good are brothers, be they Hindoos or Mussulmans. Idolatry and everything which approaches to it or may suggest it is severely condemned. The temple ought to be only a house of prayer. He tolerates among his disciples neither practice that are too demonstrative nor irregularities of custom, nor any of those external marks which are the distinctive badge of the Hindoo sects, and which serve only to divide men. Yet not to scandalize a neighbour, he enjoins on them conformity to usage in indifferent matters, he recommends renunciation and contemplative life; but he demands, above all, moral purity. And does not restrict it to one particular kind of life. All authority in the matter of faith and morals belong to the Guru. Yet obedience to his commands must not be blind obedience, and a reservation is expressly made on behalf of the rights and conscience of the believer. Of these features taken separately, there are not many which we do not meet with again more or less elsewhere in the past history of the sectarian religions. But the whole is new, and singularly recalls the quetism of the Moslem. This resemblance has been recognized in India itself. But Mahammedans claim Kabir as one of themselves, and among the Hindoos there is a widespread tradition which represents him as a converted Mussulman. One thing is certain, that Kabir was much occupied with Islam. His aim obviously was to found a unitary religion which would unite in the same faith the Hindoos and the followers of the Prophet; and with that view he assailed the intolerance of the Koran and the fanaticism of the *Molahs* with no less vigour that the prejudices of his compatriots. We cannot doubt that the spectacle of Islam with its triumphant monotheism, its severely spiritualistic worship, its large fraternity and its morality practically so incontestably superior to Hindooism, left a very deep impression on his mind. At the same time this impression appears to have been only quite general. Kabir was indifferently acquainted with the Mussulman theology; his god is neither that of the Koran, nor that of Suffism, nor that of the Vedanta. The mantra of initiation with which he receives his disciples is in the name of Rama; and notwithstanding the very exquisite profession which he makes of monotheism, he seems to have himself admitted, anyhow those who believed in him afterwards admitted, the majority of the personifications of Hindooism. The numbers of this sect, the Kabirpanthis, those who follow the path of Kabir, form at present twelve principal branches, which have remained in communion with one another inspite of sundry differences with regard to both doctrine and practice and their centre is at Benares; but we meet with them throughout the whole presidency of Bengal, in Gujarat, in Central India, and far as the Deccan. Their number, difficult to estimate because

> of the pains they take to conform to the customs in the midst of which they live, appears to be pretty considerable. At the end of last century, their religions order by itself alone contributed, it is said, 35,000 of those who took part in a mela held at Benares; and they are still more influential than numerous. Kabir himself is revered as a saint by forming sects and his influence is visible in all of them. [48]

The following extracts are taken from a memorandum on the Kabirpanthis by Mr. Sadashiv Vithal, an Inspector of schools in the Chhindwara district of the present Chhattisgarh as attached in the report of this Census.

> The head-quarters of the Kabirpanthi sect, in the Chhindwara district, are at Singhori, a fair-sized village on the Narsimghpur road, about 14 miles north of Chhindwara, where Anandi Das, the Mahant of prior, with a following of 12 byragees or priests, lives. This is the village where the head of the faith, at present resident at Kawardha, is said to have resided before removing to Bilaspur .... Kabir aimed at bringing all, Hindu and Mussulman (sic) alike, within the pale of the new faith. The date of the appearance of Kabir is given in the Suksit Dhyan (one of the books kept at Singhori) as Samvat 1524 or AD 1467. Kabir seems to have been the followers of Ramanand, who is said (Arya Darpan, September 1880, page 209) to have had 12 disciples, among whom were Rohidas Chamar and Kabir Julaha. The latter, however, went much further than his master, and discarded all the Hindu incarnations, teaching the worship of Nirankar, or the formless being. He denounced as false both the

teaching of the Purans and Vedas, and also the teachings of Mahomed. At present the chief ordinances of the faith as preached and practised in this district are–(1) to avoid idol worship; (2) to perform no pilgrimages to Hindu holy places; (3) not to touch any spirituous liquor or flesh. The prohibition of the use of tobacco (Betul Settlement Report) does not seem to be known in the district, so far as the laity are concerned and intermarriages and funeral services are conducted according to caste rules. There is no prohibition against the admission of any caste into the faith; and as a matter of fact there is a considerable number of Koshtis, Kunbis, Telis, Gaolis, Sonars, Mahesris and Chamars (besides other castes), who are Kabirpanthis, and also a few Mussulmans. The tendency now, however, is towards excluding some of the lower castes; and the Singhori priest informs me that the conversion of Chamars is neither attempted, nor, indeed, allowed in this district. Also, though theoretically there is no distinction of caste among Kabirpanthis in all but the name. The ceremony of initiation is very simple. Persons who wish to be ordinary Kabirpanthis and the orthodox of the same caste eat together and intermarry. The ceremony of initiation is very simple. Persons who wish to be ordinary Kabirpanthis are generally admitted to the faith at the residence of the Mahant, though this is not essential. The only necessaries are that a small the password (mantra) is then blown, in the orthodox manner, into the ear of the convert and he is presented with some betel leaves and sweetmeats; a necklace of...[49]

The recognition of the Kabirpanth was further underlined by adding an account of 'Kabirpanthism', furnished by Babu Tarudas Banerjee, a pleader at Raipur, and printed in the Central Provinces Report;-

> "According to the Kabirpanthis, Kabir, whom they call 'Sahib,' first appeared as a boy at Mathura and was not born of woman. From Mathura he proceeded to Benares and thence to Jagganath, performing miracles all the way. One coming to a place called Bando, he made Dharamdas a Kasundia-*Bania*, his chela or disciple, and it was this man who, on the death of Kabir, became the head of the Kabirpanthis and settled at Kawardha, where his family still continue on the gadi (throne) as the hereditary Gurus (high priests) of the sect. According to Kabir, no caste distinction are allowed; every man, irrespective of his colour or creed, is eligible to Kabirism and Hindus and Mahammedans partake of food from each others' hands after initation. Kindness to life in all forms is inculcated. But on the death of Kabir, at Mugher, the religion promulgated by him underwent those changes that have given it elasticity and life. Renunciation of caste ceased to be a *sine quo non* preliminary of system untouched and called on his followers only to worship Kabir, and to abstain from killing animals. From Gawadhan upwards all ceremonies are performed by Hindu priests, according to established ritual, without creating any scandal amongst the Kabiris. It is this spirit of compromise and tolerance which has spread Kabirism thoughout the greater part of India.

The Hierarchy—-" The chief Guru lives at Kawardha, in Zilla Bilaspur. He does not appear to be more learned than his disciples, and is more careful of his own secular concerns than of the spiritual welfare of his followers. He appoints a certain number of deputies called bhandaries and mahants from the more advanced of his followers, who, after paying a good amount for the privilege, go on recouping themselves from contribution by their own disciples, of whom they always manage to get together a good number. They are not bound to observe celibacy, but a good many assume that state for the peculiar sanctity that is always ascribed by the multitude to it. The Guru resides at Kawardha, but his mahants are spread all over the country. Besides these mahants and bhandaries there are a number of hereditary 'gadiwalas,' the principal of whom live at Kudhurmal, in the Korba Zemindari, in Bilaspur, and at Bangoli, in Tehsili Simga. Every one of these has to send a certain amount to the Sahiv according to his income, but they always retain a good round sum for themselves. The lineal descendants of Dharmadas are called 'Gadiwalas,' and have always the word 'nam' annexed to their names, e.g., 'Ugranam,' 'Sheshnam,' & c., whereas the word 'nam' annexed to their names, e.g., 'Ugranam,' Sheshnam,' & c., whereas the collateral branches, a good many of whom live at Dargaon, Tahsil Durg, in Raipur, are called 'Shakha Banda,' and have the affix 'Das' attached to their names. According to no reliance can be placed on these numbers. One of these' Shakha Bansis,' at Dhamtari, has thrown off his allegiance to the 'Sahib' at

Kawardha, and has proclaimed himself a 'Sahiv.' He has got a good many followers on that side of the district, but his celebrity is but a local one, he and his followers being considered by the generality of the orthodox Kabiris nothing but heretics.

Sadhus : Unlike the Chamars, all of whom follow some sort of secular profession or other, the Kabirpanthis have got a pretty large body amongst them, who, though not professing celibacy like the Hindu Byragees, yet resemble them a good deal in their habits and customs. Dressed in a peculiar style, they go about in pairs begging from door to door, reciting moral precepts in verse to the accompaniment of a single-stringed instrument resembling a guitar, and two pieces of black wood beaten one against the other to keep time. They profess allegiance to the 'Sahib' at Kawardha, but keep their earnings to themselves. They are generally well versed in the doctrines of other sects, when they defend and elucidate their positions by quotations from the metrical polemics of Kabir. It is thus that a good many people belonging to the lower orders of Hindus are annually converted to Kabirism, but the substantial benefit of the conversion is reaped by the nearest gadivwala or mahant, as the Sadhus cannot make chelas except by special permission of the 'Sahib' at Kawardha. It is worthy of note that in the Central Provinces almost the whole of the Kabirpanthis are *Gharbaris*, i.e, married people, whereas in Northern India the greater part of them are Nihangs, i.e., devotees vowed to celibacy, who go about the country with a sort of roving commission.

> **Principal Castes** : The largest number of Kabirpanthis in Chhatisgarh are Telis, Gandas and Pakas, which classes have en masse adopted Kabirism. But other castes also occur in numbers, Brahmins (rare), Chhatris, *Bania*s, Naus, Dhobis and Mahammedans, all classes were invited to join the fraternity. The Chhatri and Brahman are expelled from caste on their conversion to Kabirpanthis of the present day recognize and retain caste distinctions as tenaciously as the most orthodox Hindus. Ordinarily no Kabirpanthis of one caste would eat food cooked by a member of another, and it is only when they meet at Kawardha on some festive occasion that the rule is somewhat relaxed for the occasion, on the same principle, perhaps that induces Hindus to partake of food brought by any one at Jaganath. The different castes of course never intermarry. It is their social relations, habits, and superstition, the Kabirpanthis differ but slightly from the Satnamis.[50]

Except the Bengal Province, we have detailed statistics on Kabirpanthis of almost all the provinces. For the United Provinces, we have further details in the enthnographic study of William Crooke:

> The sect is open to both Hindus and Musalmans, and perhaps in consequence of this it is not a favourite with men of high caste. Most of its adherents, in these Provinces at least, are drawn from most of its adherents, in these provinces at least, are drawn from the inferior castes, as the lower Banyas, Sunars, Lohars, Koiris, Koris, Kachhis, Kumhars, Barhais,

Chamars and Julahas. Among the weaving castes it is, as has been said already, extremely popular. There is no regular formula of initiation (mantra). The introduction of a neophyte is performed in this way. A piece of ground in the monastery or in the house of the candidate is carefully cleaned and plastered. In this is placed a pitcher full of water, in the mouth of which are fixed some mango twigs (palao); on the pitcher a lamp is lighted with ghi and an offering is made consisting of sandal, holy rice (achchat) and flowers and incense is burned. A garland of flowers is placed round the neck of the pitcher and the core of a cocoa-nut with some *batasha* sweetmeats is offered. Some camphor is burnt and the neophyte sits in the holy square before the Guru, who makes him say the words:-

'*Satya purusha ko swans se hriday men japo.*' "Repeat the name of the true being within you with breath."

The disciple then with his joined hands thrice makes obeisance to the Guru and utters thrice the words, Bandagi Sahib! "My service to the Master." This is the common form, but the ritual with the more learned Mahants is of an elaborate type. After this, the Guru teaches the disciple the Gayatri or Morning Prayer and the Sandhya Sumiran or evening prayer. This Gayatri is not the usual Hindu form –'Tat savitar varenyam bhargo devasya dhimahi dhiyo yo nah prachodayat'- "Let us mediatate on that excellent glory of the Divine Vivifying Sun: may he enlighten our understanding." The Kabirpanthi Gayatri is a song (*bani*) composed by Kabir himself and runs as follows:-

Kabir din duni darbesha dwar salamat lekha; Tum rund mund men pira;Tum phaka, phakkar phakira; Tum chalo kaun ki chal;Tum ramo kaun ki nal; Tum sarbangi sahjer men, tum ko war na par. Sakal nirantar tum ramo tumhare gahar ganbhir. Khali Khalak mujh Mahin you Guru Kahain Kabir. Satya nam ki arti nirmal bhaya shareer. Dharm Das loke chale guru bahiyan mile Kabir.[51]

We can see the distribution of the Kabir Panthis in the United Provinces, according to the Census of 1891 in the following table.[52]

District	*Number*	*District*	*Number*
Dehra Dun	34	Fatehpur	9
Muzaffarnagar	6	Hamirpur	8
Bulandshahr	258	Allahabad	12
Aligarh	114	Jhansi	8
Agra	8	Jalaun	3
Farrukhabad	2	Ghazipur	209
Bareilly	15	Gorakhpur	40
Bijnor	2	Basti	8
Moradabad	36	Tarai	4
Shahjahanpur	57	Lucknow	16
Pilibhit	72	Faizabad	16
Cawnpur	18	**Total**	955

It appears that the gradual migration of the skilled and semi-skilled labours had also led groups of the

Kabirpanthis to spread in farthest parts of colonial India by the end of the nineteenth century. The census of 1901 had noted a number of Kabir followers called Kabber in Bombay province as a main caste totalling 27,330; in the island of Andamans, Bengal and Rajputana, the total number of Kabirpanthis professing it as their caste was 932. In the Madras Presidency alone, Kabbera caste had 19774 in numbers.[53]

Both the premier cities of the British India, Bomaby and Delhi had already centres of the panth in this century as I have discovered in my study. Although we presently do not have definitive evidences to reconstruct their exact history, but oral traditions aver that the oldest Kabir centre in Bomaby was well established on the Grant Road in Dadar.[54] As the present Mahant of the Math, Gobind Das, is embroiled in too many civil and revenue cases, he deliberately avoided to provide any supporting documents on its history. Some of its followers who are members of its managing trust recall that Kabir Badi Math came under the control of Surat Math in the late nineteenth century and since then this Math has remained an associate of the the former. The influence of the Surat Mahant had increased in the course of his mediation in the then raging disputes at the Kabir Badi Math when it was associated with the Dharmdasi branch. It became independent of the Dharmdasi vansh *gaddi* branch during the early 20th century.

The role of Makanji is often recalled in the growing popularity of the Kabir Badi math of Mumbai. Makanji Kuber Macwana,[55] born in Ahmedabad in 1849, had amassed so much wealth and fame as an artist that he had become a very famous Kabirpanthi in Surat and Bombay. His fame had brought him to Bombay which in itself was a fastly growing industrial city of the British India. He and his leadership seems to be a substantial factor in bringing the Kabir Badi Math under the influence of the Surat Mahant. Makanji himself was a Kabirpanthi from the lowest caste of the Hindu society, yet he became popular as Sethji Makanji Kuber (Kabir). Most of his written works related to the life and teachings of Kabir were published during the early 20th century. Although his mother tongue was Gujarati, he had acquired proficiency in Marathi, Hindi and Sanskrit. According to Y.A. Parmar, it was he who had constructed a building for the Kabir Ashram in Bombay during the end of the century. It is said before his death in 1924, he and his works had become famous from Bomaby to Karanchi, where a number of Mahyavanshi Kabirpanthis had for years, been running a Kabir centre. He is also said to have been a major influence in the popularity of the Kabir Panth in the Karachi and Sindh areas of present Pakistan.

It is noteworthy that Balaghat earlier formed part of the same Mandala kingdom which had once offered strong support to the Dharmdasi branch during its heyday in the seventeenth century. Present-day Maharashtra's state boundary co-exists with this part of Chhattisgarh. Even the present Mahant has formerly been a disciple and a care-taker of the Surat Kabir Math, Gujarat. Being an inhabitant of a *qasba* in Maharashtra near Nagpur, the present Mahant himself has recently developed another Kabir Mandir at his native place in 2004. In this region, the census of 1881 returned with the total number of 8574 Kabirpanthis in the district of Balaghat alone, out of its total population of 3,48554.

Delhi's earliest math too seems to have been built sometime in the nineteenth century. Its history faces grievous challenge from two sides–one, the present Mahant tries to hide the fact that the existing building of the Kabir Math has been a religious site. Very few members of the Kabirpanthis in Delhi are presently aware that Paharganj, one of the most crowded public places in Delhi, houses a Kabir Math as well. In course of my field works among the Jagodasi branch, I was told authoritatively by Ram Dayal Das, 87, the Jagodasi Acharya, that one of his sub-branches exist in Delhi, although he has virtually no control over it. On my repeated visits to find out its present history and condition, I could finally succeed in locating this Math's building despite the Mahant's frantic efforts to misguide me from its exact location.[56] The Math's building looks like an old structure of the late nineteenth or early 20th century, mentioning its date of construction on the front wall of the entry, but so blurred that it has become indecipherable. Yet a will paper of the preceding Mahant offers us some idea of its past.

The will-paper states that the present Mahant would succeed Manohar Das, who had also been heading a Kabir Math at Nawala near Muzaffarabad in the present Uttar Pradesh. It is said that the Nawala Math too was a sub-branch of the Jagodasi branch.[57]

Towards the western part of the United Provinces when the Westcott brothers came particularly to Kanpur in 1889, the town was still struggling to overcome the trauma of the Mutiny.[58] Canon George Herbert Westcott was sent by the Society for the Propagation of the Gospel to Kanpur. He was an Anglican and as such represented the majority of the protestant Christian Denominations in Cawnpore (Kanpur). But he and his brother set out to be 'clergymen of all citizens of Cawnpore', which gained them tremendous popularity. Altogether George Herbert spent twenty-one years of his life in Kanpur. Well-versed in Hindi and Urdu, he took a keen interest in the religious orientation of the lower classes, which led to the publication of *Kabir and the Kabir Panth* in 1907. Preface to the first edition of the book[59], makes it clear that it had taken Westcott about 10 years to complete this work, implying thereby, his accounts on the panth also pertained to the closing years of the nineteenth century. In the introduction to the book, he states: "For help in this undertaking, I am principally indebted to my *Mali*, Badlu Dass, who is himself a member of the Panth. He has visited all places of interest in connection with the Panth and introduced me to many Mahants and conducted inquiries with great intelligence."[60] If Westcott relied for his research on the knowledge of the local Kabir-panthis, Kanpur itself must have had a substantial number of them. The number of Kabirpanthis can well be imagined as there are still four Kabir Mandirs in Kanpur despite the fact that only two of these are presently active.

George Herbert Westcott still remains unforgotten. Highly educated middle class of Kanpur knows him as the founder of Christ Church College and even the common man is familiar with the 'Westcott' building next to the college. But even among local intellectuals, it was not known that Westcott wrote a book on Kabir, although

Kabir commands high respect amongst Kanpur's Kabirpanthis.

In Kanpur, already there were a few Kabir Maths. According to our informants, the oldest Kabir centre in Kanpur city has been at Karbala but presumably in a defunct state. Actually, it was the home of the renowned Mahant Sevak Das, who was one of the Westcott's informants. His grave is on Sanval Das Ghat, constructed in the 1880s by the rich tannery owner, leather merchant and Kabir-Panthi Sanval Das (1864-1908). He was a Chamar by caste, and his wealth, generosity and benevolence were so great that he even found mention in N.P. Arora's *Kanpur Ka Itihas.*[61]

We have further evidences from the then United provinces, of which Kanpur was one of the industrial towns, that premier towns of the region were already having Kabir centres in this part too. Shri Kabir Ashram, Basaha, in Lucknow[62] has been an early nineteenth century math. The ashram belongs to the Jagodasi branch and has been connected to Bidupur *sthan,* Bihar. According to the present Mahant, the ashram was established by one Mayadas around the year 1800. Being a household Math, it was since then maintained by the descendants of Mayadas Ji. As for historic value, the present Mahant has just one document written in the form of a *doha (Couplet).* Even though the writer's name has not been mentioned, it is the sole document which provides details of the successive Mahants who ran the ashram. The present Mahant of this ashram is Yogendra Das.

In another part of Lucknow city where a Kabir Math had been active for the last 100 years or so, there also, the Math seems to have been facing some revenue litigations by 1862. One of the judgement papers written in *Persian*[63] signed by Mr. Morris, Assistant Commissioner, district Sultanpur, indicate that the then Mahant Govind Das was implicated in disputed transactions of land involving Rani Sahiba, a lady of royal family, and a few other loanees of Mahant living in the neighbourhood.

Saharanpur, one of the oldest cities of United Provinces, adjacent to the present-day Haryana, came to have a resourceful Kabirpanth centre, known as Kabir-Chaura Math founded by one Chhajju Das at Chilakana Road in Dara Kotatala area of the town.[64] For sure, Chaajju Das belonged to a Brahmin family and was a householder. There is, however, uncertainty about Chhajju's whereabouts–one section believes that he was a native of Saharanpur itself, some others believe that he came from outside Uttar Pradesh and got settled in Saharanpur in early 1850s. Uncertainty about Chhajju Das's life and the opening of the Kabir-Chaura Math in Saharanpur is dispelled by the judgement of the Allahabad High Court in Oct. 1979, which had decided upon the civil appeal filed by the contesting groups of the Math in 1977.[65] The judgement paper describes that the Kabir Chaura Math has been in operation in Saharanpur at least for the last 117 years, which was opened by Chhajju Das, who had donated his entire paternal property to the cause of Kabir, his *sadguru*. The antiquity of present Maths situated at Saharanpur is also attested by the *guru-Pranali* and certain land records suggesting their existence at least since 19th century.

The Saharanpur Math acquires significance for the expansion of the Dharmdasi Kabirpanth in the interior parts of Multan[66] and Karanchi[67], integral parts of the British India as well. It is said that Chhaju Das, the founder of the Saharanpur Math was having marital ties in Multan, forming part of the old Panjab. Oral tradition and census report provide us sufficient evidence to believe the presence of the sizeable number of Kabir followers in Multan too.

A resourceful *Kutiya* (centre) at the outskirt of Ludhiana, as an offshoot of the Garibdasi Kabirpanth also, struck roots in the late 19th century. However till the end of the century, it operated from a *kuchcha* house. It was primarily the efforts of one Bhuriwale Sahib, who added a new impetus to its growth both materially and religiously. Bhurewale's original name was Brahm Sagar.[68] He was born at village Rampur in the Roopnagar district of Panjab in 1862. Brahm Sagar was elevated to the seat of Mahant of the Garibdasi Math at Chuddani as its third Mahant. During his *gaddi*, it is said the Kabirpanth took great strides in terms of followers as well as prosperity. Village Rampur is religiously called Rampur Sahib following the tradition of the Sikhs who usually add sahib to the places of their religious significance. He laid the foundation of the present splendid ashram situated in the suburb of Ludhiana. It is said he became famous as Bhuriwale because he always used to cover himself by a blanket of the ochre-colour i.e '*bhure*'. He is said to have died at Jaloor, religiously called Jaloor Sahib by his disciples, in 1947. They have preserved his *Samadhi* at Jaloor in the present Sangrur district of Punjab and treat it as an object of worship. Around the same time, another Garibdasi *Kutiya* (humbler word for a Math) came to be formed at Mullapur situated in the vicinity of Chandigarh.

In the central India however splitting tendency within the Dharmdasi branch remained unabated. Consequently, a resourceful Math of the panth came into existence at Burhanpur in the Central Provinces.[69] This Math has developed into one of the most resourceful Kabirpanth centres in India since the last century. Both oral and hagiographic texts trace its origin to the life of one Puran Das, who is said to have founded this center. The Dharmdasi texts describe Puran Das as one of the eminent disciples of its Kawardha Math during the Acharyaship of Paknam.[70] Puran is however said to have spent most of his time as a leading member at the Kawardha Math, the headquarters of the Dharmdasi branch before changing his allegiance from the latter, during the major part of the nineteenth century.

The rival group[71] of the Dharmdasi branch alleges that it was mainly Paknam's act of cruelty that had finally compelled Puran Das to abandon Kawardha center forever. Most of these informants attribute rising popularity and respect of Puran Das among the associated disciples with the Kawardha Math in particular and Kabirpanth followers, in general, which had made Puran Das suspicious in the eyes of Paknam. Puran Das, to them, had been a sadhu of high spiritual degree. When Paknam Sahib, the then Acharya, found his own position threatened by Puran Das's gaining popularity, it is alleged that Paknam, finding all other available means in his armoury ineffective, locked Puran

Das in a narrow room as a punishment. Puran's alleged crime, precipitating a harsh punishment, according to the official version of the Dharmdasi spokesperson, was initiation of disciples by him, without the clear-cut sanction of the Acharya at Kawardha. While going through the ordeal inside a locked room, one day Puran is said to have escaped and fled away to Burhanpur *qasba*.

Puran Das escapade from Kawardha has a different version too, particularly by the exponents of the Dharmdasi branch.[72] A group of informants, presently known as Parakh-Panthis, describe difference of ideological orientation as the main reason of the rift between the Dharmdasi Acharya and Puran Das. Elaborating their views, they point out that the spiritual growth of Puran had transformed him into a true sadhu, who did not appreciate the hereditary traditions of the Dharmadhasi *gaddi* at Kawardha. He had his own insight and despite all pressure and restriction imposed by the *Vansh gaddi* Acharya and his coterie, Puran Das did not distract from his *Parakhi* insight. Opposed to the spiritual insight of Puran, the Acharya took all measures to keep *Vansh* tradition intact even at the cost of expelling a true sadhu from his hereditary (*Vansh*) centres. Puran Das preferred to abandon the allegiance to the *Vansh gaddi* rather than succumbing to the spurious Kabirpaanthi traditions then pursued at Kawardha.

The Parakhi group cites a specific event to illustrate the ideological differences being the root cause of parting ways of Puran Das. It is said that Puran Das had compiled a number of devotional texts, *Trijya*, commentary on the

Bijak, just being the one among some others. He had an intense desire to get his commentary approved and signed by Paknam, but Paknam declined to approve and sign the text outrightly on the ground that the text was not conforming to the interpretation of the *Bijak* as it was being interpreted by the orthodox Dharmadasi exponents of the time.

Whatever be the fact, Puran Das himself has described his early connection with the Dharmdasi branch in *Nirnay Saar*, one of his most quoted texts. He was born in a Kshatriya family of the district Jalgaon forming part of present Maharashtra. It is said that he drew towards religious pursuits at an early age and became disciple of Sukhlal Das at Rewa, in the central provinces. He describes himself, in this text, as the disciple of a Sukhlal Das, a sadhu of the Dharmdasi line. To quote him: *Parakh Guru kabir Kahave, Parakh Dharmdas Batlawe.Parakh mein sab Sant Kahae, Parakh Amardas Guru Bhae.Tahawan Te Sukhlal Kripanidhi, Parakh Pay Sakal Bijak Vidhi. Puran Tinaka Charan Ko chero, Kripa drishti Unhin Prabhu herau..*[73]

He is said to have died at an early age of 32 in 1836, the year which one finds inscribed on the *Samadhi* of Puran Das, still preserved in the complex of Burhanpur Math.[74] He is credited to have written a number of religious texts relating to the Kabirpanth; such as, *Vairagya Shatak*, in addition to the above-mentioned texts etc, during his short-lived life. He was succeeded by his closest disciple. Hans Das at Burhanpur Math.The genealogy of Burhanpur *gaddi* [75] includes the list of 9 Mahants having succeeded there till the present Mahant– i. Hans Das, ii. Santosh Das, iii. Sri Ram Sukh Das,

iv. Narottam Das, v. Kashi Das, vi. Chhote Balak Das, and lastly vii. Ram Swarup Das and viii. Present Mahant Mohan Das.

Being resourceful and active centre of Kabirpanth, the Math management has succeeded in keeping some textual evidences in support of its history. The *guru-pranali* as preserved in the Math mentions the year 1853 of Hans's death. Upon his death, Santosh succeeded at the *gaddi* of Burhanpur and continued to remain at the helm of affairs there till his death in 1863 (v.s.1920). Sri Ram Sahib took over the *gaddi* as he was, till then, the lone survivor among the closest disciples of Hans Das, the second Mahant of this Math.

Ram Sahib[76] is said to have been an expert of religious debates and speculation; his sharp ability succeeded in drawing into his fold a number of educated disciples who later wrote on Kabir's teachings. Sri Ram Sahib himself is stated to have written a short religious text titled as *Ekkis Prashn* dilating on the spiritual quest of an initiate into the Kabirpanth. He breathed his last at Burhanpur itself in 1896 (v.s.1953).

According to the dates mentioned in the genealogy of the Burhanpur *gaddi*, Narottam Das took over the *gaddi* in 1896. His predecessor Mahant Ram Sukh Das had taken tours towards Konkan regions and succeeded in bringing into his panth followers like Kashi Das Konkan in Maharshtra. Hailing in a Konkani Brahmin family, Kashi Das was well educated. Kashi Das had become a pre-eminent disciple at Burahanpur during Ram Das life-time. Kashi was an employee of the colonial government and working as a railway station master at Galhan, near Jalgaon before he took to the Kabirpanth.[77]

His regular employment in the railways, in fact, had delayed his active participation for a considerable time to get full-time responsibility in the Kabirpanth. He later became sixth Mahant of the Burhanpur Math.

Our informants also hint at some of the issues the Burhanpur Math had begun to face towards the end of the nineteenth century. One of these issues was of the shameless character of a Mahant named Kalyan Das who was allegedly having an illicit relation with a lady disciple. He was the fifth Mahant at Burhanpur ashram, but as the charges levelled on him was against the basic tenets of the Burhanpur *gaddi*, which had already adopted a *virakta* principle for Mahant, he was forced to give up the *gaddi*. Instead Narottam was selected as the fifth Mahant. On the completion of the enquiry in which all the charges against Kalyan were found correct, he had to leave Burhanpur ashram forever. He went back to his native place, Singhkheda, in present Madhya Pradesh and remained there till the fag end of his life. His expulsion caused first split in the emerging Burhanpur Math.

One of the pre-eminent disciples, inspired by the Burhanpur Math, from the Central Provinces has been recalled as Lal Sahib. His childhood name was Ram Vidhata Prasad Chaube and born in a Brahmin family of village Hatiya-Khamhariya in Satna district. Although he was initiated into the Kabirpanth by Mahant Hanuman Das of the Rewa Math, he remained deeply indebted to the Burhanpur Math where he is said to have developed spiritual insight. For a short period, he took upon his shoulder the *gaddi* of Mahant of a Math at Bharara near Rewa, but he could not continue there for long and finally shifted to Burhanpur Math.

Further west in Gujarat, Jeevan Das[78] who had taken over the *gaddi* of Jamnagar Math in 1799, as described in my last book (2016), continued to dedicate his life in the service of the Kabirpanth almost for the half century. He is said to have travelled very widely in parts of Gujarat, resulting in the panth's expansion upto parts of Kathiawad and Porbandar, the region where Mahatma Gandhi was born in 1869. Putlibae, Gandhiji's mother, became one of the disciples of the panth, as Gandhi himself revealed in a public meeting at Kashi in 1934, a fact which is commonly ignored by most of the biographers of Gandhi.[79] Moreover, Gandhi himself admits humbly that he has been a worshipper of Kabir. Most of the biographers do relate Gandhi's household to the Pran Nathi *sampraday*, yet without highlighting its legacy to Kabir and Kabirpanth. Pran Nathi sect in some scriptures of the panth, has been shown as an offshoot of the Kabirpanth as the Garibdasi Kabirpanthis,

श्रीमती कस्तूर बा अस्वस्थ

कबीर मठमें गांधीजी

हरिजन बस्तियोंका निरीक्षण

A news clipping from Aaj, the Hindi daily

After Jeevan Das's death, Mohan Das succeeded him as the fifth *Mahant* of the Jamnagar ashram in 1849 and made great contribution to the prosperity of the ashram. It is said by the time Mohan Das died, Jamnagar ashram had emerged as the most prosperous Kabir ashram in western Gujarat region. It had acquired landed property at Dwarka and had opened a centre there to take care of the landed property. Before his death, he appointed Amar Das as his successor Mahant in 1881. But he died within two years of his selection. In the circumstance, Amar Das, one of his close disciples was chosen as the sixth Mahant of Kabir Ashram, Jamnagar in 1883.

The site where the old Ashram at Jamnagar was initially started had become inadequate because of the growing number of the followers from the surrounding areas. At that time Sant Ramdas, a disciple of Purushottam Das, had earned the respect of the local ruling family. Jam Vibhaji II (1852-1895), then head of the Jamnagar estate is said to have donated the entire land plot on which the present site of the Ashram was rebuilt in 1894.[80]

In the then Bengal Province, perhaps another centre of the Kabirpanth was being founded at Rosara in the second decade of the nineteenth century, which gradually emerged as an Acharya *Gaddi* and played a considerable role in panth expansion further east and north-east India. Its founder was Krishna Karakh, an inhabitant of Rosara itself.[81] About the Math as well as the man there is a divergent view of followers. However, all my informants agreed that he was the son of Braj Mohan Karakh and was a *grihastha* (married man with a family). His wife had died shortly after his marriage and, then, he had started to live with his brother's widow.

Some disciples said that Krishna Karakh was initially a disciple of Bagicha Kabir Math, Rosara; but his uncommon lifestyle, and his aversion to the growing Brahminical dominance at Bagicha Math, compelled the then Mahant of this Math to disown him as his disciple. In their version, Krishna Karakh, was, in fact, the leader of a Kabirpanthi group which broke off its relation with the then functionaries of Bagicha Math. Krishna Karakh was one of the eminent disciples who did not get as much respect from the authorities there as he deserved. Consequently, Krishna Karakh and his supporters were quite unhappy about the increasing arrogance of upper caste Mahants at Bagicha Math till then. Attempts were foiled by the concerted counter-measures taken by the Bagicha Math's authorities, most of whom came from upper castes. Frustrated, Krishna Karakh initiated another Kabirpanthi branch in Rosara in 1814. To legitimize the foundation of his Math, he chose one of the Mahants in Orissa as his guru who, in turn, authorized him to run a Math. It is presently known as Krishna Karakhi Vachan *Vanshi* Mahdeo Math at Rosara.

Another version tells us a different story.[82] According to it, Krishna, the first part of his name was the name of the widow with whom he was living. She used to accompany him even at market places, where Karakh Das used to go as a seller of rice and pulse. Both were famous *Bhajan* (devotional song) singers as well and often used to perform in religion gatherings. His growing popularity, as a singer and a devotee, helped him in attracting large crowds. Subsequently, he founded Mahadeo Math at Rosara, encouraged by these admirers.

Whatever be the fact, the followers and Mahants associated with the Krishna Karakhi branch do not accept the above versions about their *adi* Acharya. They narrate the story in a different way. According to them, Krishna Karakh was a true devotee of Kabir and, in an hour of deep meditation, Kabir found in him love and devotion equal in measure to that attained by Dharamdas, who was Kabir's immediate disciples. So Kabir blessed Krishna Karakh with the *Vachan* to begin a new branch for the panth. Thereafter, Krishna Karakh formed an independent branch which came to be known as the Krishna Karakhi *Vachan-Vanshi* branch centred at Rosara. They do not agree to the belief that Krishna Karakh was ever related to the Bagicha Math.

Panji Panth Prakash, one of the didactic texts published by this branch, also describes the beliefs of associated disciples about him. According to it, Krishna Karakh was born in the late eighteenth century. It came to be known as the *Vachan Vanshi* branch, characterized by the 'Vachan' (sacred words) earlier given to Dharam Das and later conferred on Krishna Karakh by Kabir himself, in a state of Karakh's deep mediation.[83]

Krishna Karakh died in 1839. Including him, this branch at Rosara has, till date, been succeeded by nine Mahants: (i) Krishna Karakh Das (ii) Dambar Das (iii) Jhakhuri Das (iv) Ram Bharos Das (v) Ram Tahal Das (vi) Baldeo Das (vii) Jeebachh Das (viii) Yadu Das and (ix) present Raj Narayan Das.[84] (Acharya Raj Narayan Das has recently died in a fatal road accident in 2017).

The clinching evidence for the Kabirpanth's background of the Radhaswami Satsang is an accomplished fact that its founder coming from United

Provinces was a Kabirpanthi, who, for reasons best known to him, formed another religious group during late 19th century. The group gradually became popular as Radhaswamis. One of its important centres later came to be formed in the Panjab.[85] Their followings drew large number from Punjab, in which many of them kept on showing their reverence to Kabir. The leading members of the *satsang* still show their gratitude to Kabir in a number of publications dedicated to him. The growth of the Radhaswami as an independent religious sect has had a definitive effect on the Kabirpanth as large number of the latter's followers are said to have shifted their religious allegiance to the Radhaswami presently centered both in Agra and Beas in Uttar Pradesh and Punjab respectively.

A contemporary accounts of Shiv Vrat Lal (1860-1939) indicates, in a definitive way, at the Radha-Swami's inspiration from Kabir and the Kabirpanth. One of the most prolific scholars and ideologues of the Radha-Swami Satsang during the early 20th century, Shiv Vrat Lal in his Kabir Yog, written originally in Urdu in 1910, clarifies the inter-relation between the two unambiguously in the following terms–"Without a close study of this book, it is impossible to know the fundamentals of various panths such as the Radhaswami, Nanak panth, Dadu Panth or any other panth. Kabir was an Adi Sant. The panth is based on his teachings...". He further clarifies that only the ignorant can have a doubt on Kabir's being the Sant Satguru. Kabir, to him, has been in the category of the incarnate greatest one (Akbar)'. He reiterates that a judicious person would never deny that no seer, pir, messenger (Paigambar) or ascetic can ever come near to Kabir's spiritual stature. He forewarns that his words ought not to be understood through narrow sectarian lenses, nor was he a Kabirpanthi as per the sectarian initiation. Instead his views are based on his vigorous studies of Kabir's qalam and their comparison with the related literatures of different dispensations. He then refers to both Guru Nanak and Huzur Saligram Sahib, the second successor of Radhaswami Satsang in Agra. He cites that Kabir had been a Ram who resides in all beings, in Guru Nanak's view. To Huzur Saligram, his own guru, the collection of Kabir's Vanis as compiled in Sant Sangrah was so precious that he had gifted it to him for regular recitation. To Shiv Vrat Lal, Huzur Sahib was not different (mukhtalif) from Kabir as such. He further highlights that Shiv Dayal Sahib, the founder of the sant mat Radhaswami himself had declared Kabir's Vanis, in his work 'Saar vachan', as the Guru-vani for all of his followers. He quotes from Shiv Dayal's above work:

> *Jo Man mein Pratit Na Dekhe, to Kabir Guru Ki Vani Pekhe*
> *Tulasi Sahebka Mat Soe, Paltu, Jagjivan kah soe*
> *En Santan Ka Du Parmana, Inki Vani Sakh bakhana.*

(If one cannot realize the knowledge, delve into the Vanis of Guru Kabir; Tulsi sahib had the same view, Paltu and Jagjivan had said the same; I have evidences of these sants, their vanis had expressed the truth, translation mine)

Shiv Vrat Lal himself recalled that his Guru Huzur Sahib, the second successor Guru of the Radha Swami

Satsang, was a devout admirer of Kabir, which was attested by the fact that Huzur Sahib had given out Kabir's granth to him for regular recitation. Furthermore, many Radha Swami followers still believe that Huzur Sahib himself was an incarnate of Kabir. Sawan Singh Maharaj of the Radhaswami chapter centred at Beas in the Punjab, the second successor, used to call Kabir as the father of Sants. It is said the founder of the Beas centre, Jaymal Singh himself had taught Sawan Singh to learn from *Anurag Sagar*, an important religious scripture of the Dharamdasi Kabirpanth, then Central Provinces.

Another contemporary missionary European scholar, J.N. Farquhar (1861-1929) offers more or less the same views regarding Kabir's elevated place in the worldview of the recently established Radhaswami followers then observed in Agra. To quote him:

> In the daily meetings of the sect, portions of their own sacred books or of the writings of Kabir and other Hindu saints are read....The affinities of the theology of the sect stand out quite clear. Most of the teaching is purely Hindu; it stands nearer to Vaishnavism than to any other part of Hinduism and is perhaps most closely allied to the teaching of Kabir. This is reflected in the practice of the sect. While they profess to find all truth in the books of their own gurus, they do use the writings of certain Hindu and Muhammadan saints and amongst these they give Kabir the highest place. (Modern Religious Movements In India, p. 170).

In the Central Provinces then the Dharmdasi *Vansh* centre having its headquarters at Kawardha, saw a major split during the late nineteenth century. During his Mahantship, Haqnam had shifted headquarters of the Dharamdasi branch at Kawadha as the head Mahant in early 1820s. According to the Dharamdasi spokespersons, Haqnam shifted to Kawardha on the repeated request of Ujiyar Singh, then local *raja* of Kawardha. Ujiyar Singh[86] had been a *raja* of Gaur dynasty centred there from 1801-1841.

Apart from Kawardha, Haqnam's *gaddi* period, as described above, had also been famous for the dissociation of Ganesh Das, the founder Mahant of Fatuha Math, from the Dharamdasi *Vansh gaddi*. However, royal favours enabled him to run his religious activities without much trouble till his death in 1833.

Haqnam could not succeeded in finding a suitable wife for himself among Kasaundhan *bania* families, the caste of Dharmdas, as he was born of the lady of a low caste at Singhori Ashram. He is, however, said to have been blessed with four sons–Paknam, Lal Das, Bhupat Das and Shital Das. He had selected Paknam, the eldest among them, as his successor at the *guru-gaddi* before his death. Accordingly, Paknam became next Acharya at Kawardha in 1833. Paknam is said to have lived till 1855. He had, according to Yuglanand Vihari, nine wives. In the passing, we may note that the soreness in relationship of Puran Das with the Dharmdas tradition actually, as described above, surfaced during Paknam's time. Pragtnam, the eldest among four of his sons, succeeded him undisputedly. He is said to have four wives. He had two sons–Dhirajnam and *Raja* Sahib. Yugalanand offers us a diferent account, which acquires significance as he was a near contemporary eye-witness of most of these events unfolding during the period. According to him, *Raja* sahib was the popular name of Dhirajnam alone, because he had been leading a royal life altogether. He had a number of wives. Before he died, his main wife had begotten a son named Ugranam. Ugranam too died at an age of 4. But destiny had something else in store for Kawardha ashram. Dhirajnam and his son, Ugranam–both had died before Pragatnam's death in 1882.[87]

Thus Kawardha ashram came to face a crisis of successor in the direct line of predecessor Mahant. Pragatnam himself died in a depressive state for want of a suitable successor. Yugalanad writes that on Pragatnam's death, widows of father and son duo, in consultation with leading members of the Dharmdasi branch tried to thrash out a solution and in the process, zeroed in on the name of Sumiran Das alias Dadi Sahib, the son of Latkan Das, the uterine brother of Pragatnam as the successor. Dadi Sahib was to succeed the *gaddi* as Dhirajnam at Kawardha, but for the fierce opposition to this decision by a prominent Mahant named Ayodhya Das. Ayodhya Das must have been in old age as he was, according to Yuglanand, a contemporary of Paknam. He contested this decision strongly and mobilized a number of Kabirpanthis from Bihar, United Provinces and Panjab and North-East to stand along with him.[88] He rather vouched for the succession of Mukund Das, an illegitimate but adopted son of Dhirajnam, falling in direct line of the previous Mahant at Kawardha.

Yugalanand ascribes Ayodhya's opposition to Dadi Sahib's candidature to personal reasons. The divided house and absence of consensus over candidature of successor finally drove Dharmdasi headquarters in a legal battle which was filed in the then Bombay High Court. The supporters of Dadi Sahib camped on the one side, comprising Mahants and followers of Kabir then living in and around Gujarat and Marathwada, whereas Ayodhya Das's group comprised followers and Mahants largely of distant regions. When the legal battle ensued against Mukund Das, rechristened as Ugranam by his camp of supporters, he had to flee away from Kawardha, as a police warrant was also issued against him. He however kept on evading the police warrant till the decision of the High court, for about 20 years and remained an absconder in the police eyes.

Yugalanand's description of the event apprises us that Mukund Das alias Ugranam had found a very reliable and trustworthy supporter in Vishnudayal, the then Mahant of Kudurmal ashram, and *Mukhiya* of the panchayat of the same name as well. Dadi Sahib' side was legally led by Jagannath Das, the local Mahant at a Bombay Math. The High Court in its decision is said to have recognized the succession of Dadi Sahib alias Dhirajnam as the legal heir of the Kawardha Math. According to the *Vansh gaddi* writings, Dadi Sahib won a degree of Rs. 45000/ in this case.[89]

Dhirajnam's death before Pragatnam goes contrary to the details provided to us by G.H. Westcott and F.E. Keay, who studied Kabirpanth contemporaneously. G.H. Westcott' description of Dharamdasi centres during last decade of the nineteenth century apprises us about the ensuing crises of succession at Kawardha. Westcott writes that:

> The father of the present Mahant died after holding office for a period of three years only, many wished that one of his disciples, Jugla Nand, should officiate as Mahant during remainder of his term of office. To this proposal, the majority of the members strongly objected on the ground that he was not a descendent of Dharm Das, and Ugranam was duly installed. His grand mother, known as Dadi Sahib, who was responsible for this proposal, still exercises authority at Koodarmal, and Ugranam reigns in the newly established Math at Damakhera. Jugla Nand with other discontented Sadhus retired to Bombay, where he has published various books bearing upon the Panth.[90]

F.E. Keay has also left an account of the schism the Dharmdasi branch then confronting after the death of Dhirajnam as follows:

> Another schism amongst the followers of the successors of Dharm Das took place in 1894. In that year Praghat Nam, the guru of the older branch, died at Kawardha, where his *gaddi* was. Ugra Nam, who was born of a woman of low caste, was acclaimed as the successor of his father, but his claim was challenged by Dhiraj Nam, whose parentage was legitimate. The dispute led to a case in the High Court at Bombay, which was decided in favour of Dhiraj Nam, who occupied the *gaddi* at Kawardha. Ugra Nam retired to Kudarmal, near Janjgir, and afterwards to a newly- founded monastery at Damakhera, in the Rajpur District. Dhiraj Nam was unpopular and little attention was paid to him. Ugra

> Nam enjoyed the real homage of the followers of the sect, who said that Dhiraj was the official guru, but Ugra the people's guru. Dhiraj Nam died shortly after. The representative of the legitimate line now has his *gaddi* at Bamni, a village only a few miles from Kawardha, but seems to have few followers and little influence. After the death of Dhiraj his mother wished that a sadhu, named Yugal Ananda, should officiate as guru during the remainder of the term of office, but the majority of the members of the Panth strongly objected, on the ground that he was not a descendant of Dharm Das. This lady was called the Dadi Sahib, and continued to exercise influence at Kudarmal. Yugalananda with other sadhus retired to Bombay, where he edited and published many Kabirpanthi works.[91]

However the sectarian publications of the Damakhera branch consider Ugranam as one of the sons of Dhirajnam. In their version, Dhirajnam's two sons had died quite early and hence he had to marry another lady who belonged to a low caste.[92] She gave birth to Mukund Das, who was anointed as Ugranam at the time of succession at the *gaddi* of Kawardha. Further they add to the fact that Dhirajnam himself could not enjoy he seat of Mahant as he died in waiting before Pragnam, his father himself died. The Damakhera version thus denies the very dispute between Dhirajnam and Ugranam.In their view, the dispute was primarily against the choice of Dadi Sahib's candidate named Yugal Anand, to whom the local Kabirpanth fraternity did not support for the seat of Mahant at Kawardha.

It is obvious however that Ugranam was a minor when he was chosen as the successor Mahant, as the Dharmdasi version dates his succession at the age of 11(1896). Dadi Sahib's preference of Yugalanand as a temporary Mahant to Ugranam was specifically for the period till the legal heir attains maturity. But this temporary arrangement too was not acceptable to the ardent believers in the *Vansh/bind* tradition of the Dharmdasi branch. Consequently a crisis of succession once again began to rattle the seat of guru at Kawardha. Pragatnam's death in 1884 marked the beginning of a legal battle crisis which resulted in a major split of the Dharmdasi *Vansh gaddi*, leading to the formation of the present headquarters of the Dharmdasi *Vansh Gaddi* at Damakheda in Chhattisgarh in 1896, while the Kawardha seat remained in the charge of Dadi Sahib and the opponents of Ugranam against whom a law suit was lodged in then High Court, then situated at Bombay.[93]

The law suit was filed against Ugranam as certain section of the Kabirpanth followers in and around Kawardha did not appreciate the candidature of Ugranam as the successor of Kawardha seat. Although, Ugranam was famous for his erudite, yet he was born of a *dasi* (servile lady disciple) also called illegitimate wife of Pragatnam in 1874. Ugranam was the only son left to Pragatnam by the time he died, for two of his sons from legitimate wives had already died at a very young age. Ugranam's childhood name was Mukund, it was rechristened Ugranam by his supporters as successor of Pragatnam.

The earliest Gazetteer of the Central Provinces of

1870,[94] too, took note of the developments taking place at the headquarters of the panth. About Kawardha then forming part of Bilaspur district, it confirms that 'the present high priest of the Kabir panthi sect also lives here and his presence attracts devotees from all parts of India.'

By the mid-nineteenth century, the Kabirpanth had already penetrated deeply into the tribal regions of the Chhotanagpur plateau adjacent to the Central Provinces. Presence of Kabirpanth activists were noted down by some anthropologists[95] and also highlighted by recent works on the spread of the Christianity in such regions of the present Jharkhand. According to a recent study,[96] four Oraons Kabirpanthis, namely; Navin Doman Tirkey, Kesho, Bandhu, and Ghuran had facilitated the initiation of the Christianity in this region, which in course of its growth, led to the conversion of a sizeable number of tribal Kabirpanthis into the Christainity. These four Oraon indigenous tribal people of Ranchi area had then vision of Jesus, which convinced them about the truth of Jesus Christ. They were baptized on 9th June 1850.[97] It is said that four Oraon were genuinely interested in what missionaries had to say about Jesus Christ. Missionaries' claim that Jesus was the Lord and he was alive, stirred the inquirers' curiosity as regards the living Lord. The four inquirers came to the missionaries seeking answer to their many questions about the new faith the missionaries were preaching. One of their fundamental questions was about the living Lord Jesus Christ as claimed by the missionaries. Their innermost desire was to see Jesus before they would commit for baptism sought by missionaries. Thus, their repeated requests to be allowed to see this Jesus live became a source of incessant nightmare for the missionaries. And as the tradition has it, after many meetings when the inquirers were not satisfied with the explanations of the missionaries, they felt let down and for them, missionaries' claim was proving hollow. And as a result, they wanted to quit. Upon the request of missionaries, they all knelt down to pray, as a prayer of departure and God's intervention. Something happened in this prayer. This was the beginning of the Church of Jesus Christ in Jharkhand.

The most prominent role in this expansion particularly towards the north-eastern India further was played by the zealous Mahants of the Krishna Karakhi branch formed, as described in previous chapter, in Rosara, Bihar during the early nineteenth century. One of the Mahants of its sub-branches at the Rajapakara *qasba,* located near Hajipur, in Bihar, is said to have first taken serious interest in bringing into his fold some of the Kabir's diciples who had already migrated to then Assam and Bengal provinces from the present eastern Uttar Pradesh as well as from parts of Bihar. Another stream of Kabirpanthis, said to have been migrating to these region, had been the Gorkhas of the Nepali origin, who came from different parts of present-day Nepal.

As per the popular memories I noted during my field works in the above regions, the Gorkhas or the so-called Nepali Kabirpanthis had been original inhabitants at several places in these regions.[98] After the treaty of Sagauli finalized in 1814 between the British rulers in India and the indigenous Gorkha rulers of Nepal, the migration of the Gorkha Kabirpanthis increased in number and expanded over a larger areas upto Sikkim and Bhutan. Tracing the history of Kabirpanth in Nepal, a book entitled *'Vachan Vansh' Kabir Panth purushdor Guru-Pranali*[99] describes that one of the earliest followers in Nepal region was one Padam Das in 1860s.

That Padam Das was the initiator of the Kabirpanth is being corroborated by one and all of the followers I met in Sikkim and West Bengal, but whether he was a Gorkha or of a non-Nepali in origin is not clear to them. However, the above text, *Vachan Vansh Guru-Pranali* locates his first meeting with his Guru, Dayadas at Adalpur in the present Bihar. Dayadas had been the Mahant of a Kabir Math opened by him at Adalpur of Vashali district, Bihar during the Guruship of Ram Bharos Das, the fourth Acharya of the Mahadeo Math, Rosara. Inspired by the magnetic personality of Dayadas, Padam Das had accepted him as his guru and got initiated into the Kabir Panth. He began to lead a life of a wondering sadhu after the initiation, and also visited a numbers of villages in the neighbouring areas of Nepal too. It is said that his religious tours in the Nepal regions were undertaken primarily on the persistent request of the locals of Hakpara, a village in the district Morang of Nepal so much so that he finally settled down there for the remaining period of his life.

As per the prevailing tradition in the parts of Darjeeling and Sikkim regions, Padam Das yet did not curtail his whirlwind tours after settling at Hakpara. It was Padam Das who is believed to have introduced Kabirpanth in the region during the 1870s. His tours in parts of Sikkim have acquired legendary character in the region. One of the legends states that Padam Das had to first face the then dominant leaders of the Hindu Jasmani sect in Sikkim. We do not have many references of the Jasmani sect of Sikkim in academic works, but a recent work of Harneet Sievers Axel[100] does refer to the conversion of some local Limbu Nepalis of Sikkim into this sect to which Padam Das, too, encountered in the region.

While touring Kalinpong and Siligudi of the present West Bengal, Padam Das had to face the challenges thrown by some Jasmani religious leaders namely, Ganpati Das and Tahal Das among some others. Jasmani sect being a devotional one also had penchant for discussion and *Satsang*; and, therefore, they first tried to defeat Padam Das in the Satsang in which Jasmani followers of the nearby villages too participated. However, Padam Das prevailed upon the Jasmani leaders and, ultimately, both Ganpati and Tahal Das decided to embrace Kabirpanth. They accepted Padam Das as their Guru, then and there, at a *qasba* named Dalpanchand in the present Sikkim. Padam Das himself is said to have instructed Ganpati Das to spread Kabir's teachings from Dalpanchand itself, and Tahal Das to work from Kalimpong. According to the '*Vachan Vansh' Guru-Pranali*, Padam Das had passed such instructions in 1876.[101]

On deputing Ganpati at Dalpanchand, Padam Das himself went back to his *gaddi* at Hakapara in the eastern Nepal. In Sikkim, a sub-branch of the Krishna Karkhi branch came into existence from 1876 onwards. *Dalpanchand* is reported to have continued as the Mahant of Dalpanchand Kabir Math till 1890. During his life, a number of the hitherto Jasmani sect followers and centers were brought into the Kabirpanth fold in the eastern Sikkim. Till 2003, Dalpanchand Math had 5 successor Mahants–1. Ganpati Das, 2. Sring Das 3. Saran Das, 4. Ashram Das, 5. Bhimadal Das.[102]

Towards the end of the nineteenth century, we have evidence to trace the extension of Kabirpanth towards the southern part of our country as well. In this process, the most prominent name of one Kanchan Das[103] comes up. What we hear from the associated disciples in Andhra Pradesh and Karnataka, suggest that Kanchan Das had been an associate of the Dhramdasi *Vansh Gaddi* Kabirpanth. He had taken to *virakta* life and is said to have dedicated his entire life to the spread of Kabir's teachings. According to the daughter of the founder Mahant of the earliest Adi Kabeer Math in Bangalore, Kanchan Das had for long lived in Hyderabad, where a Math still stands named after Kanchan Das in old Hyderabad area. An epitaph inscribed on the stone slab of a *Samadhi* inside the Kanchan Das Kabir Ashram, situated at Roop Lal Bazar, Shah Ali Banda, Hyderabad-5, mentions the name of Kishan Das[104] who is said to have been a successor Mahant after the former's death. Kanchan Das Samadhi is, however, preserved in a cave still preserved at a Adi Kabir Math in Bangaluru (Bangalore), the capital city of Karnataka.

The existing evidences suggest that Hyderabad had emerged as the most flourishing place for the growth of the Kabirpanth towards the end of the nineteenth century, for another centre of Kabir had also been in the making under the leadership of one Kailash Giriji in the growing city of Hyderabad. He opened a Kabir *dera* in the Chandan Badi area of *Gosha –Mahal* (secluded palace for ladies) Baradari, once housing the lone Qutub shahi palace, before it was destroyed by Aurangzeb.[105] It is said that it was the rule of the Hyderabad Nizam, when, the larger part of the open area in front of the Goshamahal, was given away to the freemasons of the locality for their rehabilitation by the turn of the 20th century. Kabir *dera* emerged as one of the beneficiaries of this act of Nizam as recalled by the maternal nephew of Kailash. Kailash Giri died in 1920 as is inscribed on his *Samadhi* preserved inside the *dera* campus itself. Kailash Giri is said to have been the disciple of Baba Sardar Giriji, who was ninth successor in their pedigree.[106] As per prevailing tradition about Giris connection with Kabir stemmed from parts of Panjab in the early part of nineteenth century and it travelled to other parts of India such as Delhi and Hyderabad.[107]

While Giri's disciple named Kailash limited himself in Hyderabad, Kanchan Das went as far as Bangalore to spread Kabir's teachings where he found a well-educated disciple in Gyan Das originally named Gyaneswar Rao,[108] who was an employee of a Bank in the then emerging city of Bangalore. It is said that Gyan Das had become an orphan at an early age, but his mother had grown deep interest in the teachings of Kabir as then being spread by Kanchan Das. Gyaneswar is said to have also been supported financially by Kanchan Das in his education, enabling him to study upto 10th standard. Kanchan Das gradually found Bangalore quite conducive to the spread of the Kabirpanth. Besides Gyan Das, three more disciples of

Kanchan Das forced Kanchan to stay for longer period in Bangalore. Persistent efforts of Kanchan Das and his disciples particularly Gyan Das finally enabled them to build the earliest Kabir Math in Bangalore in the early part of 20th century.

Apart from its geographical expansion, Kabirpanth came to face hostile forces posing a threat to it in a totally new fashion and phraseology in this period. We have stray reports of emerging conflicts between the modern reform organizations and the medieval reformative Kabirpanth. The Mahants of Kabirpanthi Maths in towns had commonly received some education. They came in contact with the members of the Brahm Samaj and the Arya Samaj at some places. There were, at least, two Mahants who recalled encounters with Arya Samaji Acharyas at Samastipur and Sonepur in Bihar.[109]

Late Madhav Goswami, Mahant of Kabir Math, Samastipur, Bihar recalled that the Arya Samaji Acharya met him for a specific reason, i.e., to seek his tacit consent and support to convert poor Kabirpanthis to the Arya Samaj. However, both the Arya Samaj and Kabirpanth tried to awaken (raise *chetana*) the lower castes of the neighbouring areas. The Acharya had been facing difficulties in converting the lower caste Kabirpanthi disciples to the Arya Samaj in the area of its influence. Recalling his early days, Madhav Goswami informed us that he repeatedly told the Acharya that true Kabirpanthis could never accept the teaching of the Arya Samaj.

Late Vishwanath Das, who was the Mahant of Math at Patna, till 1999, recalled an event in which his father, Bulakan Das, challenged Ram Narayan Shastri, an Arya

Samaji acharya, at Sonepur[110] towards the end of the nineteenth century, at a meeting organised by local Arya Samaji leaders. A large crowd is said to have gathered to attend the event. Bulakan Das also came out from his own camp (*Chhawani*). When Ram Narayan Shastri, one of the speakers, addressed Kabir as an ass (*Gadha*) who could not understand and appreciate the significance of the *Vedas*, Bulakan Das challenged Shastri on the spot. He lost his temper and asked Shastri, 'Who could understand the words of an 'ass' (i.e. Kabir)?' Shastri was stunned, as he had not expected such a queer reaction from the audience. *impromptu* He was unable to reply to Bulkan Das, upon which the latter pointed out that if Kabir was an ass in Shastri's estimation, Shastri, too, must be an ass, for the language of an ass could be understood properly by one of its kind alone. While some Kabirpathis remained critical to the Arya Samaji belief in the *Veda*, many others, particularly in Punjab, were successfully converted to the emerging Arya Samaj towards the end of the nineteenth century.

Such encounters with Arya Samaji leaders do indicate that Kabirpanthis, especially those in urban areas, were becoming sensitive to the preachings of modern reform associations. Yugalanand Bihari, who testifies to this development, wrote in the preface to *Anurag Sagar* how he was inspired to begin a vigorous campaign among Kabirpanthis in 1895. Recalling the context of his compaign, he wrote that, "On the one side, due to the negligence of Kabir Sahib's preachings, *Vansh* was on decline; one the other, the movement for publishing Veda itself was spreading fast. Due to the rapid spread of Arya Samajis, no religious sect of India could progress..."[111] (Translation mine)

More significant than these encounters was the adoption of modern methods by the Kabirpanthis to propagate their message. We have evidence of the publication of Kabirpanthi religious texts which are said to have been circulated widely in the late nineteenth and the early 20th century. Some of the late nineteenth and the early 20th century published texts of the Kabirpanth included *Bijak, Kabir Mansur, Anurag Sagar, Bavan Kasni Ka Janjira* etc.[112]

As has been described above, apart from varying details about the state of the Kabirpanth, we also note a kind of concerted attempt, in particular made by a group of Christian Missionaries through their writings, at proving that the Kabirpanth belonged within Christian fold. The faint attempt at Christianization of the Kabirpanth, however, can be found in the *Memoirs sur les Kabir-panthis*, of General Harriott,[113] published in 1832 in French, in which he compares it with the *Quakers*. He reports that he had many conversations with Kabirpanthis in 'Bihar and Malawi'. I discuss in the next chapter some of the significant elements of the Kabirpanth, which these Christian scholars, namely G.H.Westcott and F.E. Keay,[114] highlighted to prove their points of resemblance between these two unequal entities: the Kabirpanth, a sect, and the Christianity, a monolithic occidental religion.

In nutshell, the foregoing descriptions suggest that colonial discourses on Kabirpanth had been multifarious. In fact, all these scholars seem to have followed varying perspectives while describing the sect of Kabirpanth. To Buchanan, however, an objective description of the panth, as he himself observed, was to take precedence in his work as he was conducting the survey on behalf of the imperial government of the Bengal province which was in the urgent need to have knowledge of the native land and people of the region. However, H.H. Wilson as a worthy successor of William Jones and Colebrooke, the Orientalists, touched upon the subject in a scholarly manner and thus also referred to a number of indigenous written and oral materials in his descriptions of the sect. The census operation which was fully controlled and executed by the colonial administrators stringently considered the panth in terms of its relative political strength.

Order of the Kabirpanth was, thus, characterized primarily by its recurring splits and intriguing schisms during the nineteenth century. Although the colonial rule remained aloof from the affairs of the religious communites; such as, Kabirpanth, but its concerted attempts to understand Indian communities in European renaissance categories, did have stirring impact on identity formation for the 'fuzzy' sectarian communities. Developing educational, judicial and police system under the colonial rule too had also begun to affect the lives of Kabirpanthis, among many others, atleast urban centres. While the Bhagodasi and Kabir-Chaura branches of the panth were pooling their resources to acquire prominence from their respective headquarters at Dhanauti, Bihar and Benares, Uttar Pradesh, the Dharamdasi *Vansh* branch lately centred at Kawardha was heading towards a major split in its history, which culminated at the very outset of the 20th century. Yet further division leading to the formation of a Krishna

Karkhi Vachan Vanshi branch at Rosara in Bihar came to play a pivotal role in the panth's expansion towards north-eastern region upto Bhutan in the coming years.

References

1. I discovered these judgement papers from the scattered debris of the Dhanauti Math, the discovery which entirely owes to Gautam Goswami, visited Dhanauti, Saran district, Bihar, 29 May, 2013. I could succeed in the translation of a very few pages by Prof. Y.A. Zaffari, 85, New Delhi. I had first got the reference of Prof. Zaffari from the Director of the Iranian Cultural Centre, New Delhi, who has shown his own inability to decipher the Persian texts developed during medieval time in India. See Annexure-1, i, ii, iii, iv.
2. We can check this *guru-pranali* as preserved by Mahant Ramrup Goswami, Chatiya-Baraharwa Math, west Champaran, Bihar. He has preserved most of the documents related to the Math at his splendid house in Bettiah town, the district headquarters; this is the house where he resides instead of the Maths mainly due to the lack of civic amenities in the areas where his Maths are situated, interviewed, in Bettiah, 30 May, 2013. Ramrup Goswami is no more, he breathed his last in 2017.
3. *Nad Vansh Ka Sankshipt Itihas,* (ed. Mahesh Das), Mangal Das, Nadiya, 1996. p.129, Annexure-2, i.
4. Description of the Pavapuri Math is based on my field data collected by me on 28 Dec. 2014 .
5. Based on the oral tradition as collected during my visit to the Bahadurpur Math, Bihar on 28 Dec. 2014, Annexure-3.
6. Based on the oral tradition as collected during my visit to the Sikandarpur math Bihar on Feb. 2014, Annexure-4, i.
7. I describe the Samanpur Math on the basis of my field data, 28 Dec. 2014
8. Nad and Bind are the symbolic Hinidi words which respectively denotes Kabir's navel point and Bind as blood relatives, of Dharmdas. For details; see, Purnendu Ranjan, *Kabirpanth till the End of Medieval India*,Gyankosh Publishers,Chandigarh, 2016
9. *Nad Vansh Ka Itihās*, op. cit., p. 137.

10. *Ibid.*, p. 139.
11. The surveys conducted by Francis Buchanan, between 1809 and 1813, is one of the most detailed sources for the social and cultural history of Bihar and eastern Uttar Pradesh in the early nineteenth century, were commissioned by the British East India Company. His survey reports were first published selectively by Montgomery Martin in 1838.
12. Francis Buchanan, *The History, Antiquities, Topography and Statistics of Eastern India, Purnea and Bhagalpur* (ed. R. Montgomery Martin), Cosmo Publications, Delhi, 1976 (1838).
13. *Ibid.*, Vol. IV, p.178.
14. *Ibid.*, Vol. II, Bhagalpur & Gorukhpoor, pp. 392-393.
15. *Ibid.*, Vol. I, Bihar (Patna City) & Sahabad, pp. 203-205.
16. Francis Buchanan, *Account of Shahabad,1812-1813,* p. 63 as quoted in William R. Pinch, *Peasants and Monks in British India,* University of California Press, Berkeley,1996, p. 33.
17. H.H.Wilson, *Religious Sects of Hindus,* (ed. Ernst R. Rost), Hard Press Publishing, Miami, 2010 (1862).
18. *Ibid.*, p. 48.
19. *Ibid.*, p. 45.
20. *Ibid.*, p. 65.
21. *Ibid.*, p. 65.
22. *Ibid.*, p. 64.
23. *Ibid.*, p. 48.
24. *Ibid.*, p. 65.
25. W. J. Wilkins, *Modern Hinduism*, Delhi Book Store, Delhi, 1975 (1887).
26. *Ibid.*, p. 178
27. *Census of British India, Report on the Census of Bengal*, 1872, Vol. I, microfiche, Bengal Secretariat Press, Calcutta, 1873, JNU, New Delhi
28. *Ibid.*, p.152.
29. *Census of British India, Report on the Census of Bengal*, 1882, Vol. I, Microfilm, NMML, New Delhi, p. 207.
30. Denzil Ibbetson, *Report on the Census of Punjab*, Vol. I, 1882,
31. *Ibid.*, p.2
32. H.A. Ross, *A Glossary of the Tribes and Castes of the Punjab and*

Nort-West Frontier Provinces, Vol. I, Language Department, Punjab, 1883, p. 368.

33. Kadar Nath Dvivedi, *Kabir aur Kabirpanth, Tulnatamak Adhyayan,* Hindi, Hindi Sahitya Sammelan, Allahabad,1995, p. 174.
34. H.A., Ross, *op. cit.*, pp. 415-416.
35. *Ibid.*, p. 415.
36. *Ibid.*, p. 414.
37. *Ibid.*, p. 415.
38. *Ibid.*, p. 418
39. Denzil Ibbetson, *op. cit.*, p. 419.
40. *Ibid.*, p. 419.
41. *Ibid.*, p. 419.
42. I have described Paramanand's birth place *as per* his own version as mentioned by him in the introductory chapter in *Kabir Mansur (Urdu)* , translated in Hindi by Madhavacharya, Lakshmi Venkateshwar Press, Bombay, Sambat 2009 (1942).
43. *Census of British India*, Report,Vol. I, *op. cit.*, p. 24.
44. *Ibid.*, p. 24.
45. *Census of British India*, 1881, *Central Provinces,* Vol. I, Education Society Press, Byculla, Bombay, 1882, pp. 26-28.
46. Robert V. Russel and Raibahadur, Hiralal, *The Tribes and Castes of the Central Provinces of India,* Vol., II, Cosmo Publications, Delhi, 1975 (1916), p. 413.
47. *Census of British India, op. cit.*, pp. 44-45.
48. *Ibid.*, pp. 45-46.
49. *Ibid.*, p. 46.
50. *Ibid.*, p. 47-48.
51. William Crooke, *Tribes and Castes of the North-West Frontier Provinces and Oudh,* Office of the Superintendent of Govt.Printing, Calcutta,1896, pp. 75-77.
52. *Ibid.*, p. 77.
53. *Census of British India*, 1901, Vol. I, pt. II, table p. 362.
54. The descriptions of Bombay and Delhi Maths are based on my own field works, visited Mumbai, 20 Oct, 2013; interviewed scores of Kabir disciples in Delhi, 7 July 2013, Annexure 5 & 6.
55. Y.A. Parmar, *The Mahyavanshi, the Success Story of a Scheduled*

Caste, Mittal Publication, Delhi, 1987, pp. 93-96.

56. Visited Paharganj Kabir Math, interviewed some of the shopkeepers running their shops in Maths building, Delhi, 7 July 2013.
57. Acharya Ram Dayal Das, Bidupur, interviewed, 1 Oct. 2014. He admits that both he himself and the preceding Acharya of the Jagodasi branch could not keep track of these sub-branches, as their own headquarters had to face unnecessary litigations. Consequently, about 100 *bighas* of landed property at qasba Nawala, near Muzaffarabad, Uttar Pradesh were sold out by the concerned authorities in connivance with the local goons, Annexure-7, i,ii,iii.
58. Maren Bellwinkel-Schempp has made an intensive study of the Kabirpanthis of Kanpur, see his article, Maren Bellwinkel-Schempp,'Kabir-Panthis in Kanpur: From Sampradaya to Dalit Identity', In Monika Horstmann (ed.), *Images of Kabir*, Manohar, New Delhi, 2002, pp. 215-232.
59. G.H. Westcott, *op. cit.*, p.I.
60. *Ibid.*, p.II.
61. N.P. Arora and L.K. Tripathi (eds.), *Kanpur ka Itihas*, (Hindi), Vol. I, Kanpur, 1950.
62. Uday Adhau, My Project Fellow, visited Lucknow and interviewed Mahant Yogendra Das, 21 March 2014.
63. We had to visit Lucknow more than once to find these Persian documents from the Mahant of Daliganj Math. I also visited and interviewed, 15 March 2015. See Annexure.8, i,ii,iii,iv.
64. Rajendar Singh, my first PF, visited and conducted fieldwork in and around Saharanpur from 16-17 May 2013, but he could not visit the oldest Kabir Math of Saharanpur for fear of lynching as he explained away his delinquency to me towards the assigned tasks. However I visited this Math and found no spectre of fear existing in the area of Tilkana Road, where the deserted Math still stands, visited and interviewed, 27 Feb, 2015.
65. I discovered a copy of the judgement paper from Shree Sadanand, a former IAS, Chandigarh. See the first page of the Order in Annexure. 9, i.
66. Most of the Dharmdasi Kabirpanthis of the Panjab region consider

Kabir ashram of Multan as the seat of their guru; however Kabirpanthis then living in Multan itself left Multan forever in the trail of partition in 1947, and settled mostly in the rehabilitation camp then opened in Delhi, where they formed their new Kabir Asram, in Jhandewalan area in 1952; Secretary of the math, Omprakash, 60, a businessman by profession, interviewed by me, 26 May 2013.

67. Karanchi Ashram is said to be have been completely abandoned due to hostile attitude of the Pakistan government as reported by Bithaldas Lakhamsi Das, 89, a Pakistani Hindu Kabirpanthi living in Toronto, Canada, interviewed, 12 Feb 2012. The ashram was known as Kabir Dharmdas Ashram situated along Rangcchod Line, Karanchi. He recalled that the ashram was looted by riotteers in the aftermath of the partition in 1947, when it was being run under the leadership of Swami Balkrishna of Baroda Kabir Ashram,Gujarat.
68. Based on the field data collected by Rajendar Singh and myself, I visited Ludhiana on 29 May 2012 and Rajendar on 7 June 2013.
69. Based on the field data collected by Uday, PF, Burhanpur, and Ludhiana, Sept. 2013.
70. Rajendra Prasad, *Kabirpanth Ka Udbhav avam Prasar,* (Hindi), Vanshavali Pratinidhi Sabha, Damakheda, 1986, pp. 65-67.
71. Rival groups here denote almost all the spokespersons of the non-Dharmdasi branches of the panth. For details see, Munishwar Ray 'Munish', *Kabirpanth Ki Jago Shakha,* (Hindi), Guru Gaddi Jagu shakha, Bidupur, 1977, p. 56. I had met and interviewed Munishwar at his Hajipur residence in 1996, while he was recuperating from his chronic illness. He was a retired headmaster of a govt. school and had authored a number of books in Hindi.
72. Rajendra Prasad, *op. cit.*, pp. 63-64.
73. Puran Das, *Nirnay Saar*, Hindi, Kabir Nirnay Mandir, Burhanpur, 1951, p. 4.
74. Uday, interviewed, 15 Sept. 2013.
75. I have taken genealogy from the legal will documents of former Mahant Ram Swarup Das of Burhanpur Math; Uday visited and interviewed at Burhanpur Math, 15 Sept. 2015, Annexure-10, i, ii, iii.
76. Abhilash Das, *Kabir Darshan,* (Hindi), Parakh Prakashan,

Allahabad, 1982, p. 314.

77. Uday, *op. cit.*, 15 Sept. 2015.
78. Based on the field data collected by myself and Uday from Jamnagar Math, visited respectively in Nov. 2012; and 3 Jan. 2014. Dates are however also tallied from their genealogy of the Mahants, Annexure-11, i,ii.
79. One can check any of the scholarly biographies of Gandhi.
80. Jam Bibhaji's name is still recalled by disciples residing close to the Jamnagar Math. The genealogy of Jamnagar rajas may be seen in *The Imperial Gazetteer of India*, Nawanagar, Vol. 18, Clarendon Press, Oxford, 1909, p. 420.
81. I had discovered a manuscript of *Panji Panth Prakash* written originally by Krishna Karakh and later added by his succeeding Mahants of Rosara Mahadeo Math. The following description is based on prevailing oral tradition, also corroborated by the *Panji Panth Prakash,* Sundar Press, Muzaffarpur, 1944. I must here acknowledge the helpful and humble demeanor of late Raj Narayan Das to whom I had met and granted favour particularly during the initial phase of my doctoral research on the Kabirpanth. His accidental death appears to be a personal loss to me in many ways.
82. This version is commonly held by the hostile group of Kabirpanthis of Rosara in particular and of other parts of India in general.
83. *Panji Panth Prakash, op. cit.*, p. 44.
84. I received a copy of *guru-pranali* from Acharaya Raj Narayan Das, interviewed, Rosara, Bihar, 12 June, 2013.
85. The description is based on the views I gathered during my field work and interviews I had among related satsangis (Radhaswami disciples) in Agra, Uttar Pradesh, 23 Oct. 2015; and at its Beas centre in Panjab, 25 Feb 2012, Anx-11A.
86. Ujjiyar Singh's contribution to the Kawardha ashram is still recalled by a number of Kabirpanthis in the locality, interviewed by Uday, 1 June 2013. Also see, Rajendra Prasad, *op. cit.*, p. 73.
87. Yugalanand Bihari (ed.), *Anurag Sagar*, Venkateshwar Press, Bombay, 1931, p. 37.
88. The account is entirely based on *Anurag Sagar*, p. 38.
89. Rajendra Prasad, *Ashirvad Shatabadi Granth*, Vanshavali

Pratinidhi Sabha, Damakheda, 2004, p. 21.

90. G.H. Westcott, *op. cit.*, p. 62.
91. F.E. Keay, *op. cit.*, p. 101.
92. Rajendra Prasad, *op. cit.*, p. 43.
93. The judgement papers are still in the possession of the *Vansh Gaddi* functionaries, but despite our repeated requests, they do not want to show these to us.
94. Charles Grant (ed.), *The Gazetteer of the Central Provinces of India*, second edition,Usha Publications, New Delhi, 1984 (1870).
95. I have consulted the works of Stephen Fuchs, *Rebellious Prophets: A Study of Massianic Movements in Indian Religions*, Asia Publishing House, Bombay, 1965.
96. Joseph Bara, "Colonialism, Christianity and the Tribes of Chotanagpur in East India, 1845-1890", *Journal of South Asian Studies* Vol. XXX No.2 (August 2007), p. 205 ff.
97. *Ibid*, p. 208.
98. I have largely relied on my field data collected from Sikkim, Darjeeling, Siligudi, New Jalpaegudi, in West Bengal and Guahati, in Assam, Shillong in Meghalaya from 26 to 29 March, 2015. During the course of field work in Sikkim discovered a didactic text written in Nepali from Bhimdas Ghimrey, Shanti Nagar, Singtam, East Sikkim, that also corroborated the prevailing tradition in the region. Anex-12, i, ii, iii, iv, v.
99. *Vachan Vansh'Kabir Panth Purushdor Guru-Pranali, Nepali,* (ed.), 2002, Anx - 12V.
100. Axel Harneite-Sievers, (ed.), *A Place in the World, New Local Historiographis from Africa and South- Asia*, Brill Leiden, Boston, 2002, p. 335.
101. *Vachan Vansh, op. cit.*, 2002, p. 36.
102. *Ibid.*, p. 41.
103. I have largely relied on my field data collected from Bengalore city and Hyderabad to describe panth's expansion; first round field-work between 7 and 8 Oct., 2014. However Gyani Das's handwritten memoirs written in Kannad by him adds and corroborates the oral tradition. I have had a photocopy of it with me. Annexure-13, i, ii, iii.
104. I have taken a snap of the date as inscribed on the *Samadhi* slab

inside the Math complex, visited, 30 May 2015. Annexure-14.

105. Aurangzeb's saga still resounds in the popular memory of the people to whom I interviewed during the field work in the area, visited and interviwed, 1 June 2014, Annexure-15, i, ii.
106. The statement is based on the memory of Giri's *bhgina* (sister's son), taking care of the ashram presently, interviewed, 1 June 2014,
107. I have, during my field works in the northern India, heard of a few Giri Mahants and Guruji who held Kabir and his followers in high esteem.
108. *Jivan Charait*, a manuscript, diary, Kannad, p. 1., Annexure-16, i, ii.
109. Madhav Goswami, interviewed, Samastipur Math, 23 May, 1996. He died in at the age of 116 in 2001, Anx-17.
110. I had interviewed Mahant Vishwanth of the Patna Math at his camp during Sonepur *Pashu mela*, on 7th Oct. 1996. Mahant Vishwanath expired in 2006.
111. Yugalanand Bihari, *op. cit.*, p. 23.
112. Parmanand, *Kabir Mansur, op. cit.*, p. 12.
113. General Harriott, *Memoirs sur les Kabir-panthis,* quoted in G.H Westcott, *Kabir and Kabir Panth, op. cit.*, p.111.
114. I describe Westcott and Keay's views on this aspect in the next chapter.

Kabirpanth in the 20th Century

By the turn of 20th century, Kabirpanth had already expanded its branches from Jammu & Kashmir to the north-eastern parts of then British India. As the century progressed, it also began to expand further towards the southern parts of India. Although it could not expand towards the extreme parts of southern India; i.e. Tamil Nadu and Kerala in a significant way, it could firmly establish itself in the capital cities of the present-day Telangana, previously part of Andhra Pradesh, and Karnataka. My field-work findings in all regions make it clear that some leading members of the north Indian Kabirpanth community had played pivotal role in its expansion across all these regions. As the Kabirpanth could not make much headway towards the extreme parts of southern India, so has been in the extreme parts of the north-eastern parts of India where it could not expand beyond Meghalaya. It could expand upto parts of Karachi in the north-western parts of the British India, while almost all the present day metropolis of Independent India already came to have centres of Kabirpanth except Thiruvananthapuram by this century.

Apart from the decennial censuses being carried by the British government, we have a few non-official English scholars who have left their account of what they saw and learnt about the Kabirpanth during the early part of this century. The earliest account of the Kabirpanthi centres existing in Banares was that of G.H.Westcott, the most widely quoted work on the history of the Kabirpanth, published in 1907. It would however be a gross mistake to consider the work of Westcott merely in terms of his Christian bias, as Kabirpanth as a historical movement has met with a fair treatment in his study. Even a cursory reading of these works makes it clear that unlike Wilson, Westcott developed his argument in favour of Kabir's Muslim or Sufi origin and considers Kabir as a historical figure, as Malcolm had earlier noted in the Punjab during his study of Sikhism in 1812. He however minces no words about his difference from Wilson here again on the division and the predominance of the Kabirpanthi branches, one over the other, during his time. To quote him:

> The division of the Panth into twelve divisions as given in Wilson, H.H. seems to be quite fanciful. There are other branches at Bombay, in Gujarat etc., but it is doubtful whether these regard themselves as independent of these two main divisions. Of these two divisions, that which bears the name of Dharam Das, though barely mentioned by Wilson, is the more influential at the present time.[1]

Unlike Wilson, Westcott further highlights Kabir's mythological birth from a Brahmin widow. He points out the nature of the panth in that 'the Kabirpanth exists as a protest against the religious exclusiveness of the twice-born castes'. He goes on to compare the practices of the Kabirpanth with *sagun* Hindu sects, and let us know that originally there was no *mandar* (temple) at Kabir Chaura but in this respect, as probably in others, they had assimilated their own arrangements to those of the Maths of other religious orders. He refers to the internal bickerings then surfacing up among different branches of the Kabirpanth. Among the most talked about dispute which had broken out on account of *Jot Prasad* between Puran Das and then Mahant of Dharamdasi section, and, henceforth, the monthly schedule of *Jot* began to be observed annually.[2]

G.H. Westcott had also noted the measure of the agricultural produce of the Kabir-Chaura Math. To cite from his work, "At another place, he points out, The Hindu Math is under the management of the Kabir Chaura Mahant. The Present Mahant, Gur Prasad Dass, is especially interested in the superintendence of agricultural operations. In the absence of the Mahant the *pujari* is placed incharge of the Kabir Chaura Math."[3] At another place, he points out, "The land is chiefly under rice cultivation. In 1900, the land at Balwa supplied the Kabir Chaura Math with 750 maunds of rice and the Magahar Math with 500 maunds".[4]

Roughly around the same period, we have interesting accounts of both the Kabir-Chaura and Dharmdasi Lahartara section of Kabirpanthi centres from Edwin Greaves. His book was published in 1909.[5] He has described Kabir-Chaura as one of the most important sites then visited by the people. To quote him:

> The followers of Kabir Das have an important centre in Benares. Their monastery is situated in Kabir Chaura Mohalla. Kabir Das was an eclectic and his one endeavour, to teach monotheism which all might

hold, though expressing it in various ways. He was neither a Hindu nor Mahommedan in his teachings, and yet at his death was claimed by both. He protested against idolatry, pronounced the spirit of religion to be more important than its form and the name by which God was called a matter of comparative indifference, so long as God was really worshipped. He taught the necessity of a good life and the broad spirit of brotherhood, insisting on these points as of far greater importance than any mere outward orthodoxy. The guru or teacher was exalted to a position of great authority, so much so that in course of time the guru has, to a large extent, assumed the status which the Brahman possesses among the ortho dox. Celibacy is insisted on for full disciples of the sect, but not for those who are adherents. In other words, it is necessary for the clergy, but not for the laity.[6]

Besides describing the then prevalent view about Kabir and the Kabirpanth, he went on to describe the specifications of the physical outlook of the Kabir-Chaura and Lahartara Dharmdasi ashrams located in Benares. To cite him:

1. *Kabir Das Ka Mandir*–This is situated in a back lane not far from the Municipal Office, in Kabir Chaura. The property covers a considerable space of ground. On one side of the lane, there is a large open court-yard with various buildings round it, a place for the "Mahant," or head of the akhara, and in a chamber are treasured the "*gaddi*"(the cushion against which a teacher leans), and sandals which

belonged to Kabir Das. In many of these so-called Reformed Sects of Hinduism the worship diverted from idols has a tendency to devolve upon the "guru" (teacher), past or present. This part of the monastery is occupied by devotees belonging to the sect, they may be continuous residents or visitors from other parts. In the court-yard are also some '*samadhis*' or tombs of deceased Mahants. Most Mahants and swamies are buried (in the ground or in the river, not cremated). On the other side of the lane there is a garden and a few small buildings. This part is apparently used as a guest-house and here married men with their wives may be accommodated. In this sect all teachers and fully initiated members must be celibates, but lay members need not be so. The two parts of the premises are connected by a small bridge passing over the lane, but they have also their separate doors.

2. *Kabir Das Ki Baithak*–This is situated at Lahartara, some distance away, but as it will not fit in with any other group, and has to do with Kabir Das is mentioned here. It lies just outside Benares near the Grand Trunk Road in the Allahabad direction, very near to the 423rd milestone. There is a neatly built temple on a bit of slightly elevated ground to the south of the road, and above a shallow but wide-spreading tank or pond. It was on this pond that Kabir Das, as a babe, is said to have been found; hence the veneration in which the spot is held. In the temple, or "mandir," as they prefer to call such buildings, is a "paduka" (footprints) of Kabir Das, or

> as his followers often speak of him "Kabir Sahib." There is apparently only one old Kabir Dasi living at the place, a courteous old fellow, but quite unread, and not knowing much about the history of Kabir Das. A few graves of deceased devotees are found in the adjoining ground.[7]

Apart from the Kabirpanth establishments, Greaves also noted the active presence of the Dadupanthis who have been indebted to Kabir since its birth. To quote him," So few Didupanthis are found in Benares that it is not necessary to devote any space to an account of the sect. Very broadly speaking it is a collateral sect working along the same lines as the Kabirdasis." [8]

In addition to these individual Erupean scholars, the early censuses conducted under British colonial rule provide some ideas about their numerical strength both at all India and provincial levels. As per the religious statistics given in the 1901 census, the total number of Kabirpanthis obtaining towards the turn of 20th century in India, as mentioned in the last chapter was 8,43,171, which included the number of those Kabirpanthis alone who declared the Kabirpanth as their religion distinct from Hindu, Muslim and Sikhs in the enumeration form circulated for the purposes of census by the related officials. Nonetheless, this total at all-India level did not include the number of the Kabipanthis of Punjab and the Bengal Provinces due to certain technical reasons. But for us that number is available both for the late 19th and early 20th centuries. In 1891, Kabirpanthis numbered 1,08,175 in the Punjab and it came down to 89,259 as per the provincial census data of Punjab in 1911.[9] According to the census of 1901, this total is distributed as follows:

Central Provinces, 493,393; United Provinces, 15,771; Central India 124,600; Bombay Presidency, 9,407.[10]

However we need to be cautious while taking these number at their face value, because doubts on the number of Kabirpanthis were expressed both by the census enumerators in their submitted reports before the government then and now also in our contemporary society of Punjab by the fellow disciples during my discussions with them. We can imagine the enumerators' confusion and under-calculated number of Kabirpanthis in the Punjab in 1881 as noted by Denzil Ibbetson, who wrote that "The Kabirpanthi will almost always describe himself as a Hindu but a certain number have returned the name as that of an independent religion and some as a sect of the Sikhs." [11] At the same time it also appears that a branch of Kabirpanthis called Dharamdasi, and a Kabirwaha Rajput, an agricultural caste of Multan did not figure up in the total number of Kabirpanthis as the Dharam Dasia, the most widespread branch of the panth presently entered themselves separately as those of Kabirwah of Multan.[12]

The Census of 1911 provides further insight into the conditions of Kabirpanthis of Punjab, which are unfortunately not available for the Kabirpanthis of then Bengal Province just because of a policy decision in 1882, as stated by the census operators, that religious groups such as the Kabirpanth having no political significance for the colonial government, deserves no specific enumeration in the future census.[13] In 1911, real Kabirpanthis in Punjab were described as Sadhus 'but most weavers call themselves by that name, without knowing much about the doctrines preached by Kabir'.[14]

Further it says that the sect does not appear to be losing much ground as their total number of 1,08,175 in 1891 had not sharply declined as their number was still reported to be 89,294 in 1911.[15] Its followers were found mainly in the eastern and southern Punjab particularly in the districts of Hissar, Gurgaon, Karnal, Jind, Rohtak, Delhi, Gurdaspur, Gujranwala and Sialkot. The statistics given in the census also provide us information about the number of female Kabirapnthis in each of these districts. The largest number of them were found in then Gurgaon district in which their number was 11,908 out of the total 2,4236.

The census of 1931 reported of another group called Karal Bansi forming part of Kabir panthis as its members were followers of Kabir Bhagats (Kabir is addressed as a bhagat in the *Guru Granth Sahib*, a fact which many devout Kabirpanth followers ardently disapprove).[16] Karal Bansis also believed in Guga, in whose name a fair was then held at Meri in the Bikaner state. In the matter of dress and food, they were akin to the people of the United Provinces, and their religious ceremonies were the same as those of other Hindus. They were found only in Hissar (*sic*) district and their occupation was shoe-making and their mother tongue was *Purbi*, a corrupt form of Urdu. But the interesting point about the Guga was that Guga came to be revered as a saint and not as the founder of a sect. His votaries therefore followed any doctrines or faith. A number of Guga worshiper belonged to Muslim religion too. Thus the reports itself make it clear that the element of Guga worship was then becoming a secondary trait of one's religious life.

More significant fact from historical point of view has been their sharply declining number at least from late 19th century onwards as the decennial census till 1931 suggest. From approximately 2 lakhs during the late 19th century, their number came down to 37111 and 12780 in 1921 and 1931 respectively, declining at the rate of more than 65% a decade.[17] We would here like to highlight the fact that during the same period, the number of the Arya Samajis and Radhaswamis, modern religious organizations, increased by more than 100% as the census reports of Punjab make these clear for us. The two remaining religious communities showing substantial increase included the Sikhs and the Muslims. Closeness of the Kabirpanth with the Radhaswamis, as described above, must have been a potent factor in drawing the former members towards the latter. At the same time expansive Akali movement, in the region, seems to have adverse impact on the panth as larger part of the social constituencies of the two had been common. According to the census of 1931. 'The Akali movement during the last decade is mainly, for the most part, comprising members of depressed classes, agriculturists and artisans in rural areas',[18] the same sections which were usually the stronghold of sects; such as, the Kabirapanth. The Sikhs, in fact, just constituted 8.2% of total population of the Colonial Punjab in 1881, which rose up to 14.3% in 1931.[19]

The number of Radhaswamis in 1911 was just 3862 while Kabirpanthis were roughly in a lakh. In 1931, the total number of Radhaswamis went upto 5386, indicating a plausible shift of the former to the latter in the region.[20]

Early 20th century district Gazetteers of the British India often took note of the then Kabir followers. Some of the *tehsils* were named after Kabir such as Kabirwala in Multan. In this district, they noted that:

> Another remarkable movement of a different character in the small tomb of Sayeed Kabir, situated in a somewhat inaccessible position in the jungle west of Sarla on the eastern boundary of the Lodhran *tehsil*. The design is a curious mixture of Saracenic and Hindu types and there are inscriptions moulded on the brick, both in Persian and in Nagri characters." [21]

In Hoshiarpur district, the compilers of the Gazetteers noticed the presence of a distinct Dadupanthis. To quote,"A peculiar Hindu sect...localized in this district is that of the Dadupanthis. There are colonies of them in at least six villages of the district. Dadu had lived at Naraina in Jaipur territory about 330 years ago."[22]

In the present, these Kabir-*vanshi* desciples of Kabir, so to say, have been the actual flag-bearers of the Kabir's teaching in the northern part of India. They are also known as Kabir Bhagats, Meghs, Dhanak Kabirpanthis– all of them have been living in different parts of Panjab, Himachal and Jammu & Kashmir.

A new centre of devotion saw its emergence at village Mekhewal Ganjiya famous as *Dera* Rampura in the present Hoshiarpur district of Panjab. One Ishardas is said to be have founded this *dera* during the early years of the 20th century. Although the *dera* have till date remained part of the Ghisadasi tradition; it associates itself with the broader framework of devotion as taught by Kabir to Ghasidas.[23]

In the Central Provinces, the centre founded by Puran Das had been acquiring prominence since the beginning of the century. The landed property of the Burhanpur Math was mostly developing in the *qasba* Sidhkhera. It has since been one of the most resourceful Kabir Math in India. By dint of ample resources and dynamic leadership, it could spread its sub-branches extensively in several states of India. To manage landed property effectively, a sub-branch was opened at Sindhkhera itself. Apart from this, we found its sub-branches operating in Karnataka, Maharashtra, Andhra Pradesh, Chhattisgarh, Madhya Pradesh so on and so forth. Most important among these sub-branches have been at Rajangarh, Chiveri, Dhetha, Doma, Siwani, Bhanpuri, Attang, Sirsida, Mahasamund, Gatapar, Ranaes, Bharara, Chriracbandh, Ambala, Nagpur, Hyderabad and Bangalore, and Khalilabad in U.P.[24]

Within the Dharamdasi *Vansh* branch lately opened at Damakheda, the seeds of discord finally resulted in its last division during early 1930s. Both the scholarly studies of G.H. Westcott and F.E. Keay predated this major split. The central issues once again too veered around the hereditary succession at the *guru-gaddi* by the celibate or the householder. Hereditary succession in itself would easily become exposed in the absence of a natural heir; i.e. if the incumbent Mahant did not have a son from his recognized wife. Absence of a natural heir, in the past had precipitated splits more than once, this time, too, it led to its complete division. Consequently, a new centre was opened by the dissident group at Kharasiya, Chhattisgarh in 1933.

In fact after the death of Dayanam, the successor son of Ugranam, in Dec. 1927, the *Vansh gaddi* at the Damakheda Math had to face the serious crisis of succession exacerbated by the recurring issue of celibate/ householder Mahant at a Kabir Math till 1935.[25] It is necessary to bear in mind that Damakheda had also been the native place of one of the three wives of Ugranam, who had died in 1913. Dayanam was born of his wife from Damakheda in 1898. However, Dayanam could not beget a son, nor could he adopt a child before his sudden death.[26] Consequently, a drastic break and vaccum in the continuity of the alleged blessings of Kabir for Guruship to the descendents of Dharmdas until the 42 generation became the rallying point of the dissident groups within the Dharmdasi branch.

The vacant seat of the Acharya at the Damakhera led to the development of a 'Kabir Council' which was formed with the objective of managing affairs of the Dharmdasi headquarters in 1928. This idea of the Kabir Council emerged during a grand *sabha* (meeting) having been organized at Koogharmal from 11 March to 26 March continuously.[27] It consisted of a Core Committee of 21 Mahants and a Management Committee of 60 Kabir followers coming from different parts of the British India. The Council came to have Ganpat Patel of Tekari, Nagpur, as its first President, Keshav Prasad Verma of Faguram, Bilaspur, as its first Secretary. The core committee of the Council itself found divided over the issue of management of the headquarters. Initially the core members tried to run the headquarters collectively and unanimously, but soon they realized that one person must be deputed on a regular basis to look after the material resources of the headquarters. Some members of the core committee, Arjun Das of Damakhera, Pancham Das of Mau-Sihiniya of the Central Provinces, and Kashi Das of Rosara, Bihar and Vichardas Shastri of Kashi, to name a few, themselves began to clamour for the coveted seat. Ultimately Kashi Das, 55, emerged victorious among all of them and hence he was finally appointed as a *Diwan or Dharmadhikari* (acting head of the headquarters). Before Kashi Das took over the charge of a Diwan/Dharmadhikari,[28] he however had to sign an affidavit at Janjgir swearing that he would stick to the provisions of the Kabir Council against all odds. The affidavit was signed by two witnesses–Tilak Das of Regnauya Math, Motihari, Bihar and Yuglanand Bihari of the Kharsiya centre, then situated in tehsil Janjgir.

Splendid building inside Acharya Gaddi, Damakhera

The first meeting of the Council after its formation took place in Bhatapara, near Raipur in May 1928. It is said that Kashi Das did not return to Damakheda after this meeting almost for next 10 months. The absence of the Diwan from the headquarters for such a long time caused a call of an early meeting of the Council at Sarahar near Korba in Oct. 1928, which insisted upon an early joining of Kashi Das at the headquarters. During the deliberations, it was noted that as the Kabir Council was not yet formally registered under the Societies Act, he was withholding exercise of his fuller involvement in the participation of Damakhera seat. Subsequently, the Kabir Council was registered at Nagpur in April 1929, upon which Kashi Das did not waste a single minute in rejoining the duty as a Diwan.[29] Yet the coterie of Dayanam's widows and their well-wishers successfully forced Kashi Das to sign another affidavit of his unflinching commitment to the principles of the Dharamdasi branch and full care of the widows of Dayanam.

However, the raging issue of celibate or householder Mahant for the headquarters still remained unresolved. Kashi Das had resigned from the Bagicha Math of Rosara, his original *gaddi*, and getting settled at Damarkheda. On the other hand, the admirers and lineage group of Dharamdas were all out to fill up unprecedented vacancy at the seat of Damakhera Math by hook or by crook. The Bombay High court had already declined to recognize the succession of Ugranam, who was born of an illegal wife of the incumbent Mahant in 1898. Taking a leaf out of this judicial strictures, the *Vansh* group came out with a novel strategm in the form of a handwritten letter stated to be written by Dayanam himself, as an official will, mentioning that the successor at the seat was to take birth in the family of Chaturbhuj Das, who was related to the Dharmdas family through

Haqnam's ancestry. The boy took birth in 1933 and immediately said to be adopted by one of the three widows of Dayanam in 1933. The 'adopted' successor was named as Grindhmuni and was declared Acharya of the Damakheda Math at the age 2 ½ in 1935. The widow of Dayanam named *mata* Kalap Devi, [30] was named as the actual care-taker till Grindhmuni was declared a full-fledged Acharya in 1952. However, the *Panja* (seal of the Dharmdasi *Vansh gaddi*) began to have the name of Grindhmuni as the Acharya since 1935 itself.

Meanwhile Kashi Das successfully executed his hidden agenda of giving formal shape of *nirvana* tradition of the seat of Dharmdasi Mahant as soon as the adoption of a newly born child became public. Before he could succeed in his game plan, he had to play his card very deftly in tandem with some eminent members of the Kabirpanth both Dharmdasi and otherwise. The group led by Kashi Das, a resourceful Mahant in his own capacity, had to face a stiff resistance from the lineage groups of Dharmdas, who could never nurse the idea of letting the Acharyship of the Dharmdasi branch go out of their families. The core group of *Vansh* family was rightfully in no position to consider Kashi Das as a successor of the *Vansh Gaddi*, as he was not a natural heir but selected by the Council. Kashi Das was thus getting alienated progressively from the family lobby all out to keep seat of Acharya within the *vansh* (dynasty) of Dharmdas. In the situation, Kashi Das was practically side-lined and clearly found his objective doomed to be defeated at Damakheda. He, in active collaboration with Yugalanand Vihari, intensified his mission of forming a distinct Dharmdasi branch, which was to follow the principle of a celibate Mahant for the Kabirpanthi Math. He already had the support of eminent Kabirpanthis; such as Baji Rao Kante of Gwalior, Vichardas Shastri of Lahartara Math Kashi, and Moti Das of Baroda Math, in this task. They all began to purchase plots of land in Kharasiya in order to open a new *nirvana/nad* centre of Kabir, different from the tradition of the Dharmdasi *Vansh* headquarters at Damkheda.

Kashi Das, the Diwan of the Damakheda *gaddi*, convnend a meeting of the core committee of the Council at Sarahar near Korba in 1931 before he was to make public his hidden agenda of opening a *nirvana* Math at Kharasiya in 1934. In the Sarhar meeting itself, *nad* group had indicated at their imminent step of separation from the *Vansh gaddi*, yet it took another two years before the *nad* group adherents formed their separate headquarters at Kharasiya. Kashi Das became the founder Acharya of this Dharmdasi *nad* branch and was rechristened as Grindhmuni. His name is said to have been proposed by one Sukhdev Das, the Mahant of Koogharmal Math, which had come under the custody of followers opposed to succession of Ugranam since late nineteenth century. All the assembled followers unanimously seconded the proposal. Vichardas Shastri who had been another active member of the *nad* group was profusely rewarded as he was simultaneously declared the successor of Kashi Das .[31]

A sizeable number of followers and Mahants of Gujarat had been supporters of the group of Kashi Das and *Virakta* Mahants required for all the Kabir centres as well. Among them, some were also Udapanthis.[32] There have been divergent views on the nomenclature of *Uda* Panthis.

To some, *Uda* denotes *Udaar* (gentle) in Hindi, implying generous and saintly nature of those who initiated this group. To some others, etymologically, the world *Uda* has its origin from a Sanskrit word *Ud* which means 'Universe' (*Brahm*), thereby reflecting upon the spiritual orientation to these followers. Oral tradition prevailing among the Udapanthis, to whom we met, have a different viewpoint on the word Uda. According to them, Udas were one of the earliest groups of Kabir followers who had shown full commitment on the path of the spiritualism as taught to them by Kabir. They never wanted to deviate even an inch from their path of spiritualism, while leading a full-fledged household life. It was primarily Udasis intense commitment and devotion to the spiritual life, without renouncing family life that distinguished them both from other groups of Kabir followers and commoners and thus, they became famous as *Uda* or *Juda* (unique) in the then community. Most of these informants live, in and around, Baroda, Surat, Ahmedabad, Mehsana and so on and so forth.

It is also said that the Ram-Kabirpanthis/Udapanthis who were living in the Surat district of Gujarat, began to extend their activities in certain parts of Chhota Nagpur districts of the present Jharkhand towards the end of the nineteenth century.[33]

The informants of F.E. Keay during the early 20th century had told that Burhanpur had been then associated with the Kabir Chaura Math, Kashi. F.E. Keay's informants might be correct considering the changing association of the Burhanpur Math since its inception. There is every possibility that functionaries of the Burhanpur Math, finding themselves alienated by the Dharmdasi authorities, gradually associated with the Kabir-Chaura, as they too had to seek affiliation and legitimacy from an exiting branch of the panth.[34] Kabir Chaura functionaries came to Burhanpur's rescue at the hour of need, at least, during its formative stage.

The element of Christian bias, however, seems to have profoundly influenced the description of the Kabirpanth by Bishop G.H. Westcott, who mentions Kabirpanth, in the preface of his work, as a religious system which owes something to 'Hindu, Mohammedans [sic] and Christian influences'. He rightfully acknowledges the assistance which he received from Rev. Pandit Walji Bhai, Rev. Ahmed Shah and Baptist Prem Chand, three of the scholarly Christian converts from India – all these three had written enough to trace the origin of Kabirpanth under the direct or indirect impact of Christianity. Pandit Walji Bhai, who served as a Pastor of the Irish Presbyterian Church at Borsad for many years in Gujarat, went on to the extent of demonstrating the very institution of the Kabirpanth itself by the Jesuits working in India! [35]

He has based his wild conclusion primarily on the basis of the similarity he noted between the 'secrecy' both Kabirpanthis and certain groups of Christianity maintain about their literature and teachings. Further, Westcott received ideological support for his Christian bias for the Kabirpanth, as he referred, to Grierson's opinion in 1907, which states that "Kabir's doctrine of the Word (*sabda*) is a remarkable copy of the opening verses of St. John's Gospel."[36] However, as an erudite scholar, Westcott himself clarifies that:

> A mind influenced by Christian thought is naturally inclined to dwell upon teaching that seems to have affinity with truths that it is in position to appreciate Passages which to the original teacher may have seemed no less important are hurriedly passed over because the reader through lack of knowledge is unable to estimate their value.[37]
>
> Then he hastens to add that while examining the teaching of Kabir, mainly from the *Bijak* and *Adi Granth*, "We shall meet with teaching which will immediately call to mind passages of the Scriptures; we shall meet with condemnations of falsehood which, as regards directness of speech, should amply satisfy the feelings of the most militant type of Missionary. [38]

Yet, he emphasized that:

> It is not improbable that this doctrine as set forth in the literature of Kabirpanth has been influenced by the writings of St. John, as is confessedly the case as regards the teaching of the Radha Swami Sect of modern origin.[39]

More interestingly Westcott, after all, finds an answer to the question that he might be seeking in sects like Kabirpanth whose followers, despite having several similarities with Christianity, did not convert to the latter *en masse*. But he ultimately found its answer in the practice of vegetarianism which, as a solemn vow of a member, occupies a sacred place in the religious doctrines of the Kabirpanth. He jumped to remark that it had been the adherence to this principle by the followers that kept them away from realizing the spirituality of Christianity. To quote him, "This belief with reference to eating flesh makes them slow to realize that Christianity, which regards such questions as matters of indifference, can be really a spiritual force."[40]

F.E. Keay in late 1920s also provides us with a detailed account on the Damakhera math, which had, as described above, recently come into existence. He noted that:

> The present headquarters of that line of the descendants of Dharm Das, which has the largest following, is a village which lies just off the main road from Raipur to Bilaspur, about midway between them, and is about sixteen miles from Bhatapara station on the main line of the Bengal–Nagpur Railway. The village is a large open one; and other besides Kabirpanthis live there. In one part of it the Hindus have a temple. The guru lives in a fair-sized house of two storeys and possesses an elephant and a motor car. Close by the gate leading to courtyard of his house is a covered platform. On this is the *gaddi*, where the guru sometimes sit to receive his followers. Adjoining the courtyard of the house is a small building something like a temple. When a *mela* is held the guru sits inside this. Apparently access to his person is not made easy even for his followers, who are always expected to bring a substantial offering. A large mela is held, at Damakhera during the month of *Magh* (February) on the day called Basant Panchami, when the guru sits on his followers. For three days, all comers are fed from the bounty of the guru. The tomb of Ugra Nam is in

> the village, not far from the guru's house, but there is nothing imposing about it. Opposite the house is an enclosure with a well, and between the two an open space, where there is also a large pipal tree sourrounded by a *chabutra* (platform). There is a Math (monastery) in the village where sadhus of the sect stay when they visit this place. It is said that there are about thirty-eight Mahants, who receive their commission from the guru at Damakhera.[41]

Besides descriptiotn of the *Vansh* headquarters, he also throws light on the condition of some prominent groups of the Kabirpanthis in the region-

> In the Central Provinces it has, however, a peculiar application; for while the *pan* tribe proper is called *Ganda* in Chhattisgarh and in the Uriya country, the Pankas form a separate division of the Gandas, consisting of those who have become members of the Kabirpanthi sect. In this way the name has been found very convenient, for since Kabir, the founder of the sect, was discovered by a weaver woman lying on the lotus leaves of a tank, like Moses in the bulrushes, and as a newly initiated convert is purified with water, so the Pankas hold that their name is *Pani Ka* or 'from water.' As far as possible then they disown their connection with the Gandas, one of the most despised castes, and say that they are a separate caste consisting of the disciples of Kabir. This has given rise to the following doggerel rhyme about them: *Pani Se Panka Bhe, bundan rache sharer, Aage aage Panka bhae, pachhe Das Kabir.* ('The Panka Indeed is born of Water, and his body is made of

drops of water, but there were Pankas before Kabir.' Or another rendering of the second line is, 'First he was a Panka and afterwards he became a disciple of Kabir.')

Nevertheless the Pankas have been successful in obtaining a somewhat higher position than the Gandas, in that their touch is not considered to convey impurity. This is therefore a new religion and thereby forming themselves into a separate caste and obtaining an advance in social position.

Of the whole caste 84 per cent are Kabirpanthis and these form one sub-caste; but there are a few others. The Manikpuria say that their ancestors came from Manikpur in Darbhanga State about three conturies ago; the Saktaha are those who profess to belong to the *Sakta* sect, which unwilling to submit to the restrictions imposed on Kabir panthis; the *Bajania* are those who play on musical instruments, an occupation which tends to lower them in Hindu eyes; and the Dom Pankas are probably a section of the Dom or sweeper caste who have somehow managed to become Pankas. The main distinction is however between the *Kabirha*, (Kabirha has at times been carrying derisive connotation spoken by the hostile groups of the Kabirpanthis in Hindi as have myself noted) who have abjured flesh and liquor and the Saktaha, who indulge in them; and the Saktaha group is naturally recruited from backsliding Kabirpanthis. Properly the *Kabirha* and *Saktaha* do not intermarry, but if a girl from either section goes to a man of the other, she will be admitted into the community and recognized as his wife, though the regular ceremony is not performed. The Saktaha worship all the ordinary village deities, but some of the *Kabirha* at any rate entirely refrain from doing so, and have no religious rites except when a priest of their sect comes round, when he gives them a discourse and they sing religious songs.

The Pankas worship only Kabir. They prepare a *Chauka* and, sitting in it, sing songs in his praise, and a coconut is afterwards broken and distributed to those who are present. The assembly is presided over by a Mahant or Priest and the *Chauka* is prepared by his subordinate called the Diwan. The offices of Mahant and Diwan are hereditary and they officiate for a collection of ten or fifteen villages. Otherwise the caste perform no special worship, but observe the full moon days of *Magh* (January), *Phagun* (February) and *Kartik* (October) as fasts in honour of Kabir. Some of the Kabirhas observe the Hindu Festivals, practices as other Hindus. They admit into the community members of most castes except the impure ones. In Chhattishgarh a new convert is shaved and the other Pankas wash their feet over him in order to purify him. He then breaks a stick in token of having given up his former caste and is invested with a necklace of tulesi beads. In Mandla, a new convert must clean and whitewash his house and then vacate it with his family while the Panch or caste committee come and stay there for some time in order to purify it. While they are there neither the owner nor any member of his family may enter the house. The *Panch* then proceed to the river side and cook food, after driving the new convert across the river by pelting him with cowdung. Here he changes his clothes and puts on new ones, and coming back again across the stream is made to stand in the chauka and sip the urine of a calf. The Chauka is then washed out and a fresh one made with lines of flour and standing in this the convert receives to drink the dal, that is, water in which a little betel, raw sugar and black pepper have been mixed and a picee of gold dipped. In the evening, the Panch again take piece of gold dipped. The Panch again take their food in the convert's house, while he eats outside it at a distance. Then he again sips the dal, (pulses) and the Mahant or priest takes him on his lap and a cloth is put over them both; the Mahant whispers the mantra or sacred verse into his ear and he is finally considered to have become a full Kabirha Panka and admitted to eat with the Panch.

The Pankas are strict vegetarians and do not drink liquor. A Kabirha Panka is put out of caste for eating flesh meat. Both men and women generally wear white clothes and men have the garland of beads round the neck. The dead are buried, being laid on the back with the head pointing to the north. After a funeral, the mourners bathe and then break a coconut over the grave and distribute it among themselves. On the tenth day they go again and break a coconut and each man buries little piece of it in the earth over the grave. A little cup made of flour containing a lamp is placed on the grave for three days afterwards and some food and water are put in a leaf cup outside the house for the same period.

During these days the family do not cook for themselves but are supplied with food by their friends. After childbirth, a mother is supposed not to eat food during the time that the midwife attends on her, on account of the impurity caused by this woman's presence in the room.

The castes are generally weavers, producing coarse country cloth and a number of them serve as village watch men, while others are cultivators and labourers. They will not grow san-hemp nor breed tasar silk cocoons. They are somewhat poorly esteemed by their neighbours, who say of them, 'Where a Panka can get a little boiled rice and a pumpkin, he will stay forever,' meaning that he is satisfied with this and will not work to get more. Another saying is, 'The Panka felt brave and thought he would go to war; but he set out to fight a frog and was beaten'; and another 'Every man tells one lie a day; but the Ahir tells sixteen, the Chamar twenty and the lies of the Panka cannot be counted.' Such gibes, however, do not really mean much. Owing to the abstinence of the Pankas from flesh and liquor they rank above the Gandas and other impure castes. In Bilaspur, they are generally held to be quiet and industrious. In Chhattisgarh, the Pankas are considered above the average in intelligence and sometimes act as spokesmen for the village people and as advisers to zamindars and village proprietors. Some of them become religious mendicants and act as gurus or preceptors to Kabirpanthis.[42]

Another group of the Kabirpanthis finding place in

Keay's account had been Raghvis of Chhattisgarh. About Raghvis he writes:

> Chhindwara, on the Satpura plateau, is supposed to have been founded by one Ratan Raghuvansi, who built the first house on the site burying a goat alive under the foundations. The goat is still worshipped as the tutelary deity of the town. The name Raghuvansi is derived from Raja Raghu, King of Ajodhia and ancestor of the great Rama, the hero of the Ramayana. In Nagpur the name has been shortened to Raghvi and the Branch of the caste settled here is some-what looked down upon by their fellows in Hoshangabad. Sir R. Craddock states that their religion is unorthodox and they have gurus or priests of their own caste, discarding Brahmans. Their names end in Deo. Their origin, however, is still plainly discernible in their height, strength of body and fair complexion. The notice continues: 'What-ever may happen to other classes, the Raghvi will never give way to the moneylender. Though he is fond of comfort, he combines a good deal of thrift with it, and the clannish spirit of the caste would prevent any oppression of Raghvi tenants by a landlord or Moneylender of their own body." In Chhindwara, Mr. Montogmerie states, they rank among the best cultivators and formerly lived in clans, holding villages on *Bhaiachari* or Communal tenure. As Malguzars or village proprietors, they are very prone to absorb tenant land into their home-farms.[43]

Koshti Kabirpanthis, a sub-caste of Julahas (weaver

caste) have been another caste group who have drawn R.V. Russell's attention in their survey published in 1916. He had been senior superintendent of the previous census by the British Government in Central Provinces. They wrote that:

> In Balaghat and Chhattisgarh many of the Koshtis belong to the Kabirpanthi sect, and these revere the special priests of the sect and abstain from the use of flesh and liquor. They are also known as *Ghati Bandhia*, from the *ghat* or string of beads of basil-wool (*tulsi*) which they tie round their necks. In Mandla, the Kabirpanthi Koshtis eat flesh and will intermarry with the others, who are known distinctively as Saktaha.[44]

In common parlance, Sankat or Sanktaha denote a person who takes non-vegetarian food.

Comparing the ritual practices of the religious groups of the Central Provinces, the ethnographic survey noted that the 'Members of the Lingayat and Kabirpanthi sects bury their dead and the other cremates them.'

Mutual relationship among the different branches of the panth also drew attention of Russel as follows:

> The numbers of this sect, the Kabirpanthis, those who follow the path of Kabir, form at present twelve principal branches, which have remained in communion with one another inspite of sundry differences with regard to both doctrine and practice, and their centre is at Benares; but we meet with them throughout the whole presidency of Bengal, in Gujarat, in Central India, and as far as the Deccan. Their number, difficult to estimate, because of the

> pains they take to conform to the customs in the midst of which they live, appears to be pretty considerable. At the end of last century their religions order by itself alone contributed, it is said, 35,000 of those who took part in a mela held at Benares; and they are still more influential than numerous. Kabir himself is revered as a saint by forming sects and his influence is visible in all of them.[45]

Russell also noted Kawardha as having been an important centre of Kabirpanth during the early 20th century, which had become less significant due to recent splits of the *vansh gaddi* at the onset of the 20th century. To quote,"Kawardha was a feudatory state in the Central Provinces,....The name is believed to be a corruption of Kabirdham or 'the seat of Kabir', and Kawardha is the official headquarters of Mahants of the Kabirpanthi sect." [46]

With regard to the district of then Raipur, the Gazetteers mention that the number of Kabirpanthis there had been 1,62,175. Apart from their numerical strength, it points out their caste bases. Kabirpanthis mainly come from Pankas or Gandas who had adopted the tenets of the sect, but several other castes also belong to it. The main distinction of a Kabirpanthi in Chhattisgarh is that he abstains from meat and liquor.[47]

While describing the Kabirpanthis of the Bilaspur district in 1908, the Gazetteer uses the data provided by the last census of 1901. It shows their number in this district as having been 99,268. In addition, it also notes of the schism the panth was then confronting in the region. In its words:

> The original headquarters of the Kabirpanth was at Kawardha, but there has now been a schism, and one of the Mahants, Ugranam Sahib, lives at Kudarmal in Bilaspur, where an annual fair attended by members of the sect is held. The caste known as Panka consists of Gandas who have adopted Kabirpanthism."Kabir Panthis of Rankhandi.[48]

Kedarnath Dvivedi had estimated the total number of these Panikas to have been about 11,000 in all during 1960s.[49] Originally these Panikas formed part of the tribal groups of the Chhattisgarh region; such as, *Bhils* and *Kols*, but, in the last 100 years or so, they have spread in different parts of the region. They too have formed their exclusive group so much so that they have emerged as distinct caste group by this name. However, it would not be fair to say that all these Panikas have been following Kabirpanth, a miniscule proportion of them openly dissociate from it. In the region, all the Panikas following Kabirpanth are known as Manikpuri Panikas and intermarry among themselves as the Ram-Kabirpanthis of Gujarat.

The 20th century census too provides us some insight into the proportion of the gender of the Kabirpanthis of this region. It can be observed, on a reference to the tables, that in Central Provinces the disparity of the sexes is much less marked than in the Northern Provinces adjoining. In the British districts, it is 5,046 males in every 10,000 of both sexes. It is a little higher in the Feudatory States under the same Administration, the males there being 5,075 to every 4,925 females. Amongst the aboriginal races known, however, the proportion is reversed and the same is observable of the Satnamis and Kabir Panthis. The proportions in these sections of the population are as follows:

Proportion of Males in every 10,000 of both Sexes[50]

	British Territory	*Feudatory States*
Aboriginals	4,976	4,989
Satnamis	4,994	5,036
Kabirpanthis	4,934	4,943

Bengal District Gazetteers, based on the survey and settlement reports of province of Orissa conducted during 1890-1900, takes note of the Kabir tomb having been in existence during that period too. To quote- 'Round the latter cluster (*Swarg Dwara*), a number of Maths or monasteries among which the Kabirpanthi and Sankaracharya are prominent.'[51]

The mention of the Kabir Math in settlement report of the late nineteenth century makes it clear that Tavernier's seventeenth century reference of the Kabir tomb existing in Puri was not only correct but also the fact that the tomb had continuously been preserved all through.

Jharkhand

As has been described in the last chapter, activities of the Kabirpanthis in the present Jharkhand region seems to have intensified and reached out to a number of emerging industrial towns in this region during the first half of the century. The fact that the first group of the Christians had come from the Kabirpanth indicates that they were spiritually sensible and hungry. A few anthropologists who had studied the Santhal tribals during the early years of the century did note the activites of the Kabirpanthis in the area.[52] In non-tribal regions of the present Jharkhand, a number of Maths had been coming into existence particularly in the upcoming industrial towns.

While some Kabirpanthis were being converted to the Christianity in tribal belts of the Jharkhand, a number of them were also involved in opening new centres of Kabir in emerging industrial centres in the region. Two such centres came into existence in Jamshedpur and Dhanbad. Presently Jamshedpur has three Maths named after Kabir.[53] In formation of all these centres, migrant followers from Chhattisgarh and Bihar in addition to the tribal Kabirpanthis are said to have played major role. Most of these migrant Kabirpanthis had come there in search of jobs in Tata Nagar, then being built as the first well planned industrial town by Jamshedji N. Tata during the early 1920s. Although some of the senior Kabir disciples recall that their fathers, who formed earliest groups of workers in the Tata Steel Company established in 1907, had migrated to the Sakshi, in search of a livelihood the area where the steel plant was first started.[54] As Sakshi area gradually developed into an industrial town, the number of followers also began to increase. The speed of migration was intensified largely due to the outbreak of a severe famine in the present district of Durg of Chhattisgarh in between 1900-1903.

Its noteworthy fact that Durg then included even parts of Kawardha, Balaghat, Bastar and Rajnandgaon etc., the places where number of the Kabirpanth followers had been quite sizeable. The life threatening famines compelled many of these followers to abandon their homeland in search of livelihood and the emerging steel plant at Tata Nagar offered them a sustainable shelter in terms of employability. While the lay-out of the planned city was being finalized, it was committed in writing by the Tata management that they would respect members of all religious groups in the planned city and provide all possible facilities in order to secure their religious pursuits without outside interference.

It is said, the Tata management of the Tata Steel itself had donated a piece of land for the establishment of the earliest Kabir ashram at Sonari, in Jamshedpur way back in 1935. According to my informants,[55] Tata management had happily donated the land at the gentle but persistent request of some Kabirpanthis employed in the newly opened TISCO after 1928.

However, Kabirpanth ashram came to witness a split in 1940s resulting in the opening of a new centre in sub-urban part of the city known as Kaela-Dangari, which is presently associated with the Burhanpur branch of the Kabirpanth.[56] The Mahant at the time of split was Narayan Das. The third centre came into existence in another part of city at Parsodih in 1968.

Another centre of the Kabirpanth came into existence in Munnidih area of Dhanbad, known as coal-capital of India. Presently the centre appears to be in shambles, however its history goes back to 1960s when a number of Kabirpanthis working in the BCCL, FCI and the CIL in the Dhanbad-Sindri area found a prominent member in Misri Das, a graduate Kabirpanthi sadhu from Patna, who led the group to form their own

Kabir ashram in Dhanbad.[57] Misri Das is said to have been associated with the Damakheda branch and following its principles, opened a *grihasth/parivarik* centre at Munidih. He got the land occupied by the centre registered in the appropriate registry office in 1966, with the financial support of Sahbir Das, an employee of the FCI, Sindri. Misri Das remained its Mahant till his death in 2000, the year the centre underwent a split. The split at the Kabir centre, Munidih, part of the present Azad Colony, was precipitated after Birju Das, a schedule caste disciple of Misri Das, decided to adapt to *Vairagi* tradition of the Math after latter's death. Sumer Das, the younger brother of Sahbir, opposed his move and mobilized the associated disciples in his support. As he was a regular employee as an ASI in the BSF, he could not actively involve himself in anti-Birju group. But after retirement from the BSF services, Sumer jumped into the fray on full time basis in 2011, was selected as a Mahant, who had already converted almost 5000 into Kabirpanth before his retirement from the CISF and BSF. Birju Das got associated with the Kabir-Chaura branch of Benares.

During this period, a number of Kabir Math opened in many parts of the present Jharkhand, such as; at Hinoo Road in Ranchi, the capital city of Jharkhand, at Babhangama, in the district Jahanabad; at Barmo in west Bokaro steel city, as well as in Gumla and Giridih districts.[58]

Slowly expanding activities of Kabirpanth also led to the opening of a Kabir Math at Gatarpara, Bhagawanpur in Kharagpur town of the West Bengal. Most of the followers who were involved in the foundation of the Kabir Math in Kharagpur were originally natives of the old Central Provinces including its founder Paraur Das, who had donated his entire property to the cause of Kabir in 1967. Paraur had come to Kharagpur in search of livelihood and found a job in the Indian Railways at Kharagpur.[59] Gradually Gatarpara area came to house a sizeable number of migrant Kabirpanthis mostly from the Chhattisgarh, and it were these residents whose religious needs the Math began to cater to.

This Math has been associated with the Burhanpur branch of the panth, and as such, follows *virakta* tradition of the Mahant succession. Beginning from its first Mahant, Vinay Das till the present Mahant, Prem Das, the third in succession at the seat of guru at Kharagpur, all have been *Vairagis*. The Math's property was added by the donation of one Khem Das of Kathmandu, Nepal who had borne the expenditure of building an additional room for the Math in 1966.[60]

During 1930s, Keay also provides brief profiles of some prominent Kabir Maths then famous among the Kabirpanthis. Kawardha Math, which had been in operation, as described in the last chapter, since the beginning of the nineteenth century, also caught attention of Keay. Over the last 100 odd years of its operation, the Kawardha Math was found as follows:

> The Kabirpanthis at Kawardha say that Haqq Nam was the first guru who had his *gaddi* there. This town is the capital of a small feudatory state in the Central Provinces and being far from the railway is not easy to reach. The name Kawardha is said to be a

> corruption of Kabirdham or Abode of Kabir, but this etymology seems doubtful. There is now no guru at Kawardha and the Mahant there apparently has relationships both with the guru at Bamni and the one at Damakhera, but it is the latter guru who seems to have the real allegiance of Kabirpanthis who live at Kawardha. The former residence of the gurus at Kawardha is in a narrow street and is not a very pretentious building. It is at present deserted and in a dilapidated state. The graves of the four gurus who are buried at Kawardha are in the courtyard of the former residence of the gurus. There is also a fifth grave, which is said to be that of the mother of Haqq Nam. All five graves are built of heavy masonry and are in a straight row, occupying the whole length of the courtyard. The grave of Haqq Nam's mother is somewhat smaller than the other four, and is the first in the row.[61]

While conducting his Ph.D. research, F.E. Keay had also visited Dhanauti Math, which has already emerged as the headquarters of the Bhagatahi branch of the Kabirpanth. His description of the physical structure and the management of the headquarters become very significant as we do not have any such contemporary accounts of the Bhagatahi headquarters of the earlier period. He writes:

> Another important division of the Panth has its headquarters at Dhanauti, in the Saran District of Bihar. According to information received there, they also do not differ in any essential points from other Kabirpanthis, though they have their own

organization. The founder of this section of Kabirpanthis was a certain Bhagwan and all the gurus of this sect, who are unmarried sadhus, are Called 'Bhakta' or 'Gosain' lived at a place called Bhaktahis. Bhagwan Gosain lived at a place called Pithaurabad in Bundelkhand. He had four disciples; three of these were named Kokil, Dhani and Sumaran. A fourth disciple (name Unknown) established himself in a village called Larhia in the Champaran District and built a monastery there. A man named Banwari became his disciple, and when Banwari succeeded his disciple and when Banwari succeeded to the guruship, he had four disciples named Bhikham, Nain, Daya and Kamal. Each of them later established monasteries at other places in Bihar. But Bhikham Gosain set up his *gaddi* at Dhanauti. He was succeeded by Bhupal Gosain and the next successor was Parameswar Gosain. Gunpal Gosain, who was the next in office, left the *gaddi* and disappeared and then Sisaman came from the monastery at Kanchanpur and occupied the *gaddi* at Dhanauti.. He was succeeded by three of his disciples in turn, whose names were Harnam, Jaiman and Swarup. Sadhu Gosain who succeeded Swarup is said to have been unsuccessful as a leader and was driven from office. He was followed by the present guru, whose name is Ram Rup. For the sake of clearness we may set out the succession of gurus at Dhanauti as follows:[62]

BHAGWAN GOSAIN

Disciple (*gaddi* at Larhia) Kokil Dhani Sumaran

Banwari

Nain Bhikhan (set up *gaddi* at Dhanauti) Daya Kamal

Bhupal

Parameswar

Gunpal

Sisaman (from Kanchanpur)

Harnam Jaiman Swarup

Sadhu

Ram Rup

Adjacent to Bihar in the United Provinces, Barabanki emerged as one of the influential Kabir centres since the early years of 20th century. The emergence of a Kabir centre in Barabanki has been associated with the life and achievement of Vishal Das, an eminent Kabirpanth follower in this region.[63] The childhood name of Vishal Das was Vairishal, born in a Kurmi family of village Jaffarpur of district Barabanki. Born in 1885, Vairishal spent his early days in Sariya, another neighbouring village where his parents had recently shifted their home.

Further weat in Gujarat, Shanti Das was appointed as the Mahant of Shree Kabir Ashram, Jamnagar in 1918. To my informant, Shanti Das was a *gyan* yogi and a *karma* yogi, he worked very hard to develop this Ashram. He was a very brave and out-spoken. It is said that he had once scolded the raja of Jamnagar in a meeting because of certain actions taken by the King against the wishes of subject of the Jamnagar estate. His life and teaching is published in the Gujarati language.[64]

In Panjab, there emerged an eminent personality named Panjabi Maharaj of Amritsar among the Dharmdasi Kabirpanthis which was closely linked to the Multan and Saharanpur centres of Chhajju Das. His original name was Gurditt Singh. He had been an influential Mahant for these followers. Some of the Sikhs also took initiation into the Kabirpanth as it was then being spread by the Mahant. One such Kabirpanthi Sikh was Panjabi Maharaj, who became one of the closest disciples of Chhajju Das, the founder of Saharanpur Math. Their closeness soon transformed into blood relationship when Chhajju Das married his daughter to the Panjabi Maharaj. Some educationally advanced disciples of the Panjabi Maharaj has tried to jolt down sketches of his charismatic life district but in a booklet form.[65] According to this booklet, Panjabi Maharaj was born in 1841 and died on 31 Dec. 1931. Punjabi Maharaj had been a successful businessman as well as a government contractor during British raj. He was awarded a contract of building a bridge over river Sindhu passing through Multan. In addition, he was also running a flourishing business of cotton weaving. It was under his auspices that Multan came to have a resourceful Kabir ashram. After his death, Balwant Singh, his grandson had succeeded on the gaddi of Mahantas Ajitsingh, Balwant's father had met an untimely death shortly after the latter's birth. Punjabi Maharaj is also credited to have compiled a devotional scripture titled *Kabir Kusumavali* originally in Urdu, which was later translated in Punjabi as well.

After 1947, almost all the Kabirpanthis living in Multan and its surroundings became refugees, many of them were rehabilitated in Delhi, while some others decided to stay in Indore, where their distant relatives were ready to support, accommodate them.[66]

A close Kabirpanth family of Bodhram, husband of Veeran Bae remained a devout disciple of Punjabi Maharaj in Multan. While Veeran Bae accompanied Maharaj as a *sevika* (care-taker) since 1919, her son Chand Ram was later deputed as Maharaj's *munshi.* As a Munshi as well as a devotee, Chand Ram had to shift, on Maharaj's instructions, to Amritsar in 1929, while Veeran Bae continued to stay in Multan ashram till 1941 even after Maharaj's death. This year she decided to join his son and family members in Amritsar as Chand Ram had become father of 5 sons but his wife, Ballo Bae had expired due to a chronic disease in 1941. Veeran Bae had to take care of all these grandsons, a responsibility she carried till her death in 1948. Chand Ram himself died in 1974, by the time all his sons were well settled in Chandigarh. We can often see all of them in the forefront of Kabirpanth activities taking place in this region.

Meghs and Batwal Kabirpanthis of the Panjab region, in particular, had to face the dual onslaughts of the intensifying Sikh Gurudwara reform movements and *Shuddhi* movements of the Arya Samajis exacerbated by the Adi Dharm movement by the turn of the 20th century. Kenneth W. Jones's classic study of the Arya Samaj movement in Panjab draws our attention to the *Shuddhi* movement in which a large number of outcastes such as Meghs had been specific targets for the active Arya Samajists. To cite from his work:

> The leaders of the Ode community located in the districts of Multan and Muzzafarnagar requested that the Samaj purify them...In 1901-1902, the Multan Samaj successfully purified several hundred families of Odes, and within the decade, Aryas reclaimed 23000 Odes in the south-western Punjab. [67]

To cite from his work specifically on Meghs, a low caste having sizable proportion of the total kabirpanthis in pre-partition Punjab who put up a valiant protest to prozelytising attempts:

> The most successful by far was the Megh purification work of the Sialkot Arya Samaj and its subsidiary branch, the *Arya Megh Uddhar Sabha* organized on April 21,1912. Aryas approached the Meghs much as Christian missionaries had, using itinerant preachers and the voluntary services of local Aryas.... "Arya Bhagats," the designation of the purified Meghs, would lead a paternally directed life under the tutelage of their enlightened Arya brethren.'[68]
> The forces which propelled both Aryas and outcastes to sustain the *Shuddhi* campaign accelerated, but opposition appeared sporadically, particularly at village level....More often clashes occurred when the purified asserted themselves and insisted on the prerogatives of their newly claimed status....In Hoshiarpur, when militant Aryas purified members of the Kabirpanthi sect who were sweepers by caste, and then publicly inter dined with them,the local

> orthodox society led a movement to outcaste all Aryas. Unlike previous converts who were almost weavers or from other relatively unobjectionable occupations, the samaj was dealing here with the lowest of social groups, with the most demeaning of professions. Throughout May 1909, the Sanatan Dharm Sabha of Hoshiarpur mobilized public opinion against Aryas and their Chamar adherents. In the long run, however they were unable to sustain this social boycott and gradually Aryas were readmitted to the normal world of social relations, while purified Chamars remained a part of the Hindu community. The Hoshiarpur experience rarely reoccurred, as Aryas refrained from purifying the lowest of the untouchables and Sanatanists did not attempt to outcaste members of the Samaj.[69]

Kenneth W. Jones's study also provides us an idea of the number of the converted Meghs in the undivided Panjab, which largely consisted of the *bhagat* Kabirpanthis of the region, according to my informants. He writes that the *shuddhi* movement had permanently altered the social composition of the Samaj.

> After a decade of near stagnation between 1891 and 1901, Samaj membership rose to 100846 in 1911. *Shuddhi* campaign contributed heavily to this rapid growth, shifting as well the geographic centre of the Samaj. Sialkot contained the greatest number of Aryas, 27910 individuals who were almost totally converted and purified Meghs....the Samaj shifted its social composition to include 34 percent

> untouchables. The most numerical caste among Aryas changed from Khatris who had held that position since the movement's beginning to Meghs.[70] The heavy influx of *Sudra* and untouchable converts enabled the Samaj to grow rapidly, but would present difficulties within the movement over the readjustment of power relations between the dominant upper castes and the newly-won adherents from the lower levels of the social scale converts. *Shuddhi* had not however focussed on the lowest levels of Punjab society, the sweepers and leather workers....but aside from one attempt to purify Kabirpanthis in 1909, refrained from *shuddhi* among the lowest of the untouchables.
>
> The *shuddhi* movement also provided impetus to Samaj growth beyond Punjab....Emigration of Punjabis into Kashmir State, particularly in the Jammu area, and the *shuddhi* provided the foundation for this growth. The Megh uplift movement spread into Jammu and in 1913 another *shuddhi* campaign,...added over 9000 converts to the Samaj by the next census.[71]

Yet Bhagat, Kabirpanthis comprising Meghs mostly in some other parts resisted attempts to conversiom by the Arya Samajis and hence opened there on centre of devotion. A number of Kabir Mandirs came to be formed by Megh and Batwal Kabirvanshis in this region. The earliest of all these was opened at Bhargav Nagar in Jalandhar town presently known as Satguru Kabir Mukh Mandir in 1924.[72] During the fieldworks in Jalandhar, we came to know that Kabirpanthis claiming themselves as *bhagat* Kabirpanthis have also got their area named as Kabir Nagar. Some of these families recall their forefathers who had fought against the onslaughts of Arya Samajis as well as radical Sikhs and yet succeeded in opening the earliest mandir in Jalandhar. In 1948, some of them started the opening of second Kabir Mandir at Kabir Nagar in Jalandhar. Similar Kabir Mandirs were gradually opened by these followers at Haripur and Majitha in present Amritsar district; at Sujanpur and Deenanagar in Gurdaspur district; and in Nakodar as well as in Pathankot.

Apart from the Arya Samajis, the *Ad Dharmi* movement engulfing major part of the then Punjab had been a huge factor behind the decline in the number of Kabir followers in the Punjab. The seminal work of Mark Jugerensmeyer on the history of the *Ad Dharmis* of the Panjab has taken note of the significance of the legacy of Kabir and Ravidas and involvement of the Kabirpanthis in the rise of the Ad Dharm movement. To cite the report of the *Ad Dharmis* from his book:

> So in the beginning of 1925, a society was formed with the name of Ad Dharm: Rishi Valmiki, Ravi Das, Kabir, and Nam Dev were named as founders. The first meeting was held in the village of Mugowal, Thana Mahalpur, tehsil Gahrshankar, Hoshiarpur district on 11-12 June 1926, under the chairmanship of Mangoo Ram. The meeting was attended by people from all sections of Punjab. All Untouchables attended: Chuhras, Chamars, Ravidasis, Sansis, Bhanjres, Ghadhilias, Burrs, Julahas, Meghs, Chambars, Kabirpanthis, Mahashas, Doms and other castes. And there were other respectable people in addition to Untouchables, people from other

> communities: Christians, Sikhs, Muslims, Arya Samajis and Sanatanis. With all groups present it was a great success. Representatives of the Untouchables presented their positions eloquently and loudly. They told about all the hypocritical religions [*mazhab*], exposing them for what they are. But the representatives of organizations from the other religion criticized the *Ad Dharmis* strongly. After a lot of debate and argument and inspired by the teachings of Rishi Valmiki, Ravi Das, Kabir and Nam Dev, they decided that the Untouchables should be called Ad Dharm. And from that day on, the organization has been called Ad Dharm.[73]

F.E. Keay's work which was, perhaps, the last one by an English scholar on the history of the Kabirpanth before 1947 thoroughly examined the works of Wilson and Westcott on the panth, besides offering further information and insights into ideological differences and its connection with the Christianity. He observed that:

> There does not seem to be any essential difference in doctrine between those Kabirpanthis who are connected with the Kabir Chaura and those groups which are organized in the Chhattishgarh area. The Kabir Chaura section does not think it right for gurus to be married men and does not recognize the gurus who claim descent from Dharm Das. Kabirpanthis of the Kabir Chaura section do not visit the holy places of the Chhattisgarh section but the followers of the Chhattisgarh gurus do visit the Kabir Chaura and Magahar.[76]

He, however, devotes a complete chapter on the connection of Kabir's teachings and the Kabirpanth with that of Christianity. In the chapter, he opines that it is difficult to prove from a few passages which seem to have close parallels with Christian teachings, that Kabir, with the doctrine of *Sabda* (or divine word), who, in Keay's words, is 'a mind naturally Christian,' was directly influenced by the Christianity. Even the reference to Adam and Eve by Kabir, in his opinion, does not indicate any connection between the two. What indeed struck Keay about the Kabirpanth in showing actual resemblance between the two, were its sacramental systems. He, however, qualifies his assertion by stating that the practice of the sacramental meal or *mahaprasad* is prevalent in other Hindu bhakti sects also. He thus concludes that if, at all Kabir was influenced by the doctrines of Christianity, it was through the mediation of its influence on the bhakti movement as such.

Yet, Keay reiterates that the Kabirpanth, after the death of Kabir, "did come in contact with a good deal of Christian influence, which may have helped in the development of their sacramental system and in other ways."[77] Then he goes on to note the comparative views of some of the Kabirpanthis on Christ's level of spirituality in that He (Christ) was still entangled in the law of Karma as the Heavenly Father, too, could not deliver Him. To the Kabirpanthi interviewees of Keay, the state of Kabir's spiritual being was thus much higher than that of Christ, as the former was entirely free from the cycle of *Karma*.[78]

Keay also leaves a graphic description of some of the important Kabir maths having been in existence for the last 300 years or so in different parts of the British India. We can have a contemporary accounts of some of these in the following:

> The Kabir Chaura, which is the headquarters of the Kabirpanth at Benares, is situated not far from the hospital and is approached by a narrow street. It consists of two courtyards, the Niru Tila, which is the traditional site of the house of Niru and Nima, and was probably the first part occupied by the panth; and the Kabir Chaura proper. Both courtyards are shaded by nim trees and surrounded by buildings, in many of which sadhus of the sect are living. The chief point of interest in the main courtyard is the shrine which is said to be built over the spot where Kabir taught. It has a pair of wooden sandals upon it to represent the feet of Kabir. On one side of the courtyard is a room which contains the *gaddi*, or state pillow, of the guru. As the *gaddi* is supposed to belong to Kabir, the present occupant of the office of guru does not sit upon it but behind it. In this room there is hanging a large picture of Kabir, which however was only placed there in 1913. Other smaller pictures, which are found there, are Kabir sitting with Surat Gopal and Dharm Das, Ramananda, Nanak, Mira Bai sitting before her guru Rai Das, Siva and Parvati, Rangi Das (a former guru of the sect) in the youth, Rangi Das as an old man, Nirmal Das (a former guru) teaching his disciples, and the present guru. Over the large picture of Kabir are hung designs to symbolise the five element of earth, air, entrance to the human body. Two vases of flowers are placed in

> front of the *gaddi* and a rosary of a thousand beads is hung upon the wall for the use of the guru. A *topi* (a cap), and a *sehli* (or woollen necklace) of Kabir are treasured at the monastery, as well as a copy of the *Bijak*. In the courtyard there are five tombs, of which four are those of former gurus and one that of a disciple of one of these. From the upper storey of one of the buildings of the main courtyard there is a bridge across a narrow street to the Niru Tila. This is a smaller enclosure with only a few buildings. In the centre are the tombs of Niru and Nima, the parents (or foster-parents) of Kabir....
>
> Two miles away from the Kabir Chaura is the Lahar Talao, a shallow tank overgrown with weeds, where according to tradition, the infant Kabir was found by Niru and Nima. A small courtyard, in which is a shrine, marks the site of the traditional spot. It is in charge of a *pujari* belonging to the Panth.[79]

In addition, he also provides interesting description of the Magahar's Kabir tomb as existing in the early 20th century:

> Another branch of the Benares section of the Panth is to be found at Maghar, the traditional site of the death of Kabir. Maghar is a villiage about sixteen miles from Gorakhpur, but in the Basti district. The Kabir Panthi sacred place here is situated on the bank of the Ami river. It consists of two portions divided from one another by a high wall. There are no striking buildings.
>
> One portion is in the hands of a family of Muhammadan weavers who claim to have had charge

of the tomb from the time of Kabir's death. It is the custom from each holder of the office to nominate his successor. He has the title of Ghani Karan Kabir. The present holder of the office is a woman, but the duties are performed by her husband. No record seems to have been kept of the names of previous holders of the office. The Muhammadans in charge of this shrine do not regard Kabir as God, but simply as a *pir*, or Muhammadan saint. They deny the legend about the heap of flowers and say that the body of Kabir was buried here in accordance with Muhammadan custom. They say that Raja Bir Sinha was away hunting when Kabir died and was buried; and that when he returned he demanded that the body of Kabir should be exhumed and cremated ; but his demand was successfully resisted.

The Mussulman shrine stands in the centre of the enclosure built like a temple and surrounded by a platform. At the right-hand corner of the shrine is a small covered building, where the custodian of the tomb has his *gaddi* during the time when melas are held. At the back of the platform, on the same side, is a much smaller shrine, which is said to be the tomb of Kamal. By the custodians of this shrine Kamal is regarded as the real son of Kabir. Over the tomb of Kabir, a white cloth is placed. Incense is burnt and flowers are strewed at this tomb. But while the rites seem to approximate to those performed at Hindu temples, they are probably only similar to those which take place at the tombs of other Muhammadan saints. In the courtyard is another smaller tomb which is said to be that of Bijli Khan, the Pathan, a

> original shrine of Kabir is said to have been much smaller and this seems likely, as the present building is certainly much later than his time.
>
> In early days it is said there was only one shrine, which both Hindus and Muhammadans visited, and a *mela* was held which lasted over a month. Later on friction arose; and this probably led to the building of the second Hindu shrine. A custodian of the Hindu shrine, named Man Das, is said to have been killed in an affray between the Hindu and Muhammadan followers of Kabir.
>
> The Hindu shrine is in the hands of a *pujari,* who is a sadhu of the Kabir Panth, and derives his authority from the Kabir Chaura at Benares. The shrine of Kabir is situated towards one side of the enclosure, and its similar to, though rather smaller than, the shrine in the Muhammadan enclosure. On the right of the platform, as one approaches the shrine of Kabir, is the shrine of Kamal. The shrine of Kabir is said to be on the spot where he sat waiting for death. It covered with a red cloth and worship takes place at the shrine every morning and evening. There is also worship at Kamal's shrine. At the full moon of the month Aghan (November-December) and the guru of the Kabir Chaura at Benares visits the shrine and administers the Jyoti Prasad, a sacramental meal. The Kabir Chaura Math possesses some property near Maghar.[80]

Keay's reference of the killing of Man Das in the infighting among Hindu and Muslim disciples at Maghar, a Hindu care-taker at Maghar, had also found support in the nineteenth century accounts of Francis Buchanan, as described in the preceding chapter, but the latter, in his accounts, had not mentioned the name of the slain *sadhu*. Yet these references lead us to relocate the history of the Kabir Samadhi, which, in all probability seems to be built lately in the late eighteenth century.

His observation of the Burhanpur Kabir Math appears as follows:

> Connected with the Kabir Chaura there are monasteries in many parts of India. Amongst these, an important one is at Burhanpur, in the west of the Central Provinces. At this monastery lived about a hundred years ago a certain Puran Sahib, who is the author of a commentary on the *Bijak*, as well as of other Kabirpanthi works.[81]

The informants of F.E. Keay had told that Burhanpur had been then associated with the Kabir-Chaura Math, Kashi. There is no reason to disbelieve F.E. Keay's informants of the time, for functionaries of the Burhanpur Math and those of the Kabir-Chaura have been ardent propagator of the principle of selection of celibate Mahants at the Kabir Maths. Ideological bond, in addition to the need of legitimization of the newly created Math might have been a potent factor in bringing Burhanpur Math close to the Kabir Chaura. Yet the new bond could not survive for long, the Burhanpur Math gradually assumed airs of independence and under the guru *gaddi* of its last Mahant Ram Swarup,[82] it has come to take on the status of an independent Acharya *Gaddi* by 1950s. We have all the evidences to establish disassociation of the Burhanpur Math from the Dharmadhasi branch due to the reasons described in the last chapter. Another group of informants presently known as the *Parakh-Panthis* in the Kabirpanth, began to showcase the Burhanpur Math as the main patron of their principles highlighting the astral body of Kabir as adorable, instead of his mortal physical being, which ultimately found formal expression in the opening of the Parakhpanthi headquarters at Allahabad during the post-Independent India.

At Burhanpur Math, according to my informants, Narottam Das was fortunate to have some influential disciples during the early period of the 20th century.[83] The names of his eminent disciples were Prem Das, Nirmal Das and Lal Sahib. None of them however could succeed Narrotam who died in 1920 (1977v.s.). Prem Das yet became famous as the writer of *Timir Bhashkar*, a Hindi religious text containing a commentary on the *sakhis* of Kabir.

In 1920, Kashi Das succeeded Narottam Das at the seat of Burhanpur Math. He did not fall in direct line of Narotam's disciples, but was a disciple of Ram Sukh Das, who was originally a disciple of Sri Ram Das. It is said that the main factor behind the selection of Kashi Das had been his erudite and profundity. A number of religious texts are credited to him–*Parakh Bodh, Panchgranthi, Sanyukt Nirnay Saar, Vairagya Shatak, Kabir-Parichay, Vivek Saar, Vivek Chandrika* etc.[84] Some of his books were later translated into many Indian languages too. Towards the end of his life, he had renounced the Burhanpur *gaddi* and had placed Chhote Balak Das as the acting Mahant. Henceforth, Kashi Sahib is said to have led a life of a wandering ascetics from one to another Kabir's centres. It was one of his tours towards Agra that he breathed his last at a village named Basal Arela in 1923, where his *Samadhi* was erected by his followers.

Chhote Balak, as the successor of Kashi Sahib, became quite popular particularly. He succeeded in winning back the trust of the functionaries of the Singhkhera Math, which was intiated by Kalyan Das, the expelled Mahant from the Burhanpur Math. He remained Mahant at Burhanpur *gaddi* till his death in 1930 (v.s 1998). Like his predecessor Mahant, he also took deep interest in literary activities. He is said to have first modified the original version of '*sakhum Bahar*' and then got it published in a printed form. '*Sandhya Path*' was his original publication. As per the prevailing tradition, he had financially contributed to Kashi Das in the publication of religious texts.

Chhote Balak ensured that Ram Swroop Das, the longest serving Mahant of Burhanpur Math, succeed him. For this purpose, Chhote Balak had declared him as the successor Mahant of the combined Burhanpur–Singhkheda Math during his life-time. Ram Swroop thereafter remained Mahant of this Math till his death in 2005. He had left a will prepared before his death, and the will itself has been a source of several informations relating to the Burhanpur Math. [85]

For further information regarding the Saharanpur Kabir-Chaura Math in the United Provinces, we can rely upon the same Allahabad High Court judgement. The judgement paper also clarifies that Chhajju Das left his ashram thus formed by him under the custody of his son named Shankar Das. Kabir Chaura, under the supervision of Shankar Das, began to be managed by a five-member committee since 1914. One of the members of this committee, named Babu Amarnath had sold out his landed property measuring 1 *bigha* 18 *biswa* to the Kabir-Chaura in July 1936.

It is stated that neither Chhajju Das nor his son Shankar Das ever began the tradition of appointing a succeeding Mahant for the Saharanpur Kabir Chaura. Upon Shankar Das death on 3rd Nov. 1938, the supervisory committee continued to run it under the guidance of Roshan Lal, the son of Shankar Das. In Dec. 1939, this Math was brought under a Trust Deed which is said to have deputed Roshan Lal as the sole Trustee of this *gaddi*.

The seed of discord at this earliest Math in Saharanpur gets planted when one Santokh Das, appeared in the close circle of the Math during Roshan Lal's life time. Santokh Das was one of the closest disciples of Shankar Das, named Saheb Das. Santokh Das had begun to play a leading role in the affairs of the Math during Roshan's trustiship so much so that Santokh often presented himself among Math's followers as the *de facto* Mahant of the Kabir Chaura *gaddi*. Santokh could easily emerge as the leading figure as Roshan Lal had been losing his interests in Math's affairs. By the time Roshan Lal had expired, Santokh Das is said to have usurped full charge of the Math in his own hand and the counsel of the trust hardly not was commonly not sought by him.

In 1970, before his death, Santokh Das got his own will deed prepared in favour of Sadhu Sharan Das as his successor after his death. Sadhu Sharan was one of his disciples, unrelated to the family of founder Chhajju Das. The managing committee of the Math was constrained to sack Sadhu Sharan from the *gaddi* of Kabir-Chaura, an act which triggered a series of the litigations in the civil law courts of Saharanpur in 1977.

According to another version, Santokh Das was appointed as the Mahant of this Math by the religious certificate (*Panja Pravana*) of the Kharasiya Math, district Raigarh, Chhattisgarh in 1935.[86] After Santokh's death on 26 Jan. 1972, Sadhu Sharan was appointed as the successor once again by the Kharasiya Math's certificate issued in 1973.[87]

Further southeast in Kanpur, another emerging industrial town of the British India, a Kabir Mandir came into existence in the Idgah Colony area. The brothers Makkan Das and Dakkan Das got it built in 1915. They were Kureels like Sanval Das, rich tannery owners and devout Kabir-panthis as well. Inside the house there is a shrine, showing Kabir with his two main disciples, Dharmdas and Surat Gopal. They were famous for the religious celebration, the *chauka* on Kabir's birthday in August. For that event, they had invited 25,000 villagers from Unnao district to attend the celebration and the following *bhandara*.

Kanpur came to have its third Kabir Mandir in Juhi Labour Colony near Swadeshi Cotton Mill. It was setup in the 1930s. It is a simple structure housing the graves of the two Mahants, Laldas and Balakdas.[88] The present Mahant is a middle aged Kabir-panthi named Shankar Das, who looks after the Mandir.

Its fourth Kabir Mandir is situated at Cooperganj,

the main grain market in Kanpur. It was setup in the 1940s with a *dharmshala* for marriage parties. It has also served as an office of the Republican Party. The Kabir Mandir is an interesting structure with a decorated front. Stretching over the well, beneath the flat roof, two friezes of male statues are to be seen approaching the oversized figure of *Satyapurus*, the primordial man, who nearly covers the whole of the front of the building. Underneath, Hanuman stretches out his arms.

Hulasi Das,[89] Munni's grandfather, has emerged as the most popular Mahant in Kanpur. He was an inhabitant of Unnao. He had left his village in Unnao at the age of ten. He entered Cooper and Allen Tannery and Leather Factory just when it was opened in 1880. Intelligent, hard working and reliable, he became a *mistri* after nine years. The expression mistri (derived from Portugnese mestre in the meaning of gentleman) is misleading, because his responsibilities far exceeded supervisory functions. He was a labour contractor, recruiting, employing and maintaining labours for the factory. He lived for his men and on them. His job was so remunerative that he was able to buy eighteen houses, which he rented out. He was a patron, looking after his workers in sickness and death, marrying off their daughters and caring for the old.

Besides, he became the disciple of Mahant Lal Das in Dalelpurwa, from whom he took the *Panja* as priest in 1903. This enabled him to resign his job, it is stated in his work certificate issued by J.H. Sannester in 1914.

> This is to certify that I have known Hulasi Dass Mahant for about 26 years. He worked under me as

> mistry for the last 17 year in Cooper & Allen Factory. I always found him honest, hard working and a man with a certain amount of tact, dealing with the men under him. I was very sorry to part with him. He left about ten years ago on his own request to take up the calling of Padri amongst his class. I very often seen him and judging by the esteem in which he is held by his followers, he must have kept up the reputation I had of him years ago.[90]

Kanpur's Kabirpanthis all belonged to the Damakhera line of the Dharmdasi branch. During the time of Westcott, there were five Maths in Kanpur which attracted substantial following among the untouchable castes, very much in line with the social composition of Kabir's following among sudras, tribal people and untouchables. The community got closely knit and strict in its commandments of honesty, faithfulness, cleanliness, vegetarianism and *ahimsa*, education and a self-reliant income. Transgressions were reprimanded and led to excommunication, even in irrelevant cases. Vegetarianism and the strict rejection of any intoxicants set the *sampradaya* very much apart from untouchable culture. In the opinion of Bellwinkel-Schempp,"Although Kabir is considered to be the pre-eminent figure of 'the transcendent and formless *nirguna* aspect of divinity' his Kanpur followers were quite evasive and blended the belief in the spiritual representation of God with worship of the Devi."[91]

Once settled, the pioneer members became a source of inspiration for several Kabirpanthis living in the far-flung area as well. Migrating from Bundelkhand, the

Koris entered the textile industry and were preferred by the British. Although they are performing a non-polluting task, in Kanpur they are still classified as untouchables.[92] The Koris considered themselves natural adherents of Kabir, as he was still followed and this they did not perceive to be in contradiction to Kabir's teachings.

Hulasi Das's only son, Prem Das, was born in 1908. Educated privately by a pandit and a *maulwi*, he was trained to become a Vaidya, which secured him an income over and above his remunerations as a Mahant in the Kabirpanth. During the Hindu-Muslim riots in Kanpur in 1931, with the power of his moral command, he saved two Muslim families from the rioters. He also put a ban on *balidan* (animal sacrifice) at the Kali-temple in Parmat, much to the dismay of his Kureel brothers.

And in 1927, Ugranam, the Acharya from Damakhera, the headquarters of the Dharmdasi branch, had orginised a big meeting in Kanpur to propagate the teachings of Kabir.[93] Since then Kanpur has become one of the most important centres of the Dharmdasi Kabirpanthis in India where Grindhmuni, the last Dharmdasi Vansh Acharya had convened an all-India Kabir Sammelan in the 1960s.

Prem Das knew that he had to lead the Kabir-Panthis out of the private realm into a public domain. Just towards the end of his life, he started a unification move amongst the sampradaya. In 1969, he called for an *Akhil Bharatiya Kabir Acharya Sammelan evam Satsang* in Kanpur.[94] It was held in the Brijendra Swarup Park, named after a leading Arya Samaji family of Kanpur. The objective was to generate equality, love and goodwill among the Acharyas, Sants and Mahants for the development of the Kabirpanth. The meeting was well attended with a great success. The second conference of the All India Kabir Panthis took place in Koogharmal in then Madhya Pardesh, the seat of the Dhamakhera gaddi, in 1971. It claims to have delegates from Maharashtra, Gujarat, Madhya Pradesh, Uttar Pardesh and Bihar. The third conference took place in New Delhi in 1973.[95] Prem Das's detailed report tells us of the difficulties he had in organizing a meeting of that significance in the capital city and of the reluctance of the Gujarat Mahants to attend.

Upto the 1960s, they still excelled in conspicuous consumption on behalf of the Kabir-Panthis. Till recent times, Krishan Kumar, their grandson, is struggling to get his harness business going.[96]Although Kabir was considered to be the 'fountainhead' of bhakti culture, within the present Dalit discourse in Kanpur, he has receded into the background.

It is said that most of the Kabir followers have left Kanpur in the last 50 years or so. They have moved to Shuklaganj on the other side of the Ganga, where the river still has water. In new suburbs *pan ka masala* is produced and plots are cheap. The Mahants followed their disciples. Mahant Jaiguru Das holds his *chauka* there. Mahant Gyan Das, a great yogi who took Samadhi for six months, has also moved to rural Unnao, just opposite the Karbala and Sanval Das Ghat.[97]

In Chamanganj Koriana area, my informants recalled that there were ten Kabirpanthi families till 1980s, but now there is none. They take 'Kabir' as their family name, like so many educated Chamars take Ambedkar's name.[98] The surname becomes a caste marker. Kabir and Ambedkar's are signifiers of dalitness among Koris and Chamars. The *Kori Samaj Seva Samiti* places Kabir, Ambedkar and Jhalkari Bae in their pantheon. Jhalkari Bae is popularly recalled as a constant body-guard of Lakshmi Bae, the legendary queen of Jhansi. She is said to have laid down her life fighting against the British troops just to protect life of Lakshmi Bae during the revolt of 1857.

The Kabir-Panthis were the puritans of the early Dalit movement. With their strict emphasis on truth, cleanliness, vegetarianism and *ahimsa*, they considered themselves the elite of their community. As long as they were rich and could give freely to their caste brothers, their moral superiority was accepted. Prem Das's life set an example in that respect. Their religion was basically inwardly oriented and there was no scope for public representation, which is essential in the present-day political discourse. Bellwinkel-Schemp opines that the uncompromising righteousness of the Kabirpanthis does not fit into modern politics, which is based on networks of shifting alliances.

Eminent members of the Jagodasi branch in Uttar Pradesh further opened a number of Maths in the post-independent period.[99] One of these was Shri Kabeer Jagu ashram of Chauksahar, Tahnandpara, district Bahraich adjacent to the Indo-Nepal border which came into existence in 1952. It was initially connected to the Shivpuri centre of the Jagu branch. But after the death of the founder Mahant Bhagirath Das, Gurdayal Das the present Mahant of the Derabassi Kabir Math in the Punjab has been handling the affairs of the ashram since

1992.

An ashram was also built by Vicharpati Saheb and his wife Shanti Das at Rukundipur, near Fardhan, in Lakhimpur-Kheri district of Uttar Pradesh. Being childless, they looked upon Gurdayal Das as their son, and handed over entire charge of the ashram to him.[100] The ashram was setup on 30 January, 1968. Since then, Gurdayal has been serving as its Mahant. Gurdayal Das is also responsible for management of two other ashrams. Therefore, his disciple Neeraj Das handles day to day affairs of the ashram in his absence.

This ashram is associated with the Jagu branch centred at Biddupur, Bihar but it is also in regular touch with the Shivpur Jagu Math, Benares. This ashram is a *virakta/nirvana* type and there are thus five *virakta* sadhus residing there.[101] Even though there is no follower of Kabirpanth in Rukundipur village, Sadhus have to live here to cultivate the land and fields of the ashram.

Besides this ashram, Gurdayal Das, also takes care of two other ashrams, namely Shri Kabeer Jagu Ashram, Mishritirth, Naimisharanya and Mishriv in district Sitapur, Uttar Pradesh. Gurdayal Das got this ashram built in 1972.[102] During *Holi Parikrama* festivities, sadhus from across the country participate in a conclave organized at Mishritirth. When Gurdayal Das constructed the ashram, he intended to make sure the holy men participating in the conclave get adequate boarding and food. It is to be noted that the conclave is meant for the entire Hindu community in general and not for Kabirpanth alone.

Rajasthan and Maharashtra

At Ajmer, in Rajasthan, a Kabir Ashram, was opened towards the turn of 20th century. There was a person from Dholabata area of Ajmer who was attached to the Kabirpanth and he also got *Pana-Parvana* from Damakheda to open a Kabir centre.[103] But no record is available these days. The followers of Kabirpanth also went in this area of Dhalabata many times and tried to inquire about this but could not get any information.

In the area of Ajmer and Pushkar around 40-50 years ago, most of the Kabirpanthis came from the lower castes. Mahant Hari Singh Rathore emerged a predominant figure in this area. In fact, it was his aunt (sister of his mother) who had first adopted Kabirpanth. It was one of her journeys to Damakheda during which she had introduced him to it. It was the time of the gaddi of Graindhmuni, the then Acharya of the Dharmdasi branch. Hari Singh took to Kabirpanth only on the inspiration of Graindhmuni, the father of Prakarshnam, the present Aeharya of the Damakhera centre.

Most of Kabirpanthis in this area are the follower of Hari Singh.[104] Hari Singh Rathore got attached to Kabir Panth for the last 40 years. He was elevated to the seat of Mahant by Grandhmuni.

One of the present Gujarat's major Kabir ashrams came into existence at Limdi in the Saurashtra region. It is associated with the Kharsiya *Tyagi Gaddi*. Mahant Charandas is handling the affairs of the ashram at present. Tradition has it that in Ayodhya, Tapsi Bapu gained Siddha at the Paltu Saheb Kabir Akhara and came to Limdi, Gujarat. In Ayodhya, Bodhi Saheb was Tapsi Bapu's guru. After completing his lessons at the age of 16, Tapsi Bapu came to Lal Darwaza Kabir Ashram at Surat in Gujarat and started living there.[105]

The Mahant of Lal Darwaza Kabir Ashram, Thakur Das is said to have hired a woman for day-to-day chores at the ashram, including cooking and washing dishes. This did not go down well with Tapsi Bapu who maintained that there was no place for a woman in an ashram associated with the *Tyagi* tradition and run by sadhus. Tapsi Bapu asked the Mahant to discontinue her services. When he did not do so, Tapsi Bapu left the ashram himself.

At present, Thakur Das is the Mahant of this ashram, which is associated with the Kharasiya *Nirwan* Dharmdasi branch. Under Thakur Das, the ashram became a *Grihasta* Math as he chose to married life. The Mahant's son, Jagdish Das, the successor Mahant, claims to be presently associated with the Damakheda family (*Vansh)* seat.

Thus, Tapsi Bapu forsook the Kabir temple at Surat. Thereafter, his journeys took him to Junagarh, Rajkot, Laktar, Surendra Nagar and eventually to Limdi. The local raja, of Limdi, Bharat Singh Dada happened to meet Tapsi Bapu.[106] At the insistence of Bharat Singh and his followers, he set up an ashram in Limdi and started living there in 1958. In this way, the ashram of Limdi was established with the active cooperation of devotees as well as Bharat Singh.

Many sadhus and associated people with the Limdi ashram recall the miracles performed by Tapsi Bapu. One of the storeies associated goes like this: once, Tapsi

Bapu organized a *bhandara* (community meal) at the ashram. But devotees thronged the ashram in large numbers and the food was inadequate to feed such a big crowd. When sadhus told Tapsi Bapu about their predicament, he went to his cave to meditate. As he was meditating, a *mahatma* came to the ashram. Someone gave him two *boondi ladoos*. The *mahatma* kept one of the *ladoos* and asked the sadhus to keep the other one in their stock of delicacies. The sadhus followed his instructions and the Mahatma left the place.

Later, Tapsi Bapu got up from his meditative pose and asked the sadhus if a mahatma had come. When the sadhus told Tapsi Bapu about the sequence of events, he asked them to go ahead and feed as many people as they wanted to. Miraculously, there was enough food for everyone. When the sadhus asked Tapsi Bapu who the Mahatma was, he said it was none other than Kabir Saheb himself. Since then, the Limdi Ashram is known as the place where Kabir Saheb appeared personally.[107]

Another well-known legend is that of Chakabal Saheb, who was lame by birth. One day, when Tapsi Bapu saw Chakabal Saheb limping around, he is said to have thrown a stick at his foot. After that, Chakabal is said to have been cured of his disability. Chakabal is still alive and lives in a village nearby with his family. Many stories of the miracles performed by Tapsi Bapu have been witnessed by the sadhus. Mahant Charandas took charge as a successor Mahant after Tapsi Bapu. He often undertakes journeys within the country and abroad to promote the panth.

Apart from Limbdi, Kabir temples, which are more than 100 years old are located in almost all districts of

Gujarat, including Vadodara, Ahmedabad, Kheda, Limdi, Rajkot, Jamnagar, Shvambhat, Porbandar, Anand, Bharuch, Dwaraka, Panwel etc.

The Ram Kabir temple in Dwaraka, the Kabir temple in Pani Gate, Vadodara and the temple at Sant Kabir Road, Vadodara are all associated with the Ram Kabir Samaj. Both the idols of Lord Rama and Kabir are installed and worshipped in these temples, and all these temples are associated with the Ram Kabir.

Some Kabirpanthis of Gujarat have also linked Kabir's temple with the idol of Krishna.[108] At the Ram Kabir temple of Dwaraka, idols of Radha and Krishna have been kept alongside those of Lord Rama and Kabir. At the Limbdi, Kabir ashram, the idol of the child Kabir strongly resembles to *Bal Gopal*. This Kabir temple in Limbdi is also known as the Krishna Kabir temple.

An interesting development has taken place in the panth at Potiyadehi in Chhattisgarh, particularly under the guidance of Abhilash Das, the founder of the Parakhpanthi branch of Kabirpanth in Allahabad. In this *ashram* only females (single women called sisters) can stay and they can conduct research studies. Presently there are 40 sisters (females) living in this ashram. This ashram is the largest ashram of this region (area-wise and number-wise) which has been developing under the overall supervision of the heads of the Allahabad branch. This Ashram was constructed in 1993 with the donations of the villagers and with the collective support of the Parakhpanthi headquarters at Allahabad.[109] From the foundation day till date Shri Kabir Brahmcharini Ashram Potiyadihi, as it has been named, is headed by *bahan* (sister) Sushila.

The annual conference, *Gurupurnima*, Kabir and the birthday of Abhilasha Sahib are the occasions of celebrations in this Ashram. The residents of the nearby villages participate and contribute in these celebrations. Male members are not allowed to saty inside the ashram.

Jammu and Kashmir

In the state of Jammu and Kashmir, we have a number of Kabir Mandirs spread over major part of the Jammu region in particular. The most prominent feature of these Mandirs has been their foundation by the *bhagats* of the Megh and Batwal castes of the region as described above. During our field works, we noted active Kabir Mandirs at Rakh Amb Tali, in Samba district, Badyal Qazian and Nandpur in the district R.S. Pura, at Kandholi on the National Highway, Jammu, at Janipur and at Hazuri Bagh. We also came to know that resourceful Kabir Mandirs have been active at Kathua, Riasi and Bishnah.[110] Some of these Mandirs are said to have been in existence since the early 20th century. The formation of the early Kabir Mandirs was necessitated by the gradual onslaughts of the Arya Samajis and the radical forces of the Gurudwara Singh Sabha, further exacerbated by the Christian Missionaries. The major initiative of the building of Mandirs among the Meghs seem to have branched off from Jalandhar, where a Kabir Mandir, as described above, was built in the early 20th century.

According to T.R. Azad,[111] a leading Ambedkarite activist from Jammu, historically the Dalits of the state, as elsewhere in India, have converted in large numbers to various religions in search of liberation from the caste system and the Brahminical religion that provides it religious sanction. Many Dalits who are today counted as Hindus follow sectarian traditions that are markedly egalitarian and anti-brahminical, such as the Ravidasi panth and the Kabirpanth. These traditions, in theory, obviate the need for the Brahamin as an intermediary, and also stress the equality of the human beings. In the case of the Kabirpanth, inter-communal harmony, between Hindus and Muslims, is also given particular stress. Rituals, while not denied, are morality and devotion to the one formless God.

Although some 2000 Dalits of the Batwal castes, formerly stated to be Kabirpanthis have converted to Bhudhism in recent years, they are said to be Buddhist only in name and to retain most of their Hindu beliefs and practices. Batwal caste has been one of those castes during the mid-nineteenth century, which according to Ibbetson, was Kabirpanth followers *en mass*.[112]

N. Kumar,[113] a school teacher from the Megh or *bhagat* (weaver) caste, who are also known as Kabirpanthis, points out that while the Meghs claim to be followers of Kabir (who was also from the weaver caste), and have several Kabir temples in Jammu, in actual fact they continue to worship the deities of the Brahminical pantheon and to employ Brahmins to officiate over their religious functions. 'This is a complete travesty of Kabir's message', he admits. The Brahminisation of the Kabirpanth tradition has gone so far, he claims, that the Meghs now consider themselves superior to the Chamars and generally refuse to eat food cooked by them. He alludes to the role of the Arya Samaj in this regard, and claims that Arya Samaji Missionaries have been actively engaged in promoting divisions between the Meghs and the other Dalits. 'They propounded and propagated the myth that the Meghs were originally Brahmins and hence superior to the Chamars, but that because they inter-dined with the Dalits, they, too, were condemned to becoming Dalits. In order to co-opt the Meghs into the Hindu fold they went about then providing them with the Brahminical thread', he told me.[114]

Critiquing the Brahminisation of their religious traditions also means retrieving what the Dalit activists see as their authentic histories, fashioning historical memory into a tool for social protest. Thus, Ravidas, so the 'Brahminised' version of the story has it, died after he was refused entry into a temple in Chittor by the Brahmins. In order to prove that he was a 'Brahmin', he tore open his heart, revealed three 'holy' threads inside his body, and then died. 'This is complete hum-bug, a myth propagated by the Brahmins in order to claim Ravidas as one of their own. Elaborating further on this issue, Ramesh informs me, "In this way they want to argue that Dalits just cannot produce such a great thinker as Ravidas. It is also a way to dilute the powerful challenge to Brahminism that Ravidas posed."[115] The same recovery of history is under way among some Kabirpanthi Meghs, who as Megh activists says, stoutly rebut the theory that Kabir was born in a Brahmin family. 'We must rewrite our traditions from the Dalit perspective, for if we lack our own histories, we will never be able to speak for ourselves', he asserts.

As the radical Kabir and the iconoclastic Ravidas have been 'spiritualised' beyond recognition, they have been turned into caste deities, functioning to symbolise caste division rather than inspiring their followers to overcome these differences. 'Both Kabir and Ravidas', says this Megh activist, 'spoke on behalf of all the oppressed, but today Ravidas has become a *chamar* deity and Kabir a Megh deity'.[116] As a result, few, if any, Chamars visit Kabir temples and hardly any Megh worship in temples dedicated to Ravidas. 'We in the Ambedkar Educational Foundation', Satindar Singh further explains, 'try and encourage Chamars and Meghs to visit each others' places of worship. That is precisely what Ravidas and Kabir would have wanted, and, besides, this sends out a powerful message to our people that we must work together.'[117]

South India

The most striking progress of the Kabirpanth was seen in the south India since the turn of the 20th century. In all probability, it took the route via Telangana territory, where a number of Kabir followers both from Gujarat and the Central Provinces were migrating. Hyderabad, the then growing city in the Telangana area, seems to have drawn the Kabirpanthis most. The earliest Math in the city was formed in the Shalar Band area of the old Hyderabad.[118] One Kanchan Das is said to have been the founder of this Math in 1887. At the same time another Ram-Kabir Mandir was also built in 1959 as it is inscribed on its front wall. The most prosperous Kabir ashram also emerged under the guruship of a Sardar Giri jee, who had become a legendary figure in the city.

In Bangalore, the earliest Math called the Adi Kabir Math was founded by a Maratha Kabirpanthi in 1925.[119]

Another splinter Adi Kabir Math was formed in another part of the city in 1934. The third one which predominantly has the followings of weaving community of Karnataka was formed in 1959. The latest one was formed in 1967 under the auspices of Mahant Ram Swarup Das of the Burhanpur Math.

Uttar Pradesh

Kabir Ashram at Basaha in Lucknow,[120] founded during the mid-nineteenth century emerged as one of the household (*parivarik*) Jagodasi sub-branches. Although the Jagodasi branch claims to be an adherent of the *virakta* tradition of Mahantship, yet the branch has had some exceptions of houseold Mahants. The genealogy of the Mahants has been well preserved. According to it, the founder Mahant died in 1918 and Sharan Das, the succeeding Mahant continued till 1947. Bhagwan Das succeded as the third Mahant but died in 1970. He was succeeded by Sukhdev Das who remained Mahant till his death in 1998. The guru of the present Mahant, Yogendra Das of the Basaha Math, Premanand Das, remained Mahant just for 5 years.

The most significant aspect of the Basaha ashram has been long association of Muslims with this ashram. There was considerable Muslim population in the two villages of Paigrame and Bhakhamo along with some Hindu Kabirpanthis. Earlier, they would often visit the ashram but with time, the number of Muslim visitors has fallen drastically. In course of its growth, Basaha Math is said to have brought into its fold a number of villagers as evident in the formation of ashrams at Mahmudpur, district Sitapur, Kateyaha and

Bhumuliyapur in district Barabanki and Akbarpur in district Bahraich.

However, the ashram is in a shambles today. The old *samadhis* (shrine) is in a dilapidated condition and work on the new one was stopped midway due to disputes within the family. Under the circumstances, the ashram is barely able to make ends meet. Even though the ashram is said to be affiliated to the Jagodasi branch, Biddupur, there is no sign of cordial relationship between both of these.

In nutshell, we can say that 20th century had been the period which offers us the most detailed information on the constituents of the Kabirpanth. Based on varying sources, we find that the panth had acquired contours of a national level religious community. Its social constituency also included people from almost all castes and religions of India–Hindu, Muslim, Sikhs and Christians; however, majority of its followers came from the lower castes of the Hindu and Muslim communities, the former having the preponderance.

After partition of India in 1947, majority of the Kabirpanthis living in Multan, Sialkot and Sindh regions left their native land and resettled at different places such as Delhi, Indore, Hathras and also established their ashram of Kabir, in their respective new shelters after rehabilitation. Yet a number of Hindu Kabirpanthis continued to live in Karanchi and Sindh regions of Pakistan. In all, the number of Muslim, Sikh and Christian Kabirpanthis had sharply declined, so much so that their number presently can be counted on fingers. In the post-independence era, Kabirpanth besides being a religious community, has emerged as the name of a scheduled caste (SC) in Panjab, Haryana, Himachal Pradesh, and Jammu and Kashmir, while in other provinces, it could not develop into a caste group. In the Chattisgarh and Maratha regions, Koshtis, Raghavis, Manikpuri Panikas and the Ram Kabirs have substantially taken on the contours of a sub-caste within the Kabirpanth community. Yet the vast majority of these devotees treat themselves as mere followers of their *sadguru* Kabir.

References

1. G.H. Westcott, *Kabir and the Kabirpanth*, Sushil Gupta, Calcutta, 1907
2. *Ibid.*, p. 62.
3. *Ibid.*, p. 58.
4. *Ibid.*, p. 58.
5. Edwin Greaves, *Kashi, the City Illustrious: or Banares*, Forgotten Books, 2015, pp. 101-102.
6. *Ibid.*, p. 61.
7. *Ibid.*, pp. 61-62.
8. *Ibid.*, p. 63.
9. Census of Punjab, 1911, p. 122.
10. Census of British India, 1901, p. 362.
11. H.A. Ross, *A Glossary of the Tribes and Castes of the Punjab and the North-West Frontier Provinces*, Vol. II, Language Deptt. Punjab, Patiala, p. 419.
12. *Ibid.*, p. 419.
13. Census of British India, Bengal, 1882, p. 87.
14. Census of Punjab, 1911,Chapter-IV, p.121.
15. *Ibid.*, p.122.
16. The Census of British India,1931, Chapter-XI, p. 302.
17. *Ibid.*, p. 301.
18. *Ibid.*, p. 304.
19. *Ibid.*, Section-IV, p. 69.
20. *Ibid.*, 301.

21. These gazetteers contain a large number of statistics from the preceding censuses undertaken by the British rulers in India.
22. *District and State Gazetteers of the Undivided Punjab (Prior to Independence)*, Vol. II, B.R. Publishing, Delhi, 1963 (1904), p. 80.
23. *Panjab District Gazetteers*, V. XIIIA, Hoshiarpur District, Pt. A, with Maps, Punjab Court Press, Lahore,1988 (1904), p.71.
24. I visited this Ghasidasi Kabir Math on 21 May 2014 and interviewed its Mahant and Resident Sadhus at Mekhowal, District Hoshiarpur, Punjab.
25. Kanchan Das Kabir Mandir has been under the control of the Burhanpur Math since 1976. Annex 18 i, ii.
26. We have succeeded in getting hold of the *Panchnama* prepared at the time of the split of the two and the date is taken from this document. Anx-19. i, ii.
27. The death of Dayaram has been explained by some scholars and informants as a case of suicide; see Minishwar Ray 'Munish', *Kabir-Panth Ki Jagushakha*, Jagushakha Guru Gadi, Bidupur, 1977, pp. 58-59.
28. The description of the council is entirely based on Rajendra Prasad, *Kabirpanth Ka Udbhav avam Prasar*, Hindi, Vanshgaddi Pratinidhi Sabha, Damakheda, 1981 pp.74-80.
29. Sewa Das, the founder of the Nadiya Math, was also designated as *Diwan/dharmadhikari* earlier by then Acharya Surat Sanehi for the Singhori headquarters, but Sewa Das finally revolted; the practice of selecting the successor Mahant as *Dharmadhikari* still continues at various maths, for instance, the Kharasiya Math Achaya Gaddi has a Dharmadhikari in his own younger brother. Anx-20.
30. Rajendra Prasad, *op. cit.*, p. 76.
31. Mata Kalap Devi, the widow of Dayanam is said to be a *bhagini (sister's daughter)* of Acharya Grindhmuni; for details see, Munishwar Ray 'Munish', *op. cit.*, p. 54.
32. Vichardas Shastri later on succeeded as the Second Acharya of Kharsiya *Nirwan Shakha* after Kashi Das's death in 1944 due to his sudden fall from the horse. Vichardas Shastri, like his predecessor was a member from an upper caste in Bihar.
33. I had met and intrviewed a strong group of Udapanthis in Los

Angeles, USA, where they have developed a huge Ram Kabir Mandir. I had visited this temple during my last trip to Los Angeles, USA, 8-9 July, 2015. Uday, PF, also conducted an intensive field works among Udapanthis in Gujarat from 21-23 Dec. 2013. Anx-21,i.

34. My statement is based on field data collected from the Ram-Kabirpanthi of Gujarat, also called *Bhagats*.
35. The present functionaries of the Burhanpur Math however deny its earlier link with the Kabir-Chaura, Varanasi, Uttar Pradesh.
36. Westcott himself acknowledges Walji Bhai's help in his study of the Kabirpanth. See G.H. Westcott, *op. cit.*, p. 4.
37. *Ibid.*, p. 82.
38. *Ibid.*, p. 107.
39. *Ibid.*, p.106.
40. *Ibid.*, p. 44.
41. *Ibid.*, p. 113.
42. F.E. Keay, *Kabir and His Followers*, Association Press, 1931, p. 102.
43. *Ibid.*, pp.108-111.
44. Robert V. Russel and Raibahadur Hiralal, *The Tribes and Castes of the Central Provinces of India,* Vol. I , Cosmo Publications, Delhi, 1975, p. 237.
45. *Ibid.*, p. 243.
46. *Ibid.*, Vol. II, p. 327.
47. *Imperial Gazetteers of India*, Central Provinces, Vol. XV, Today and Tomorrow Publishers, New Delhi, 1908, p. 193.
48. *Ibid.*, vol. XXI, p. 52.
49. *Imperial Gazetteers of India, Central Provinces to Coompta,* Vol. XXI, Today and Tomorrow Publishers, New Delhi, 1908.
50. *Ibid.*, Bilaspur, p. 221.
51. Kedarnath Dvivedi, *op. cit.*, p. 162.
52. I have taken this table from the *Census of India, Central Provinces,*1931, p. 333.
53. *Bengal District Gazetteers*, Govt. Secretariate Press, Calcutta, 1909, p. 176.
54. I have relied on the information about the history of the Tata Nagar (Jamshedpur) as posted on Google by the Tata Steel Establishment.

55. Description of Jamshedpur Maths is entirely based on my field works conducted on 30-31 Dec. 2013.
56. Tata Management,*op. cit.*
57. Mahant Sukhdev Das, interviewed, Jamshedpur, 31 Dec. 2013.
58. Mahant interviewed, Kaela Dangari, Jamshedpur, 31 Dec. 2013.
59. Based on my field works conducted in Dhanbad city, 1 Jan. 2014.
60. We could not personally visit these centres; however, I conducted a field work in Giridih city, Jharkhand on 2 Jan. 2014, where a Kabir Math, has been working since 1996. Sadhvi Gyananand, the head of the math, was, on a religious tour, hence I could not interview her. Anx-22, i, ii.
61. Based on my field work in Kharagpur and surrounding villages, 10 Jan 2014.
62. Khem Das's name is still inscribed on the front wall of the Math. Anx-23.
63. F. E. Keay, *op. cit.*, p.105.
64. *Ibid.*, pp.105-107. The diagramic sketch of successive gurus is also taken from F.E. Keay, *Ibid.*, 106.
65. Based on my field works in Barabanki on 26 June, 2013.
66. The present Mahant of the Jamnagar Math was unable to provide us the book.
67. I have based my account on the extensive field works we conducted in several parts of present Panjab; we heard of Panjabi Maharaj for the first time in the field, 1-3 July, 2013. The booklet is published under the title of *Sadguru Kabir Gaurav Gatha*, Srichanda Ram Charitable & Educational Trust, Chandigarh, 1998. Anx-24.
68. Kenneth W. Jones, *Arya Dharm, Hindu Consciusness in 19th-century Punjab*, University of California Press, Berkeley, 1976, p. 212.
69. *Ibid.*, p. 307.
70. *Ibid.*, p. 308.
71. *Ibid.*, p. 310.
72. *Ibid.*, p. 311.
73. I conducted field works in Jallundhar, Amritsar, Gurdaspur, and Pathankot areas over different period of time in 2013 and 2014.
74. Marc Juergensmeyer, *Religious Rebels in the Punjab, The Ad Dharm Challenge to Caste*, Navayana, New Delhi, 2009 (1982), pp. 298-299

75. Madhav Goswami, cited in Purnendu Ranjan, *History of Kabirpanth, A regional Process*, Anamika Publications, New Delhi, 2008, p. 198.
76. Visheshwar Das, quoted in *Ibid.*, p.199.
77. F.E.Keay, *op. cit.*, p.105.
78. *Ibid.*, p. 105.
79. *Ibid.*, pp. 94-95.
80. *Ibid.*, pp. 95-96.
81. *Ibid.*, pp. 97.
82. *Ibid.*, p. 97.
83. Based on Mahant Ram Swarup' s written will papers obtained from the Mahant of Kabir Math in Nagpur city, Maharashtra, by Uday, PF. Ann-25-i, ii.
84. Uday, PF's field notes and interviews, Burhanpur, 18 Nov., 2013.
85. Abhilash Das, *Kabir Darshan, op. cit.*, pp. 316-321.
86. Kharasiya Nirwan Math is presently divided into two. The split is said to have occurred around year 2000, resulting in the formation of a Chhota Math at the distance of about 2 Km. from the previous one.
87. This is the version of present incharge of the Saharanpur Math, Gursharan Das, an appointee of the Kaharsiya Acharya Gaddi, living in Saharanpur since 1999.
88. Based on the field notes I collected in Kanpur on 23 Jan. 2014.
89. I had visited this Math during my field work. Anx. 26, i.
90. Munni, interviewed, Kanpur, 23 Jan. 2014.
91. This certificate is cited in Maren Bellwinkel-Schempp, 'Kabir-Panthis in Kanpur: From Sampradaya to Dalit Identity', in Monika Horstman, *Images of Kabir*, Manohar, Delhi, p. 217.
92. *Ibid.*, p. 228.
93. Koris are one of the scheduled castes of Uttar Pradesh, while OBCs in Bihar, however they are known as Sainis in Haryana, Punjab and Himachal Pradesh.
94. Kanpur is believed to be a powerful centre of the Dharmdasi *Vansh gaddi* till date. In most of the *melas* organized at Damakheda, the followers of the city register their presence in sizeable number.
95. The years of meetings I have taken from Rajendra Prasad, *op. cit.*, 1981, pp. 73-78.

96. For details on Prem Das's report, see Maren Bellwinkel-Schempp, 'Kabir-Panthis in Kanpur: From Sampradaya to Dalit Identity', In Monika Horstmann (ed.), *op. cit.*, 218.
97. Krishna Kumar, interviewed, Kanpur, 23 Jan. 2014.
98. Unnao has been a strong centre of Pran Nathi Kabirpanthis as well.
99. I noted a number of erstwhile Kabirpanthis during my field work, active in the Dalit movement, under the banner of Ambedkar, both in Kanpur, and Jammu, visited, 23 Dec. 2015.
100. Uday, P.F., conducted field works in this region, thanks to the unstinted support from Gurdayal Das, the Mahant of Derabassi, from 7 to 8 June, 2013.
101. Based on the interview of Gurdayal Das, by Uday, PF.
102. Uday found these sadhus, during his field work, living there.
103. Uday, visited Ajmer Saharif Math, 16 Aug, 2013.
104. Based on Uday's field-reports collected in Rajasthan, 17 Aug. 2013.
105. Hari Singh, interviewed by Uday, 14 Aug. 2013.
106. Uday conducted field work in Limbdi, Gujarat, January 29, 2014. Anx-27.
107. *Ibid.*
108. *Ibid.*
109. Very few scholars on Kabirpanth had earlier noted the worship of the Krishna's idol in Kabir temples. Our field works in Gujarat has brought this fact into academic focus.
110. Parakhpanthis have now taken up independent stance and operates centrally from Allahabad Parkh Sansthan. Its founder Abhilash Das took Samadhi (died) in 2006. Annx-28-i, ii.
111. I have myself conducted field trips in Jammu region from 5 to 6 Sept. 2014. The details of the region are based on my field notes.
112. T.R. Azad, interviewed, Jammu, 5 Sept. 2014.
113. Ibbetson, *op. cit.*, p. 97.
114. Nand Kumar, interviewed, Katra, Jammu, 6 Sept. 2014.
115. *Ibid.*
116. Ramesh, interviewed, RS Pura, 6 Sept. 2014.
117. My informant is basically a political activist from the BJP in Jammu, interviewed, 5 Sept. 2014.
118. I interviewed Ajnala, 45, who has been an active Kabirpanthi in

Hyderabad, 1 June 2014. The first Kabirpanthi in his family was his grand-father, and Kanchan Das is said to have initiated him.

119. I had second round of field work in Bangalore from 2 to 3 June 2014 during which I could get hold of the Gyan Das's diary and got it photocopied.

120. The account of the Kabir Ashram, Basaha, Lucknow is entirely based on the field notes of Uday, PF, visited, 27 March 2014, Anx. 29, i, ii.

Kabirpanth Abroad

Kabirpanth as a religious community, unevenly spread over more than 18 Indian provinces, has witnessed recurring instances of diasporas of its sizeable followers particularly during its growth over the last 200 years. Named after Kabir, a 15th century devotional mystic saint, the Kabirpanth, has been divided into several branches and sub-branches in the process of expansion. It has simultaneously distanced itself from a number of apparently similar looking devotional sects developed in the period. Surprisingly there is, till date, no specific work written in India that dwells on the compelling factors leading to the particular diasporas of the Kabirpanth followers in more than a dozen countries of the African, American and the European continents. Yet it is a noteworthy fact that the Kabirpanth's multi-national presence owes solely to these diasporas whose historical trajectory is yet to be known in its entirety.

The following account is based primarily on the findings of my recently completed research work among the Kabirpanth followers living in India as well as abroad.[1] I make use of the findings I could procure from a few relatives of the indentured families who had then left India and several others to whom I had occasions to interview face-to-face in Canada, London and the USA and still others, through e-mails and audio-visual communications. I also consult some of the contemporary scholarly works available on indentured labourers once living outside India.[2] Based on these sources, I then address some of the key issues relating to the diasporic communities; such as, the impact and invisibility of the diasporas on the receiving countries and their respective homes left behind.

The diaspora of the Kabirpanth followers is said to have begun initially during the pre-colonial time when a sizeable number of them had migrated from Saurastra and Kutch regions lying in the present Gujarat province of India to the African countries.[3] However, we do not have a definitive account of these followers who formed part of the larger trading communities that had left their homeland for overseas having better prospect of monetary benefits. But the reliable account available to us relates to the subsequent phase of their diaspora beginning from the mid-nineteenth century onwards till 1917 when indenture system was finally abolished by the British rule.[4] The massive diaspora mainly occurred in the trail of the indentured system which was introduced by the British rulers during the early nineteenth century. The indenture system, as is widely known to us, had been a system of hiring manual and skilled labours for placing them as substitute cheap labour forces in foreign enterprises of the colonial establishments, where, for various reasons, labour forces were in short supply soon after the end of the slavery system in African and the Caribbean countries in 1832.[5] The second phase had been the period during which a huge number of the Kabir's followers seems to have settled on foreign lands.

Most of these labour forces were recruited from the eastern and western parts of the British India, covering roughly present parts of Uttar Pradesh, Bihar and Gujarat. Significantly enough, these two parts have also been traditional stronghold of Kabir followers for centuries as my findings suggest.[6] It is said that most of the immigrants from the Gujarat region settled in different parts of the British colonies in Africa; whereas those of Uttar Pradesh and Bihar were shipped mostly to Mauritius, the Caribbean countries, British Guyana, Dutch Guyana and Fiji.[7]

Kabirpanth diaspora seems to have found its first homes in Mauritius and British Guyana, which were the earliest countries to have indentured labourers from British India, way back in 1838. It is estimated that the largest number of Kabirpanthis, among all the recipient countries, have been living in Mauritius. According to my informants[8], the numerical strength of the Kabir devotees in Mauritius came down sharply from about 20,000 in 1901 to 6000 in the present, as many of them gradually got converted by the Arya Samaj from 1910 onwards. Presently the country has about six Kabir centres and most famous of these are situated in Vacoas and Grand Boi. Puran Daas, one of the Mahants in Mauritus, apprises us that they have been running an organization called the Kabirpanth Federation in order to consolidate devotees spread in its different parts since 1941.[9]

Roughly around the same time, another batch of these followers, among many others, began to settle in the Caribbean countries, at least, from 1840 onwards. Out of the total 2.4 lakh indentured labourers, there had at least been 40 thousand Kabir followers. My informant, Jagessar Das, one of the oldest survivors among them, recalls that his parents were shipped there in 1910, the year as mentioned in the Emigration Pass. As a youngster in early 1940s, he would often find himself in the religious gatherings of his 150-200 co-religionists, but in the present, he does not hear of anyone following Kabirpanth's principles there. It is said that these followers failed to develop any specific Kabir centre there as all the *panth* activities used to be organized at their own houses. Most of the remaining followers may have left British Guyana in the aftermath of their freedom struggle during 1960s. Jagessar Das, the among then, himself left Guyana in 1954. To quote him:

> Kabir Panthis in Guyana, among Hindus and Muslims, were taken as indentured labourers to work on the sugar plantations owned by the British. The majority of the Indians in Guyana, during my youth, were the ones who chose to stay and to do farming on this small farm allotted to them. My parents were indentured in 1910, i.e. they were taken from India to Guyana on a ship named the Indus. When I was born my parents were already free from indentureship and opted to stay in Guyana. They had a small piece of land on which they did mixed farming including rice paddy, fruit and root vegetables for home consumption and extras that were sold at a farmers' market.
>
> The Kabir Panth was a minority group among the indentured labourers. They brought their religious

> practices to Guyana. Among them there were Mahants who conducted religious ceremonies for the other Kabir Panthis. My father was a Diwan or an assistant to a Mahant.
>
> The Kabir Panthis in Guyana were scattered sparsely in two counties: Demerara and Berbice. I am referring to the 1930s and1940s. Travel between these places for religious functions were by train, bus or on foot. In case of a death, we had to reach a Mahant by sending a telegram through the post office. The religious functions that required the services of a Mahant were the *chowkaarati* and funerals. As a Diwan, my father could perform all the necessary religious functions.
>
> Over the years very few Kabir Panthis became Mahants or Diwan, as a result when a death occurred amongst them there were hardly any replacements. The last Mahant in Guyana immigrated to Canada and at present living in the United States. This has created a void in Guyana and for approximately the last 15 years there is no Mahant in Guyana. The Kabir Panthis also decreased in number as the older generations passed away and the younger generations had no leadership. A few of them adopted other religions.[10]

British Guyana appears to be the lone country, from where almost all the Kabir followers are reported to have either re-migrated or converted to the Arya Samaj or to the Sanatan Dharma.

An interesting piece of information about the *panth* in Trinidad and Tobago, is also available in a memorandum which was submitted before the British officials by Philip Ramkissun, a converted Christian, in 1893.[11] He points out that the Kabeer-Phunt (sic) was introduced in Trinidad and Tobago by one Meethoodass, who was a Chamar by caste. He is said to have come there from Demerara (British Guyana). Apart from Kabirpanth, there also existed three other religious panths; namely Ramanund, Owghur and Sewnarain (sic). According to Haridas[12],an informant from Trinidad, one of the earliest batches of the indentured labourers were shipped to Trinidad in 1845, comprising of 225 persons, which included some Kabir followers too.

As per the prevailing tradition, the first centre of the *panth* in Trinidad was opened at Arima in 1880. By 1891, the total number of these followers reached 150. According to a rough estimate, about 1.5 lakh Indian labourers, in all, had been brought there on contract of 5 to 10 years.[13] Most of the Kabir devotees, among them, who had opted to stay put in Trinidad and Tobago, formed an umbrella organization being called the Kabir Panth Association. They got it formally registered in 1932. In addition, those who have migrated in recent years have formed another association called Satya Kabir Nidhi. At present we do not have exact idea about the numerical strength of these followers but my informants estimate it to be not less than 20,000 out of the total Hindu population of about 2 lakh 50 thousand in Trinidad. They can be seen living in various places; such as, Penal, La Cuasa, Williams Ville, Freeport, Siparia, Guece, Manzanilla, Barrakpore, Chaguanas, Fishing Pond etc. They constitute one of the four main groups of the Indians living in Trinidad. However, Tobago presently has negligible number of Kabir's followers.

During early 1860s, another group of the Kabirpanth followers known as the 'Ram-Kabirs' inhabiting in most parts of the present southern Gujarat of India, had begun to migrate as indentured labourers to different parts of the British colonies in the mainland African continent. Between 1860 and 1911, the Colony of Natal imported 1,52,184 Indians to work primarily on the sugar plantations.[14] They gradually came to settle in areas presently known as South Africa, East Africa, Ghana, Nigeria, Kenya and Rhodesia. A sizeable number of them are said to be Kabir followers. Many of them, after the end of colonial rule in these countries, were forced to leave these countries for ever due to unfavourable political condition and subsequently re-migrated to the USA and the UK instead of their homeland India even after 1950. A very miniscule number of the followers are still said to be living in these countries. According to the Mahant of Jamnagar Math, the total number of Kabir's followers presently in these African countries must not be less than 10,000.[15]

Surinam has been one of those countries where first batch of the Kabirpanthis, among many others, had begun to settle in 1883. Recalling the predicament of their predecessors, Chand Sitaram,[16] one of the Kabirpanthis in Holland, informs us that the very eagerness of their forefathers to work in Surinam first emerged out of a verbal confusion over the name of Surinam; they mistook it as Sri Ram, implying the land of Sri Ram, one of the popular Hindu Gods in India, where they were then being shipped to. Till 1916, the total number of such indentured labourers reached 35,000 and a sizeable number among them belonged to the Kabirpanth. As per the prevailing tradition, the first Kabirpanth Guru who arrived there was Bhagawan Das. They succeeded in forming their first Kabir Mandir of Surinam in 1958. Most of these followers were forced to stay there till Surinam's independence in 1975. In the changed political scenario, majority of the Kabir devotees decided to leave Surinam and decided to re-migrate to get settled in the main cities of Holland, the actual homeland of their colonial master. It took them another five years to regroup together as Kabir followers when they organized a national level body called Kabir-Satsang in 1980.

Fiji is one of those countries about which we have interesting contemporary accounts of their activities. A Kabirpanth diaspora, in Fiji, began immediately after the introduction of the indenture system in 1879. Totaram Sandhyay, an indentured labourer, who had lived there almost 20 years in between 1893-1914, offers us valuable details on the origin and internal feuds arising within the *panth.* He wrote that:

> In December, 1894, Baba Oridas founded this *akhada* in Manipatu. He initiated about 200 devoted disciples into this sect. Oridas was an employee of the police department. As he was well liked by his disciples, the number of his devotees increased to one thousand. Every fortnight, *bhajans* and prayer meetings were held at this place... Eventually, he left for India, entrusting his sect to Baba Dalbhanjandas, his favourite disciple.[17]

Significantly enough, Kabirpanth's chequered expansion took an interesting turn in the mid-20th century particularly, a period during which a number of these colonies hitherto having indentured labours either became independent or were to gain it. Instead of coming back to India, during early 1960's, several adventurous followers from above-mentioned countries, began to re-migrate and settle in England, New Zealand, Australia, Netherlands, Panama, Mexico, Canada as well as the USA.

The largest number of them are said to have settled in Canada and the USA. Majority of followers coming from Mauritius, Trinidad, British Guyana, and, in recent times from India, too, re-migrated to the metropolises of Toronto and Vancouver in Canada. They later formed a pan-Canada association called the Canada Association of Kabir, having its headquarters in Surrey, Vancouver in 1884, under the capable leadership of Dr. Jagessar Das, a retired medical practitioner, and its sister organization called the Kabir Association of Toronto, Toronto under Mahant Jay Juggesur, an immigrant from Mauritius settled in Toronto. They have been running an exclusive Kabir Mandir in Surrey, Vancouver since 1996. Recalling his journey in Canada, Jagessar Das pointed out:

> My experience as a devotee of Kabir in Canada has been similar. In 1976, Shri Hazur Udit Nam Saheb visited us in Canada and ordained my brother as a Mahant and me as *dharmadhikari*. As the devotees of Kabir from Guyana, we held *satsangs* at one another's homes. We sang *bhajans*, studied the teachings of Kabir, performed *arati* and shared *Prasad*. We also observed the *purnima* fasting and recited the *purnima katha*. In 1984, we formed the Kabir Association of Canada and in 1996, we purchased a unit in a

> commercial complex where we held all of our religious functions. We held educational seminars, musical concerts and cultural functions.
> In Canada, the Kabir Association also produced three TV programs observing Kabir Saheb's *Jayanti*. I give talks on the teachings of Kabir Saheb at our Sunday *satsangs*. I also delivered teachings of Kabir in Trinidad, Los Angeles, New York and Toronto. I was also interviewed several times on ethnic TV, and a few of my talks are on YouTube. For several years I produced a journal entitled: *The Kabir Voice*. This journal was dedicated to the teachings and philosophy of Kabir Saheb. I have also created a webpage through a webmaster that contains many of Kabir Saheb's teachings. The webpage is www.kabir.ca.[18]

The history of the small Kabirpanth community in the United Kingdom cannot be traced earlier than mid-1970s. It coincides with its expansion in the USA. According to one of my informants, Arajan Kushwaha, to whom I met and interviewed during my last visit to the UK in April 2015, 'First known Kabirpanthi disciple in the UK arrived in mid-seventies (1970s) via Eastern Africa particularly from Uganda and Kenya.' Arajan Keshwaha was born and spent his youth in Jamnagar, Gujarat but has been settled in the UK since 1977. Arajan was however a Kabirpanthi before he arrived in the UK.

In UK, most Kabirpanth followers are attached to Jamnagar Kabir Ashram. Ramswarup Das and Shanti Das, former Mahants of the Jamnagar Ashram would travel frequently to Kenya and Uganda during 1960s and 70s, and later to UK, USA and Canada too. Jagdish Das ji, the successor Mahant had inspired Arajan and other Kabir devotees to start the *Sadguru Kabir Seva Samaj* (SKSS), UK in 2001.

Initially Lilaben Odedra and her mother, brothers and sisters from Leicester; Bhupendrabhai from Kingsbury in London, Bharatbhai from St. Albans, and Arajan from Basildon, Essex started the tasks of charity. Currently of the original Trustees, only Arajan, Bhupedrabhai and Bharatbhai are engaged in running SKSS under guidance from Mahant Rameshwar Das, then Mahant of Jamnagar Ashram in 2015. The main aims of this association have been to support the Samarpan Hospital, Jamnagar, *Goushala* (cow-shred) and Jamanagar Kabir Ashram–all located in the central parts of the city.

According to Bhupendrabhai, Kabirpanth has given him a lot of social recognition and satisfaction that he had been able to help and meet other like-minded people to serve Kabir Ashram, Jamnagar and local community in the UK. There is no political recognition of the Kabir Panthis in the UK, they do not seek active recognition to this aspect, however, they wish they should try a bit harder to get recognised,which they may pursue in future as a post-retirement project.

Kabirpanth has seen ups and downs in the UK during the 20 years of the formation of association. At present, as Arajan laments, they could have achieved a lot more, if they had more volunteers. However, the current Trustees feel that they would only undertake a project where they can support hundred per cent They all are full-time employees/or running their own business and short of time. Every time Guruji from Jamnagar visits UK, they welcome him with open arms and heart and be there to take care of him and organise fund-raising activities.

In the USA, many Bhakta families (as Gujarati Kabir followers called themselves) began to settle first in San Francisco, while some others also settled in parts of its Eastern coast. The arrival of Chhaganbhai Bhulabhai Bhakta there from England for higher studies is said to have ushered them in a new phase of the Kabirpanth's entry in California. It is he who is said to have established the *Bhakta* Society of USA in 1973 with its avowed objectives of preserving and promoting Kabir's teachings, at least, among the Bhakta families then living overseas. Since then, this society has progressed both in number, and resources as well. My informants[19] emphasize some important milestones the Society has crossed in its ongoing progressive march; such as, its success in obtaining a tax-exempt status under section 501 C 3, as a religious organization active within the USA, its re-naming as the Ramkabir Bhakta Samaj and gradual formation of the distinct chapters of the Samaj across almost all the states of the USA. The *Samaj* also took upon itself the publication tasks of religious books and *Bhakta* Directory, and also formed an Education *Corpus* Fund for assisting needy students of its community in higher education within the USA.

Within Indian sub-continent, Kabirpanthis can be seen living in different parts of Bangladesh, Bhutan, Nepal and Pakistan. Although I could not visit due to paucity of resources any of these countries except Nepal, I could get substantial information about Kabir followers either through migrant followers living in

Euro-American countries or my online interviews with some of them. During my last visit to Canada, I had met and interviewed in Toronto a Pakistani Hindu Kabirpanthi family hailing from Karanchi in 2012, but having permanent residency of Canada. According to the eldest member of this family, aged 81, almost all the Kabir centres which had been active during his young age in Karanchi region, had either been closed by force or were on the verge of closure. While he was in Karanchi till 2002, the Kabir Ashram situated there on the bank of river Indus was in existence just for name. He suspected that by now it must have been shut down. However, recent audio-visual documentary on Kabir produced by Shabnam Birmani financed by the Ford Foundation makes it clear that a sizeable number of Kabir followers still reside in and around Karanchi.

It appears that most of the Kabir followers of this town were originally Gujarati as my Canadian informant led me to believe. His information is further corroborated by a bi-monthly magazine named *Swa-Samved* in Hindi, begun to be published from Baroda, Gujarat, in 1934. In its November-December issue of the first year itself, the magazine contains a 2 page report on the origin and activities of the Karanchi ashram. It reports that Balkrishna Das, a Diwan from Baroda Kabir Ashram, had been staying there along with his Bhandari named Srikrishna Das for three months. The report written by Dahyabhae Lavajibahe, a mechanic working at the cast Iron Foundry, Lawrence Road, Karanchi traces its origin in about 1830s, founded by a Mahant Mangal Das of Baroda (see, page to 210, 211 and 212). But the century-old Kabir Mandir came to be closed in the1910s due to inefficient succeeding Mahants of the centre, as he describes. In the circumstances, once again, the Mahants and leading members of the panth from Baroda and Surat, reinforced their efforts to re-establish a fresh centre in Karanchi and they formed an association called *Satya Kabir Satsang Mandal* in 1930. They also arranged a rented hall for regular *satasang* to be continued for the local followers in the town.

Their efforts got a fillip once Mahants of Rajkot Kabir ashram and Morbi also came forward to do their bit in the task during 1932-33, when Manekdas and Madhav Das, Mahants of Rajkot and Morbi Kabir ashrams personally visited and stayed among the followers living in Karanchi almost for two months at a stretch. Finally their efforts bore fruits and another Kabir Ashram was opened in Ranchhod Line area in 1937, on a land plot which was purchased at the cost of Rs. 3000/ collected from the resourceful followers of the region. This information makes it clear that most of the followers in this region had their roots in trading community of Gujarat, who had earlier migrated to Karanchi and its neighbourhood. After the partition of India in 1947, many of them were forced to go back to India. However, those who decided to stay back there are said to have continued their nirgun bhakti alive, but could not keep it going in the face of growing militancy in Pakistan. Many of them left for foreign lands and a few who still live there succumbed to the adverse circumstances and have forgotten the path of Kabir. The same ashram thus built according to my informant had remained active till the end of the 20th century, but now it has become totally defunct and its building has also fallen apart.

करात्री में कबीर धर्मस्थान और हमारा कर्तव्य ।

आज लगभग तीन महिना होते हैं, श्रीमान् स्वामीश्री बालकृष्णदासजी साहेब भंडारी श्रीकृष्णदासजी साहब के साथ करांची में पधारे हुए हैं। जब से आप पधारे हैं तबसे करांची की कबीरपंथी जनता में अपूर्व उत्साह छाया हुआ है और आपके सदुपदेशों के कारण नईर सद्भावनायें यहांकी धर्मप्राण जनता में जागृत हो रही हैं।

सौ वर्ष पहिले की बात है कि महात्मा महंतश्री मंगलदासजी साहब ने सिंध-करांची में पदार्पण कर सद्गुरु कबीर धर्मदास साहेब के सद्धर्म का प्रचार कर सत्नाम का झंडा गाड़ा। आप चमत्कारी सिद्ध महात्मा थे। आपने करांची में एक मंदिर बनवाया। और अनेक संतमहात्मा वहां आने जाने लगे तथा साधुसेवा का कार्यभार वहांकी धर्मप्राण कबीरपंथी जनता ने सहर्ष उठाया और अबतक उठाती आ रही है। इस सेवा में बाधा उपस्थित हुई और आज बीस वर्ष हुए मंदिर, उत्तराधिकारी के अयोग्य निकलने से, बिक गया और प्रेमीभक्तों का दर्शन-सत्संग का आधार टूट गया। तब से करांची के कबीरधर्मानुयी निराधार हो गये। किन्तु श्रद्धा भक्ति अटूट रही। इसीकारण संवत् १९८७ के दूसरे श्रावण में बडीदा के श्रीमान् १०८ महंतश्री बालकदासजी साहेब तथा दिवान श्री बालकृष्णदासदासजी साहेब, पं. मोतीदासजी, भंडारी कृष्णदासजी, श्रीदलालदासजी तथा भंगीदासजी के साथ आग्रह से पधारे और उपदेशपूर्ण कथा-सत्संग से बहुत ही अच्छा प्रभाव पडा और 'सत्य कबीर सत्संग मंडल' की स्थापना हुई। सत्संग का कार्य किराये के मकान पर चलने लगा। किन्तु अपना स्थान न होने की कमी सबके हृदय में दुःख पहुंचाती रही। फिरसे संवत् १९८९ के आषाढ मास में बडौदा के श्रीमान् महंत बालकदासजी साहेब, सुरत सगरामपुरा के महंतश्री मोहंगदासजी साहेब, पं. भू. महंतश्री विचारदासजी साहेब शास्त्री, दिवान श्रीबालकृष्णदासजी साहेब, पं. मोतीदासजी तथा कपिलदासजी पधारे और धर्मप्रचार का शुभ कार्य शुरू हुआ और अपूर्व जागृति आयी। उसी अरसे में राजकोट के छोटे महंतश्री माणेकदासजी साहेब अपनी संत मंडली के साथ पधारे। इससे और भी अधिक प्रभाव पड़ा। संवत् १९९० के भादों में मोरबी के महंतश्री माधवदासजी साहेब अपनी संत मंडली के साथ पधारे। आपने भी दो मासतक रहकर धर्मप्रचार किया।

इस प्रकार एक दो वर्ष के बाद करांची की कबीर पंथी जनता को धर्मलाभ होता ही रहता था। किन्तु अपना स्थान न होने की कमी दुःख देती ही रहती थी। वह भी सद्गुरु की दया से अब दूर हो गई है। अभी गत श्रावण मास में (सं. १९९३) बड़ौदे से पूज्य स्वामीश्री बालकृष्णदासजी साहेब, भंडारी कृष्णदासजी के साथ करांची पधारे। आपके सदुपदेश पूर्ण व्याख्यानों से बहुत ही धर्मजागृति और शुभ कार्य के लिये उत्साह पैदा हुआ है।

ालस्वरूप करांची के रणछोडलाइन मुहल्ले में ।२० वार सम चौरस जमीन रु० ३०००) ीन हजार में खरीद करने की लिखापढी ो चुकी है और बडे उत्साह और प्रेम से हां के परमोत्साही धर्मानुरागी श्रीयुत् मीस्त्री डाह्याभाई लवजीभाई, श्रीयुत् छगनभाई जीवाभाई नागर, सवजीभाई तुलसीभाई आदि भाई स्वामीश्रीबालकृष्णदासजी साहेब की आज्ञानुसार कार्य में संलग्न हैं। इन भाइयों ने अपनी धर्मवीरता का बहुत सुंदर परिचय दिया है। मीस्त्री डाह्याभाई लवजीभाई, छगन-भाई इन दोनोंने ५०१) रुपया करांचीमें कबीर धर्मस्थान के लिये प्रदान किये हैं। औरर भाई बहिन भी कोई सौ तो कोई एकावन, इस प्रकार बड़े उत्साह और लगन से सद्गुरु सेवा के पवित्र कार्य में संलग्न हैं। यह सब संतमहात्माओं के सत्संग का, विशेष में स्वामीश्री बालकृष्णदासजी साहेब के प्रभावशाली सदुपदेश तथा पू. स्वामीजी के अपने निर्मल व्यक्तित्व का प्रभाव है। और आशा है कि, निकट भविष्य में करांची में एक नूतन कबीर धर्मस्थान आधुनिक शैली पर प्रतिष्ठित हो जायगा। पूज्य स्वामीश्री बालकृष्णदासजी साहेब तथा मीस्त्री डाह्याभाई, छगनभाई, सवजीभाई तथा अन्य सब भाई हमारे हार्दिक धन्यवाद के पात्र हैं। सद्गुरु! शीघ्र करांची की जनता को इससे लाभान्वित करें यही हमारी विनम्र प्रार्थना है।

स्वसंवेद के प्रिय पाठक वर्ग, माननीय महंत साहेबो, संत महात्माओ तथा धर्मप्रेमी सज्जनों से साग्रह विनंति है कि आप साहेब भी अपनीर यथाशक्ति मदद जरूर पहुंचावें। हमारे में संगठन शक्ति का जो अभाव दीखता है उसको इस कार्य को अपना कर दूर कर दीजिए। हमको चाहिए कि हम एक दूसरे को मदद करें और इस प्रकार सारा पंथ संगठन के सूत्र में बंध जाय। धनी मानी महंत संत तथा सज्जनों से हमारी सादर अपील है कि आप सब करांची में तैयार होते हुए कबीर धर्मस्थान को जरूर मदद पहुंचावें। मदद पहुंचाने का पता यह है:—

श्रीयुत मीस्त्री डाह्याभाई लवजीभाई,
धी कास्ट आयर्न फाउन्डरी, लोरेन्स रोड,
मु०, पो०, **करांची** (सिंध)

नागपूर में दूसरी बार भक्त कबीर टोकीज बंद।

स्वसंवेद के पाठकगण तथा संत महात्माओं को विदित होगा कि, पिछले साल ता० १६–१०–१९३३ को **कबीर कमाल** फिल्म नागपूर में बंद हुई थी। अभी फिर से यहां के सुप्रसिद्ध रिजन्ट टॉकीज में **ऑरिएन्टल टॉकीज** की '**भक्त कबीर**' बोलती फिल्म ता. ७–१०–१९३६ से शुरू होनेवाली थी। अतः यहां के सद्धर्मप्रचारक कबीर समाज के उत्साही कार्यकर्ता श्रीमहंत हीरादासजी साहब, दि० रामदासजी साहब, श्री बलीरामजी पोदार, नीलकंठरावजी ईले ठेकेदार शामरावजी मालोकर, कोठीराम ढोबळे, रामराव ढोबळे इत्यादि के प्रयत्न से मे० डिप्युटी कमिश्नर साहेब ने बंद करवा दिया। यहां पर शहर में बहुत ही कोलाहल मच गया है।

२१० स्व-संवेद । [वर्ष ५

करांची श्रीकबीर धर्मस्थान ।

करांची श्री कबीर धर्मस्थान में सद्गुरु प्राकट्य महोत्सव इस वर्ष भी उसी अपूर्वता के साथ मनाया गया जैसा कि प्रतिवर्ष मनाया जाता है। ता. १८-६-४० बुधवार को करांची के भूतपूर्व मेयर रा. सा. जमशेदजी महेता की अध्यक्षता में सुप्रसिद्ध विद्वानों के व्याख्यान हुए। और ता. १९-५-४० गुरुवार को सिंध के सुप्रसिद्ध विद्वान साधु टी. एल. वासवानी की अध्यक्षता में महोत्सव का कार्य बड़े समारोह के साथ संपन्न हुआ। करांची की प्रत्येक कौम के प्रतिष्ठित व्यक्तियों ने बड़े प्रेम और आदर के साथ महोत्सव में भाग लेकर सद्गुरु के प्रति अपनी श्रद्धा और भक्ति प्रगट की। बड़े २ विद्वानों ने भी सद्गुरु के प्रति अपनी पूर्ण निष्ठा प्रदर्शित करते हुए जनता के कल्याण के लिये इसके अधिकाधिक प्रचार की आवश्यकता पर भार दिया। करांची अपनी विशेषता के लिये हमारे पंथ में सुप्रसिद्ध ही है। करांची के श्री कबीर धर्मस्थान के संस्थापक श्रीमान १०८ महंत साहेब स्वामीश्री बालकृष्णदासजी साहेब और धर्मस्थान की कमेटी के मेम्बर और वहांके भक्तजन प्रतिवर्ष एक प्राण होकर प्राकट्य महोत्सव को अपूर्व बना देते हैं। इस वर्ष भी आप लोगों ने यह प्रणाली कायम रखी और 'सद्गुरु कबीर साहेब और उनका सिद्धान्त' नामक क्राउन सोलह पेजी साइज की ६४ पृष्ठ की पुस्तिका सबको मुफ्त वितरण की और स्वसंवेद के प्रिय पाठकों को भी इसका लाभ दिया। इस पुस्तिका की एक हजार कापी निकालने में आपको करीब सौ रुपया खर्चना पड़ा। तौभी आपने इसे अमूल्य वितरण करना ही निश्चय किया है। आपकी प्रकाशित की हुई यह पुस्तिका बहुत लोकप्रिय हुई है। और इसकी बहुत जोरोंसे मांग आ रही है। इस महती साहित्य सेवा के लिये माननीय महंत साहेब स्वामीश्री बालकृष्णदासजी साहेब, कबीर धर्मस्थान कमिटी के मेम्बर एवं करांची की धर्मप्राण और श्रद्धालु कबीरपंथी जनता हमारे अनेकानेक हार्दिक धन्यवाद और अभिनंदनार्ह है।

हम आशा करते हैं कि हमारे पंथ के अन्य महंत साहेब भी धर्मवृद्धि में तन, मन, धन से इस प्रकार आगे बढ़ेंगे।

पं. मोतीदास.

As has been described in the last chapter, most of the Kabirpanthis particularly Hindus are said to have left Multan and Sialkot areas of the present Pakistan, in the midst of bloodshed witnessed in the aftermath of the partition of India in 1947. After the death of the Punjabi Maharaj, who had laid the foundation of a Kabir ashram in Multan town in the early years of 20th century, continued to function under the able leadership of his son Balwant Singh, as his successor till 1947. But it had to be closed down once almost all the Kabir followers had to flee away from the town in no time. According to Om Prakash, my informant in Delhi, whose parents and kinsmen had survived the bloodshed of the partition, they had tried to carry along whatever they could from the ashram in Multan, but for fear of death, they had to leave Multan instantly abandoning the ashram at its own fate. A large group of Megh and Batwal Kabirpanthis left the Sialkot region and came to settle at Jallundhar, Meerut and Ludhiana. They had become popular as Bhagats of Kabir, as Kabir himself has been shown as a Bhagat in the Guru Granth Sahib. Except Karanchi, it appears most of the Kabir followers had *en masse* left Pakistan by the end of 1947.

But in Nepal, the number of Kabirpanthis has been in thousands, being served by a number of Kabir ashrams belonging mainly to the Bhagodasi, Jagodasi and Krishna Karakhi *Vachanvanshi* branches. The followings of the panth include both Nepali Gorkhas and the *Madheshi* Hindus. They have kept aloft the flag of Kabir and his panth in several parts of the country; such as, Hakpara, Kathmandu, Thakale Basti, Malangawa, Pokharwinda etc., at least since mid-nineteenth century. As my study demonstrates, expansion of the Kabirpanth in parts of Bhutan, Darjeeling, Sikkim and Meghalaya owe in its earliest stage to the Gorkha converts, whose descendants carry forward the tradition even after their migration towards these regions. One of the oldest sub-branches of the Bhagatahi branch situated at Etiahi in the district Birganj is still active.

According to Rajendra Sunuwar, a non-resident Bhutanese living in Calagary, Alberta, Canada, 'there must not be less than 500 followers of Kabir in a Buddhist-dominated country'. A memorial of the royal family member of Bhutan built at the Mahadeo Kabir Math, Rosara, Bihar has been a striking testimony of the spread of Kabirpanth in Bhutan.

However, I could not gather any substantial

information regarding the actual location of Kabir followers in Bangladesh. Some informants in the West Bengal stated that a small number of Kabir followers still exist among the Bihari Bengaladeshis.

In the process, their invisibility in a foreign land is also said to have given way to a growing recognition as the believer of the secular messages of Kabir. The emerging faint visibility has found expression in their services to the victims of the natural disasters occurred in the USA, India and some other countries in recent times. They have asserted their presence by owning a property in Norwalk, California where presently the Bhakta Cultural Centre after Kabir's name was built in 2002. It was inaugurated by Maa Sarveshwari, a woman Mahant of Gujarat region. Simultaneous with the organizational development has been considerable increase in the diasporic Kabir *bhagat* community as well. It is said the total number of ongoing diasporas of these followers has been not less than 50,000 alone from the Gujarat region during the last 40 years. Main reason leading to the latest diasporas, in Mahant Ram Swarup Das's opinion, has been the preference of the Bhagat parents in the USA for a Gujarati bride and bridegroom for their sons and daughters over non-Gujarati or American or European life-partners. However, better prospect of jobs there has been an added allurement for them.

In terms of the issue of the invisibility of certain diasporas, the existing evidences suggest that the diasporas of the Kabir followers was actively made invisible in two main ways: first, their sectarian identity was not taken into account at the time of their recruitment as an indenture labour. Instead, most of them were inducted as a member coming from the greater traditions of the Hindu, Muslim or the Sikh religions; second, almost all the scholars who have studied, Kabir followers except a few of the scholarly fellows, have treated them merely as a part of the homogenous indenture Indian labour force. Combined with these two factors, its high concentration among the low Hindu and Muslim castes, and abysmally lower level of educational growth among them had made their invisibility all the more entrenched. Nonetheless, the role of the existence of other groups of diasporic communities and their relative smaller number in the same colonies cannot be ignored in making them invisible. In all probability, their invisibility was consequent upon a number of historical factors then prevailing in the colonial era, but by the turn of the 21st century, the layer of invisibility has gradually been getting thinner in the face of the growing awakening among these followers themselves, accompanied by the expanding print, electronic and network of the web world among many other media. This process has got further stimulus at the time when ethnicity and identity has come to acquire centre stage in these erstwhile British colonies. In addition, increasing level of educated persons in the community has enabled a few of them to pen down their own trials and tribulations in their respective countries. Presently we can easily find information regarding their activities and the programmes on their respective web pages. Jagessar Das finds the usefulness of the Kabir centers (ashram) not just for the Kabirpanthis but for the entire communities of Canada. In his own words:

> The problems in Canadian cities are similar to problems in any city. There are domestic violence, drug problems and violent gangs, murders and racial conflicts. There is inequality in economic status. Kabir Saheb's teachings are relevant in that he taught against illicit drugs, tobacco, alcohol and non-violence. He taught love, respect and equality of all based on the fact that we need to see God in all beings. He taught against racism and casteism and avoidance of conflicts based on religious differences. His teachings will benefit all people of Canadian cities in curbing problems[20].

Along with their settlement in varied colonies belonging to the British, French and Dutch imperial powers, there also began the opening of devotional centres exclusively meant for the Kabirpanth in their respective regions. Opening of such centres has not followed an even pattern. While in mainland Africa, British Guyana, England, Netherlands and New Zealand, these followers, till date, have not been able to open an exclusive centre of devotion; in Mauritius, Surinam, Trinidad, Canada and the USA, they have built up their own exclusive Kabir centres. The successful attempts to open exclusive centres are commonly attributed to the resourcefulness of the related groups of followers; these also reflect their emerging visibility among competing Hindu sects as well as majority groups of the Christianity predominant in those countries. These centres have also come to fill the glaring need of a sacred space they had been missing out in countries where they had decided to settle down permanently. In these acts, we often notice that they actively supported each other while living on different islands of their settlement. For instance, Tota Ram account of Fiji specifically mentions that the first centre of Kabirpanth in Fiji was opened by one Mitthudas who had come there from Damerera in the British Guyana. In other countries, such as; Trinidad, we are informed by Philip Ramkrishnan that regular advice and support from a guru, living in Banaras, India was sought not only to open centres but also to resolve their internal disputes. The present wide network of the *panth* across four continents appears to be the net results of the then initiatives taken by these followers working as indentured labourers.

Over the last two centuries, overseas devotees of Kabir seem to have undergone certain changes in their religious practices in alien situations, wherein they have been living a life of a minority Indian community. As mentioned above, while the caste considerations, at least, guide their marital affairs, and thus, have been a potent factor in sustaining their Indian connection amidst incongenial circumstances rituals are said have become prominent among most of these devotees. Elaborating on the increasing ritualistic trend, some informants further cite the instances of the often seen wide publicity over radio and television for an extended period, of the cases of death taking place in a Kabir family and then preservation of a dead bodies for days together, before their final funeral, a practice not observed among Kabir followers any where in India. In African countries except Mauritius, these followers have placed Kabir's statues by the side of a Hindu deity, within the same complex of a Hindu temple, following the footsteps of the Ram Kabirpanthis of Gujarat. Such developments are seen by many followers in India, as going against the basic tenets of Kabir, their *Sadguru* (the true master). Vivek Das,[21] the present Mahant of Kabir-Chaura Math, Varanasi, thus justifies his recently launched specific campaigns targeted particularly against the increasingly ritualistic developments in Kabirpanth both within India and abroad. Jagessar Das, as a scholarly Kabirpanth leader draws our attention to another dimension of the problem Kabirpanthis in diaspora has been facing:

> The Kabir Panthis in the diaspora are nearly all in English speaking countries. They are at a disadvantage since the link with the central body in India is weak. Their positions will be greatly improved if knowledgeable Kabir Panth scholars, versed in English, were to visit periodically and strengthen relationships with India. There is also need for such scholars to write informative books in English on Kabir Saheb's philosophy and even comparing it with the Vedantic philosophy, the Upanishads, Gita, Brahmasutras etc. Scholarly books on the *Nirgun Bhakti* of Kabir Saheb, his karma yoga and his teaching of Sahaj Samadhi are important subjects. How does his philosophy compare with the others in India and abroad. There is need of scholarly works and they can be translated into other languages and be widely circulated.[22]

Yet we must note that, besides adding an international

dimension to the Kabirpanth, the diasporic followers have immensely contributed not only to the financial betterment of the community in India but has also added to the growing recognition of Kabir and Kabirpanth worldwide, as being indicated by the fact that a number of American and European scholars have drawn their attention towards the study of Kabir and the Kabirpanth in recent times.

References

1. I had completed a Major Research Project on re-writing the Kabirpanth history, financed by the University Grants Commission, New Delhi in Jily 2015. I had proposed in the project to devote a chapter on the overseas expansion of the *panth.*
2. For the history of the indentured labourers, I have mainly consulted works of Peter van der Veer (ed.), *Nation and Migration:The Politics of Space in South Asian Diasporas,* University of Pensylvania Press, Philadelphia, 1995; Steven Vertovec, *Hindu Diasporas: Comparative Patterns,* Routledge, London, 2000; Brij. V. Lal,(ed.), *Girmitiyas: The Origins of the Fiji Indians,* Australian National University Press, Canberra, 1997; Steven Vertovec, 'Hinduism in Diaspora: The Transformation of Tradition in Trinidad', In Gunther-Dietz Sontheimer and Hermann Kulke (eds.), *Hinduism Reconsidered,* Manohar Publications, N. Delhi, 1997, pp. 265-293; Yogendra Malik, *East Indian in Trinidad,* Oxford University Press, London and Chandra Jayawardena, 'Religious Beliefs and Social Change: Aspects of the Development of Hinduism in British Guinea', In *Comparative Studies in Society and History,* vol-8, 1966, pp. 211-240; Joanne Punzo Waghorne, *Diasporas of Gods, Modern Hindu Temples in an Urban Middle Class World,* Oxford University Press, New York,2004, unless otherwise mentioned.
3. I was informed about the earliest exodus of Kabirpanth disciples of Gujarat by Mahant Rameshwar Das, Kabir Ashram, Jamnagar, India, interviewed, 10 Jan. 2014; and Mahant Gokul Das, Kabir Ashram, Kharasiya, Ahmedabad, interviewed, 17th January, 2014.

For reason unknown to me, Rameshwar Das is reported to have been sacked from Jamnagar Ashram in early 2017.

4. Indenture system was introduced in the British India way back in 1828, but its proper execution began only after 1835 onwards; for details, see, David Northrup, *Indentured Labour in the Age of Imperialism,1834-1922*, Cambridge University Press, New York, 1995, and also, Peter van der Veer (ed.), *op. cit.*
5. Acute labour shortage had crippling effects on the emerging sugar plants being run in almost all these colonies where slavery system was abolished in 1827. Local labour forces were found reluctant to work at these sites forcing colonial powers to procur them from vast colonies, such as, British India.
6. For details on the origin and spread of the Kabirpanth, one can consult scholarly works of David N. Lorenzen (ed.), *Religious Change and Cultural Domination*, El Colegio de Mexico, Mexico, 1981; Kedarnath Dviwedi, *Kabir Aur Kabir Panth*, (Hindi), Hindi Sahitya Sammelan, Allahabad,1965; Parashuram Chaturvedi, *Uttar Bharat ki Sant Parampara,* (Hindi), Bharati Bhandar, Allahabad, 1964; also my work, Purnendu Ranjan, *History of Kabirpanth, A Regional Process*, Anamika Publications, New Delhi, 2008 and *Kabirpanth till the End of Medieval India*, Gyankosh Publishers, 2016.
7. The description of regional pattern of the Kabirpanth diasporas is based on my interviews with the related informants coming from the USA, Canada, Trinidad, Mauritius and also frequent visitors from India to the overseas devotees; their oral testimonies regarding regions of their domicile also find support in all the above scholarly works on the indentured labours.
8. I have based my account of Mauritius mainly on the Sudhakar Das Shastri (*Dharmadhikari*), interviewed, Varanasi, 3rd January, 2014, Mahant Puran Das, interviewed, Delhi, 5 Feb., 2014. Puran Das belongs to the fourth generation of the Kabirpanth family who had migrated to Mauritius from present Bihar in India. Dharmadhikari Sahib, who is successor designate of the Acharya *Gaddi*, Dharamdasi Kharsiya *Gaddi*, Chhattisgarh, has visited Kabirpanth centres in Mauritius twice in 1998 and 2002.
9. Puran Das recalls the year as it is mentioned in the registration

certificate of the Federation. I succeeded in tracing the kinsmen of Puran Das at village Dhanauti, district-Saran, Bihar; most of his kinsmen still profess Kabirpanth.

10. Mahant Jagessar Das was born in British Guyana in 1931. His father was an assistant (*Dewan*) of a Mahant famous all over the country during 1930s. As a young student, he however re-migrated to Canada in search of livelihood in 1957 and since then has continued there as a medical practitioner. He also provided for me a copy of the Emigration Pass of his parents issued in 1912. Dr. Jagessur Das, interviewed, Surrey, Vancouver, Canada, 3 Feb., 2012; See Anx -30, i, ii, iii, iv the copy of Emigration papers of Jagessar and his wife's parents, given to me by him.
11. Ramkissun's memorandum was sent to India by Surgeon Major D.W.D. Comins who was then working in Trinidad; see,'Note on the Emigration from India to Trinidad', Home Department File, Bengal Secretariat Press, Calcutta, 1893, pp. 38-39. I found this file preserved in the National Archives, New Delhi.
12. Haridas has been an active and educated Kabir follower in Trinidad to whom I had met in Varanasi during his India tour in 2007. The following details about Trinidad is partly based on his writings and largely on what he shared with me on 6th June, 2007, Varanasi, India. One of his articles on the activities of the Kabirpanth in Trinidad and Tobago is also published; see, Haridas, '*Divyalokki Sanniddhi Mein Gujare Do Din*', *Siddhapeeth Kabir-Chaura*, (Hindi), Kabir-Vani Prakashan, Varanasi, 2007, pp. 80-84.
13. Contract for indentured labourers were usually given for 5 years renewable maximum for 10 years, but very small number of them could come back from the intricate system to India. These details are mainly based on interviews of Acharya Vivek Das,Varanasi, interviewed, 16 March 2014, and Haridas, *op. cit.*
14. David Northrup, *op. cit.*, p. 61.
15. Rameshwar Das, then Mahant of Jamnagar Kabir Mandir, Uday Abhau, interviewed, 11 Aug, 2014.
16. The following account of Surinam is based on Chand Sitaram's memories; he was born in Surinam but immigrated to Holland in 1976. Chand Sitaram, interviewed, Varanasi, 2006. Also see, Chand Sitaram, 'Dhanp Na Sake Badal Jahan Sach Ke Badalko',

(Hindi), In *Siddhpeeth Kabir Chaura, op. cit.*, 2007, pp.75-79.

17. Brij V. Lal and Yogender Yadav (eds.), *Bhut Len Ki Katha,Totaram Sanadhya Ka Fiji* (The Story of the Haunted Lane: Totaram Sanadhya's Fiji), Saraswati Press, New Delhi,1994, p. 247. Totaram had been one of the prominent indentured labourers in Fiji who had succeeded in returning to India. Later, he spent most of his life in Gandhi's Sabarmati Ashram, Ahmedabad, to whom he knew since his days in Fiji.
18. Dr. Jagessar Das, *op. cit.*
19. These information I have gathered through e-mails from Mahant Arun Battan Das, Portland, USA dated 29 March 2014; Rakeshbhai Sanmukhbhai Bhakta, Secretary, Shri Ram-Kabir Bhakta Samaj, Los Angeles, USA, dated 2 April, 2014. Anx. 31, i.
20. I include Dr. J. Das, Jay Juggessur, Haridas and Chand Sitaram among the highly educated followers. Dr. Das has translated Kabir's *Bijak* in English apart from his other writings. Jay Juggessur edits the annual magazine which is published by the Toronto Kabir Association, Canada, Jagessar Das, interviewed, *op. cit.*
21. Acharya Vivek Das has perhaps been the lone Mahant within the Kabirpanth who has been opposing increasing ritualization of Kabirpanth in recent times both in India and abroad. He has been exposing such practices through his writings as well. Some of the educated followers, however, read into his criticism a reflection of the growing infighting between the Dharamdasi and the Kabir-Chaura branches of the Kabirpanth.
22. Jagessar Das, Interviewed, *op. cit.*

Kabir Panthis of Rankhandi

Unlike the Kabir Panthis of Chattisgarh, those in Uttar Predesh are not associated with a specific caste, but are comprised of several castes. The U.P., Kabir Panthis are connected with the Kabir Chaura in Benares. However, except for the center in Benares itself, little information is available on their organization. The only information I could get on village Kabir Panthis was in unpublished field notes. These notes were taken by anthropologists from 1954-1956 on a research project sponsored by Cornell University under the direction of Dr. Morris Opler[1]. Rankhandi is a village in Saharanpur district, U.P. The dominant caste group is Rajput.

There were about thirty families who belonged to the Kabir Panth in 1954. According to one informant, the list according to caste is:

4 Vaish (merchant)
5 Budhi (artisans)
10 Kumhar (potter)
1 Nai (barber
1 Julaha (weaver)
6 Rajputs (landowners, "warriors")
1 Dhobi (washerman)
1 Gaririya (herders)

1 Siani (Muslim caretakers of religious shrines)
1 Brahmin[2]

According to another informant, the Dhiman Brahmans also had a few families in the Kabir Panth.[3]

In 1956, fifteen Julaha families were listed as Kabir Panthis. The Kabir Panthi Julahas are a separate group from the so-called Kori Julahas and the Camar Julahas (Camars who turned to the weaving profession) who live in different neighborhoods and do not interumarry[4]. Apparently, there are also Muslim Julahas in the village[5] as in most villages in the plains of North India.

The distinctive characteristics of the Rankhandi Kabir Panthis are: (1) they do not (at least theoretically) worship idols or believe in amulets or spirits;[6] (2) they do not eat meat or harm animals[7] (3) they do not drink liquor; (4) they believe in the equality of Castes. One of the books they use is the Kabir Sahab ka Mukhia Granth-Mul Bijak, published in Sambat 1984 (A.D.1927) by Lakshmi Venketeshwar Kalyan, Bombay. This is a reprint of the Purandas edition of the Bijak. They follow a "Guru" (Mahant) who lives in Saharanpur where there is a Kabir Panthi Math. A few members meet every night for kirtan, a larger group on Tuesdays for satsang, and the whole group on *puranmashi* (full moon) for a *katha* (reading from scriptures and puja).[8] Various members of the group read at these meetings, or a Mahant if one happens to be visiting. No Brahmins are employed for these meetings. The Kabir Panthis of Rankhandi do not practice caste inter-marriage but are somewhat relaxed in matters of commensality and do not practice untouchability. An active Vaish Kabir Panthi was quoted as saying that the Kabir Panth does not discriminate against human beings either on the basis of religion or caste, going on to say.

There are Kabir Panthis in the village belonging to various castes except Bhangis and Camars[9] (two of the lowest castes). I for one have taken my food at the houses of different members of the Kabir Panth irrespective of their caste. I may even take food in the house of a Harijan untouchable provided he has a sense of cleanliness. On the other hand, I may not take food at the house of a Rajput if he has no sense of cleanliness.[10]

Another Kabir Panthi, a Kumhar, stated that his idea of untouchability was that one should not touch anyone who ate meat or drank liquor, but that it was all right to touch anyone who did not. This particular informant also stated that the difference between the Kabir Panth and the Arya Samaj (another influential reform sect in the area) was that the Arya Samajists do not practice what they preach.[11]

No cauka ceremony or initiation was described in the field notes, but in 1954, a visiting Mahant held a satsang in the Kumhar basti (neighbourhood). About twenty-eight people, including a few women, attended. The Mahant, dressed in saffron robes, sat on a carpoy in the middle of the room, while the others sat on the floor. He was reading from a book. He would read a stanza and then comment on it.

The three things he emphasized were ahimsa, love of human beings and Mercy. He talked about the permanence of the soul and the impermanence of the body, saying that the soul does not die with the body, but comes back in another body. It may be born into any caste, creed or nationality. Therefore, there should be no discrimination among human beings, since people are all one.

In discussing ahimsa, the sadhu said that those who eat meat are like the devil. God exists in all living creatures. If you kill an animal and eat it, you are defying God. Since there are other things to eat, human beings should not eat meat. For wild animals like the lion, there is some excuse for meat eating because they cannot produce anything and their nature is such that they must not eat meat to live. But human beings should not kill other creatures.

The sadhu said that those who want salvation should follow Kabir's teachings as true devotees of God. They should love all beings, be merciful, and protect the weak. They should obey their parents and teachers. One should always be careful of one's actions as one is responsible for them (karma).

While the sadhu was reading and explaining the text, other people in the room nodded in agreement. Occasionally, one man would recite one or two additional stanzas to support what the sadhu had read[12].

Two years later, another Kabir Panthi Mahant from Saharanpur visited Rankhandi and stayed with the same Kumhar family. He wore a white robe and was about 100 years old. He was accompanied by a disciple wearing a saffron robe. During his visit, a satsang was held at the house of a Dhiman Brahman. There, the Kabir Panthis sang bhajans, read from the scripture and had a religious discussion with the Mahant[13].

The Kabir Panthis seem to be well integrated into village life, despite their somewhat different religious practices. They participate in most of the major festivals, such as Karva Cauth, but they do not celebrate payta or kanagats (ancestor worship). In Rankhandi, the Kahir Panth appears to be more concerned with religious activity than with social reform. It is not a radical organization. It may happen that a family has some Kabir Panthi members while others remain orthodox Hindus. According to a male Rajput informant, the Kabir Panth is not at all popular with Rajput women inspite of the seven or eight men who are followers of Kabir. Their wives follow the religious practices of other Rajput women of the village.[14]

The Kabir Panthis are a well developed sect in this area. A study of their particular beliefs and rituals would certainly shed light on Indian folk religion and sectarian organization in general. This sketchy description is intended to provide some idea of village Kabir Panthis and to show the need for further studies.

References

1. All citations in this appendix refer to notes in this collection. They may be found in Dr. J. Michael Mahan's office at The University of Arizona, Department of Oriental Studies. Citations include the initials of the fieldworker (s), the code number and the date of collection
2. V.M. 9 79-210, April 23, 1956.
3. M.M., R.J., 79-214, November 20, 1954.
4. P.M.M., U.B., 56-60, January 3, 1956.
5. H.S.S., 56-437, July 20, 1954.
6. A leading Kumhar Kabir Panthi stated that Kabir Panthis do not worship Johar Divan (a local deity) but that he himself accepted things offered at the shrine because members of his caste traditionally do so. (P.M.M,, U.B., 56-224, February·27, 1956).

7. They also decided after a meeting that smoking was *pap* (sin).
8. In 1976, a new temple (mandir) was built for the Kabir Panthis of Rankhandi; previously members had met at private home so the money for building materials was provided by the village pancayat (J. Michael Mahar, personal communication, May 24, 1977).
9. When asked if Bhangis and Camars could belong to the sect, another Kabir Panthi (Kumhar) replied, "Yes, but *(they)* do not believe in Kabir. (M. M., R.J.,79 - 214, November 20,1954.
10. V.M. 79-208, April 22 , 1956. flies, insects, and mice die in the syrup that is put on tobacco.
11. P.M.M., U.B., 77-14, March 31, 1956.
12. M.M., R.J., 79-214, November 20, 1954.
13. V.M., 79-187, April 22, 1956.
14. H.S.S., 56-437, July 7, 1954.

Kabirpanth in and Around Taraiya

A micro-study, as conducted by me, to understand the processes of the expansion of the Kabirpanth in a village community does help us to have a clear picture of how this movement had been operational at least until the end of the 20th century. For the purpose I had selected a village named Taraiya and its neighbourhood situated in the present Madhubani district of Bihar. Taraiya is situated in between two rivers–Dhaus and Paini, tributaries of the river Kamala. Their annual flood during the monsoons would bring rich alluvial soil for the agricultural lands till about 30 years ago. Both these rivers are important constituents of the *Adhawara* group of rivers flowing in northernmost Bihar.

Culturally, village Taraiya lies in the central part of Mithila[1] which has been offering some interesting topics of studies to scholars for a considerable period of time. Since the ancient period, this region had been fertile enough to give birth to legendary figures such as, Raja Janak, Yagyavalkya, Kapil, Vishawamitra and Kalidas besides many other personalities. All these personalities have been recognized as contributors to the legendry culture of the people and the Maithil society. During the sixth century B.C., it could emerge as the most powerful principality by bringing the confederacy of Vrijji's under its suzerainty.

Passing through several vicissitudes in the medieval period, it was brought by Akbar under the direct rule of the Darbhanga Raj, and he declared the Raj as a *subah* of his empire. After the medieval period, Britishers' increasing hold over the Indian territory and their land settlement policy facilitated the Raj to function as a forceful 'Raja' of the British empire all through the colonial era. Underneath these political changes, people's socio-religious attitude and inclination underwent certain changes and the advent of the Kabirpanth in the region represents one strand among many other changes. Of course, Kabir and Kabirpanth have been traced back to the medieval period of Indian history, but its spread in the area of my intensive case study in and around Taraiya cannot be located so far back. At the most, it can be traced back to the mid-19th century according to the current oral traditions prevailing there.

Village Taraiya, divided into two sides by Dhaus, is basically inhabited by a peasant community. During the major part of the year Dhaus is dry, only during the flood seasons, wooden boats were arranged by the villagers to cross rivers, now mostly replaced by permanent iron or cemented bridges. The villagers produce three main crops annually: Rice, Wheat and *Marua*, (ragi) the last one almost becoming a vanishing crop by now. In addition, till 50 years back, they used to produce both cash crops like sugarcane and oilseeds and leguminous plants like gram, *khesari* and peas, meeting the villagers' daily needs in the agrarian community itself. The rain-fed rivers, Dhaus and Paini, used to supply water regularly till a decade ago and, hence, the farmers had no need to seek any alternate forms for irrigating their fields: but for the last ten years, they have been victim to the irregular supply of water in the river and as I was told, even the annual visits of floods have become an irregular feature in Dhaus. Peasant attributed this change to factors unknown to them, while the more orthodox reply related it to the divine punishment inflicted upon the degrading society.

This particular disturbance in the agrarian life of Taraiya has affected the peasant community in many ways. Effects of this change are reflected in the changing status of the relatively rich peasant families of the village which have to look for the money to keep their fields cultivated from sources other than their own produce. Increasing dependence on modern pumping sets and chemical fertilizers has compelled peasant families to seek loans from others in the village who have earnings from outside, a troublesome situation for the peasants. The effect of these developments is also noticed in the shrinking of *per capita* land cultivated by the peasant families and in their increasing inclination towards occupations other than farming agriculture which is often seen as an unproductive one.

The impact of this type of shift in peasant community can't be discussed here.[2] In what follows I discuss the beginning of village settlement at Taraiya and emerging interests of some of villagers in the Kabirpanth during modern period.

I was told by many informants that the original inhabitants of Taraiya were Dhanuks, comprised of two groups. The earliest inhabitants were the Dudhiwara

Dhanuks, situated on the western side of the village, but the dominant group in the village is Silaut Dhanuks who were migrants from a certain village, now recalled by Siyadhari Das (78) as Rupawara in the present Sitamarhi district of the north Bihar.[3] According to him, almost two hundred years ago, his forefathers had fallen out with some agents of zamindar at Rupawara where the majority of inhabitants were upper caste. An internecine quarrel had ensued in the trail and his forefathers had murdered not less than four close aides of the zamindars. But they could not face the consequent revenge and hence had decided to disappear from the village forever.

The arrival of Silaut Dhanuks added a lot to the numerical strength of the Dhanuks previously settled at Taraiya. Soon after their arrival in Taraiya, came a sub-caste of Vaishyas called Sibahare. As one of the Sibahares remembers, his forefathers were itinerant banias, acting under the guidance of the Darbhanga Maharaja in the early nineteenth century. Around the mid-19th century, according to him, his forefathers had to face heavy losses, so they had to sell all their property at village Dima of the Jale Block in the former Darbhanga district.

Both the migrant groups, Silaut Dhanuk and Sibahare settled on the western side of Taraiya. On the eastern side, the centre of activity was the working of a *kachahari* (a functional seat of zamindar) which is still known by the same name, though now under the possession of a Dhanuk family. According to one of my informants, the first batch of Sibahare family was the forefathers of late Sri Jhari Lal Sahu which could accumulate considerable wealth from their prosperous business. Since the beginning of 20th century late Jhari Lal and his family members exercised full control over transaction in the agricultural surplus of the village. Even items like *Gunrra* (unrefined sugar) prepared from sugarcane grown in the Sibahare's own fileds and other item prepared by the Telis (oil-crushers) of Taraiya could be sold through them. The increasing profits from business enabled this family to purchase the maximum land at Taraiya. Another informant told me that it was not just fair business of Sri Jhari Lal but their usurious practices that many small landholders in the village had to first mortgage and then surrender their land to Mahajans (Sibahare).

Whatever be the case, the family under late Jhari Lal acquired the name of 'Mahajan' (literally indicates the greatness of a person but here only denotes a money-lender. A moderate version of the estimate of their landed properties indicate these having gone up to 100 acres by the mid-20th century. But the growth and subsequent breakup of the joint family led to distribution of the property into four equal parts, possessed separately by the four brothers.

Under the guidance of the Mahajan's family almost all other Sibahare families of Taraiya had been doing their small businesses, supplying villagers' everyday necessities.

One of the oldest men at Taraiya reported that Sibahare have found themselves in a difficult situation, for, inspite of their better economic condition than those of other castes, they have never been able to overcome the numerical strength of the dominant caste Dhanuk at Taraiya. Dhanuks are one of the *shudra* castes in the Hindu caste system and they were associated with activities like palanquin–bearing and cleaning of dirty plates on the occasions of the collective feasts in some villages. But unlike other villages , no family of Dhanuks is said to have been engaged in these activities at Taraiya particularly. Siyadhari Das, a Silaut Dhanuk, told me that it was his forefathers who, almost two hundred years ago, had migrated to Taraiya. He was, during my case study, the eldest surving member of his family, because his eldest brother, Buddhi Lal had died way back in 1991. According to him, his forefathers did not have much difficulty to come to fair terms with the Dudhiwara Dhanuks, the former inhabitants of Taraiya . Any sort of conflict that arose at Taraiya began only after the arrival of other castes like *Kumahars* (potters), *Telis* (oil-men), *Lohar* (iron-smith) and *Mallahas* (fishermen). All the interviewees were unanimous on one point that Silaut Dhanuks gradually emerged the most dominant group in the village.

The Silaut Dhanuks under the active leadership of the late Bhutta Das, the father of Siyadhari, emerged as the most powerful group at Taraiya during the first decade of 20th century. But the emergence of Bhutta Das has also been related closely to the expansion of Kabirpanth therein. Siyadhari Das remembers that his grandfather's father was the first Kabirpanth follower of Taraiya. I was told that late Girdhari Das (the first follower) was a muscleman and had been exercising powerful control over his caste, in particular, and over others, in general. He, along with his family members was initated by Kunji Parein, then Mahant of Kurthaiya Math.[4]

Late Kunji Parein was an inhabitant of Siriyapur in the Benipatti Block almost 20 kms. from Taraiya. Siriyapur was under the jurisdiction of a zamindar located at a qasba named Khirahar, where both Kunji Parein and Girdhari Das used to meet as some of their relatives lived there. Kunji Parein was a Bhumihar (a landowning upper caste in north Bihar) by caste. Girdhari Das's mother-in-law was a widow there who had become a Kabirpanth follower, and it was her persuasive influence that had initially drawn Girdhari Das towards Kunji Parein. In course of time, Kunji got himself settled at Kurthaiya and founded a math there presently called the *pachhiari patti* Math. His permanent residence at Kurthaiya as the founder Mahant made it a sacred Math for the Kabirpanthis of Taraiya .

The formation of a devotional centre at Kurthaiya called *pachchiari patti* Math can be traced back to the latter half of 19th century during which the first group of Taraiya's Kabirpanth followers got initiated in the panth. Their conversion to Kabirpanth brought other groups too in its fold. First, Girdhari Das tried to infuse a sense of solidarity among the Dhanuks who were a scattered lot, and pulled apart in varying directions, by other privileged groups like zamindar's agents and the rich family of Mahajans. I was told that Girdhari Das could not convert any of his caste fellows to Kabirpanth, but, to a great extent, was successful in making Dhanuks realize the significance of unity, for it was during his life-time that, for the first time, all the Dhanuks were brought under a *Miejan*, a head of entire caste, usually chosen separately by each caste in a village community, a custom currently in outdated mode in the 21st century.

The panth is said to have grown substantially during the life-time of late Bhutta Das, the grandson of Girdhari Das. He played a crucial role in spreading the Kabirpanth teachings at Taraiya and its nearby villages in the region. He is said to have had the combined gifts of singing and dancing together to the tune of nirgun *bhajans* in the gatherings of Kabirpanth. His life-time (1886-1966) was reported to have witnessed the conversion of all Dhanuk families into this panth. His influence did not remain confined only to the Dhanuks, rather he succeeded in drawing even the families of Mahajan to get converted to the panth. The conversion of the Mahajan family, in turn, helped Bhutta Das to acquire prominent position in other fields of village life also.

The Mahajan's turn to Kabirpanth led to a cordial and commensal relationship between the two families of the two different castes–Sibahare and Dhanuk. The religious bond between Mahajan and Bhutta Das's families still lingers on, athough has lost its vigour, in the recent years, consequent upon several non-religious factors. On the other hand, inter-caste commensal relationship between the two premier families affected the other group in more than a way. Henceforth these two families, united, could establish unchallenged leadership over the inhabitants of Taraiya. Certain constructive works like the foundation of primary school, library and the digging of common pond could be successfully constructed only under the concerted efforts of Bhutta Das and Jhari Lal families. I was told that the land for the school was donated by Jhari Lal while Buddhi Lal, the eldest son of Bhutta Das, offered his multi-faceted academic excellence in these tasks. Even the land for library was donated by the same Jhari Lal whose name is still engraved on a dilapidated wall of the non-functional library house. This library is said to have been washed away in the current of a heavy flood that had visited this village in 2003.

Bhutta Das himself had a little formal education but he had memorized hundreds of Kabir *bhajans*. He had five sons out of whom the eldest and the youngest passed away in 1991 and 1983 respectively. These two of his sons were the first graduates of the village and the eldest, late Buddhi Lal was, perhaps, the first matriculate of Madhawapur Block and the first graduate of village Taraiya; and the youngest son, Sonelal was its second graduate till the pre-independence time. Bhutta Das, besides being gifted with intelligent sons, had also acquired reputation in politics as well. In 1928, he became a member of *Anchal* Congress Committee, the first person from Taraiya to get that position. Subsequently he could gain some say in local political matters. Simultaneously, the increasing stature of Bhutta Das came into clash with the interests of Zamindar's *Kachahari* located on the eastern side of Taraiya. Many of the interviewees in their 70s remembered that the agents of the zamindar used to just place their orders, and these were binding to the hapless villagers. The zamindar's land was cultivated by the villager's oxen, free of cost, whenever such service was needed, the *diwan* of the Zamindar would come and take the oxen from anybody's house. Some blacksmiths (*lohar*) reported that they had to abide by the calls of the zamindar even if there were urgent circumstances at home requiring their presence. Literally, it was difficult to keep anything valuable in their own houses; for instance, if a family had a turnip on the roof-top of his/her *kachha* houses, as soon as it comes to the notice of the zamindar's agents, it would be taken to the Zamindar's kitchen unhesitatingly.

But I was told by Subodh Das, the third son of late Bhutta Das, that 'the application of forceful orders was not for all. In practice, the families of Bhutta Das, Jhari Lal and some others in those days, would also supply '*lathaits*' and as collaborators proved to be social and political buttresses for the zamindar at least at the times of crises. They were usually spared the maltreatment meted out to the labouring mass which included many Dhanuks also. More so, since the political and religious association of Bhutta Das with the Congress and the Kabirpanth had begun to strengthen solidarity among the Dhanuks, in the main.

Around 1910' the tenurial rights over about an acre of land were asserted by the family of Bhutta Das who had been in possession of the disputed land for several years. According to late Subodh Das, the zamindar had assumed the ownership of those land plots just because his ancestors had failed to return debts in time. The zamindar acted as if he was the real owner of the land and had allowed Bhutta Das's family to till the land on rental basis. The dispute became sharper when the first case against a member of Bhutta Das family was filed in 1920. Then the *diwan* of zamindar was severely beaten up while defecating in an open field, an age-old practice commonly prevalent even after the introduction of safety latrines particularly in the village community of our country towards the end of the 20th century. Recalling the immediate cause of this event, Subodh Das informed me that it was the forceful exactions of the *Malguzari* demand whose fixed rate was not accepted by the Zamindar. Left with no other option, one of his uncles resorted to the violent step to revenge upon the diwan. He remembered a few more civil and criminal cases were also filed against them but ultimately the district Diwani court of Darbhanga gave its final judgement in favour of Bhutta Das's family in 1928.

In the same period, some members of Bhutta Das family conspired to beat up the Diwan of the local zamindar as noted above. This was the period of Non-cooperation movement in India, but its happenings at micro-level are generally not minutely reported by the contemporary officials, so in the absence of any written reports, I had to bank upon the information furnished by my interviewees.

From 1920 onwards, it was not easy for the zamindar to overlook the interests of Bhutta Das and his family whose multi–faceted stature could be felt. Being Dhanuk by caste, he could easily gather the labourers of the village, who were also the potential muscle power at Taraiya. Almost all of them had turned to Kabirpanth under the influence of Bhutta Das. So his appeals, in the dual capacities of a political and religious leader, had generally unfailing impact. Given the fact that a majority of the inhabitants on both sides of Taraiya, were Dhanuks. Bhutta Das's role in contemporary village affairs became more crucial. On the eastern side of Taraiya, besides the Kachahari of zamindar, who was a Bhumihar, there are *Dhanuks, Koiri, Sibahare, Kayasthas, Barae, Dusadha, Hazam, Goar* and *Chamar* castes. At present the *Kachahari* site is in the possession of late Surat Mandal Das, the Sarpanch of erstwhile Vishanapur Panchayat in which Taraiya lay till the turn of the 21st century. He told me that his father was the junior *diwan* of the zamindar, and all the Dhanuks of his *tola* (hamlet) had become the yes-men of the zamindar under his influence.

In return, his *tola* was never coerced into acquiescence. The servant and *malik* relationship between his father and the zamindar had won many rewards for him, including the gift of *Kachahari* land to his father at a nominal price. Almost all the families living around *Kachahari* were patronised by the zamindar so that they would stand by the side of the zamindar in an adverse eventuality at any given time.

The second group of beneficiaries on the eastern side of Taraiya was the *Kayasthas,* whose selected members had been serving as the *munsif* at the *Kachahari*. Their sincere service to the Zamindar, I was informed, resulted in a substatntial accumulation of land tracts for the *munsif*'s family after the abolition of the Zamindari system in our country .

An informant among *Koiri caste* told me that other groups in the village had to accept the dominance of these groups, closely attached to the zamindar. By 1920s, almost all the Dhanuks, a majority of Sibahare and some of the potters and Telis were also converted to the Kabirpanth under the influence of late Bhutta Das alone. But this movement was resisted by the zamindar, who did not like the assembly of labourers, workers and tenants at the same place, a common feature of any Kabirpanth gatherings. Bhutta Das, being affiliated to the Congress (INC) politically, had to move secretly from one village to another. In fact, as some of the interviewees recalled, the activities of Kabirpanth followers had to go underground during this phase of the British rule. Chalittar Das had told me that most of the time, they had to move around during the night and they would make all efforts to conceal their gathering from other Panthis, particularly the Ramanandis (Worshippers of Ram) in the region. Those found participating in Kabirpanth activities were often punished by the Zamindar. The punishment varied from person to person and, in some cases, the cattle property of the "guilty" was also taken away. I was even told that some of the followers were forced to look up at the scorching sun without batting their eyelids, often leading to blindness to the victim. Amidst such adverse conditions, the Kabirpanth followers of Taraiya had to keep up their spirit high and carry on their activities.

Even then it was the formative phase for Kabirpanth in the region, as my interviewees in villages surrounding Taraiya made it clear. One of the sons of Bhutta Das, Shobhit Das, 99, presently the most famous Kabirpanth singers in the region, informed me that the first batch of the Kabirpanth singers comprised of half a dozen persons was formed during the late 1920s under Bhutta Das. He is the oldest Kabirpanth leader and the lone survivng son of Bhutta Das in 2017. Bhutta Das is said to have selected all of them from his own caste. The chief instruments used by singers were *tabala*, harmonium, *Jhal, Tanpura* and *Kharuki*, the last item made of thin leather covering a small cylindrical wooden shaft, about 5 inches high, was played by Bhutta Das himself. All of them are dead now, except Shobhit Das, who, had acquired just primary education without any formal training in music, were inducted in the band during 1940s. (P.S. by the time the book goes to print, Shobhit is reported to have expirded)

These two sons, Subodh Das and Shobhit Das, apprised me that the band of singers, under Bhutta Das, was the chief means of spreading Kabir's message and his panth. Till 2005, the Kabirpanth band of bhajan singers had been active under Shobhit Das, and had been one of the most reputed among the Kabirpanth followers of the region. During the second and third decades of 20th century, this band used to visit the followers' families of different villages on invitation. Bhutta Das used to sing the answer queries from the audience. Among other groups of singers is one under Chalittar Das, a Koiri by caste, at eastern Taraiya, who admitted his inspiration from late Bhutta Das; however, he mostly used to sing the bhajans of Paltu Das, the eighteenth century disciple of Kabir.

Shobhit Das said that his songs have not *been Kirtans* which are sung by the Ramanandis and similar *Sagun* panthis; his are *bhajans* sung in the spirit of devotion to the divinity, not to any formal God. To him, *Kirtans* are eulogies bestowed on God. He said that the songs sung by him are the best means to pass the message to illiterate mass, for bhajans in a musical form, leave an impeccable impact even if their meanings are not understood by the audience. He added that while singing he always keeps in mind the mental bent of the concerned group. For instance, when he gets invitation from the scheduled caste followers, he tries to sing only those bhajans which reflect Kabir's great concern for the depressed class; if the audience comprises mostly of women, he picks up the *bhajans* on the tune of *Sohar* and *Samadaun* which are sung by women in marriage ceremonies in Mithila. At the close of the programme, he invites queries from the audience and tries to satisfy them with his 'little knowledge' of *adhyatma* as (spiritualism) preached by *nirgun* sants.

Shobhit Das has memorized, he claims, not less than 3000 *bhajans*, drawn from several sources of Kabirpanth and other bhakti texts. He had passed IIIrd standard at the Taraiya school but the domestic pressures on his father compelled his three brothers to drop their studies in childhood. Just his eldest and youngest sons could pursue higher studies in college. Shobhit Das attributes all his memorization of the bhajans to the 'she-buffalo' whom he used to take to the pasture lands every morning and evening. This occupation offered him a lot of spare time for memorizing the bhajans, while the she-buffalo would graze over the pasture lands.

The movement of Bhutta Das and his band was attested by interviewees in different villages. Most of them got inspired by his bhajans in 1930s and turned to the Kabirpanth. All the villages around Taraiya, namely, Pakari, and Pakarisama on the east, Parari on the west, Balasa-Baramotara on the south and Sakaram on the north came in contact with the panth during this period

But before discussing the spread of the movement in other villages I would present the caste configuration of Taraiya towards the end of the 20th century (see Table 1).

Name of the Caste	*Numbers of Taraiya*	*Number of Household*	*Kabirpanthi followers*
Dhanuks	800	125	Almost all
Koiri	100	18	60
Sibahare	175	32	100
Kayastha	90	14	None
Mallah	100	18	None
Teli	50	8	30
Goar	75	11	25
Lohar	50	9	11
Chamar	200	35	50
Dusadh	125	22	50
Hazam	50	8	10
Barae	100	18	50
Kumhar	200	35	30

The tabular presentation of the caste and the Kabirpanthi followers among them makes it clear that the village is populated entirely by the lower castes except Kayathas on the eastern side. According to the *District Censes Handbook*, 1981,[5] the total area of Taraiya is 234-31 hectares, with a population of 1,972. The figure for caste distribution rests on oral estimates of the members of different caste groups and was cross-checked by me with the voters' list and with the information at the village ration shop. We notice that more than half of the population at Taraiya comprised of Kabirpanth till the end of the last century. Most of them were *Kanthidhari* (initiated) followers. The panth had spread most among Dhanuks whose numerical strength, economic and political dominance and modern education and occupations make them a 'dominant caste' in the village.

Dhanuks have been Panchayat Sarpanchs continually till the reorganization of the Vishanpur Panchayat and a new Panchayat named after Taraiya formed in 2002. I was told that the total Dhanuks land-holdings exceed those of any other castes of Taraiya. Dhanuks' ritual practice is emulated in many respects, their rights and rituals are imitated by other castes at Taraiya except by the Kayasthas who see themselves as being upper castes. The impurity attached to Dhanuks in the orthodox Hindu caste hierarchy is not observed at Taraiya, for the village consists of the lower caste alone, except a marginal group of Kayasthas, most of whose members stay outside the village in urban centres where they have jobs. In the absence of upper castes, Dhanuks do not have to face the Brahmanical unwanted intereference in the village.

In this particular village, Dhanuks have acquired the higher ritual status and being a Kabir's followers, they consider themselves equal in ritual status to any upper castes. In fact, all the spokespersons of Dhanuks stated that they do not have any regard for the Brahmanical caste hierarchy, as they in no way, lead less sacred life than those of the upper castes.

Educationally, not less then fifteen Dhanuks from the village are graduates; and out of them nine are already employed as government servants. There are, at least, 3 persons who had to drop their studies after 12th standard and apart from them, almost a dozen others had to drop out either near matriculation or after passing it. Except government servents, all Dhanuks are engaged in agricultural activities, most of them are agricultural wage-earners in the field, either of their own caste fellows or of others. This way, M.N. Srinivas's four criteria[6], necessary for the emergence of a dominant caste in a village community, namely, the numerical strength, economic and political power, ritual status, and western education and occupations were found to be fulfilled by the Dhanuks of Taraiya.

Comparatively seen, the Kayasthas of Taraiya have almost the same number of educated persons, but their numerical, political and economic conditions are dissimilar to the Dhanuks; and hence they fail to play a dominant role in the village. Among the Sibahare there are only four graduates, four other young boys have recently succeeded in securing jobs in the government sector during 2010s. In their relatively lower educational level, combined with smaller numbers despite their sound economic condition, they lag behind the dominant position of the Dhanuk Kabirpanthis.

Among all other castes, both the educational and economic condition are very poor. Very few of them are even a matriculate. Of late, the younger generation of these castes has been sending its children to the middle school at Taraiya.

About non-cooperation movement at Taraiya and its neighbouring villages, we have no official information or written evidence, forcing us to rely totally on the oral history as narrated to me by my informants. According to them, despite all efforts of zamindar to check agrarian tensions, these grew. Siyadhari Das recalled that Kabirpanthis being the most powerful group at Taraiya, turned out to be the main target of the zamindar, for Kabirpanthis in general were going against his interests in two ways. First, it stands for the establishment of an egalitarian society, allowing no discrimination on any grounds and accepting the equality of every human being irrespective of castes. Second, most of them were the *raiyats*, most of whom had a large number of grudges against the zamindari exploitation. An official report about agrarian unrest of north Bihar mentions the tenants' no-tax campaign which had turned violent at several places. The Commissioner of Tirhut which included Taraiya, wrote in 1921, 'Nor is the rest for the division free from excitement and the possibility of trouble.'[7] The tenants unitedly looted the house of a *munsif* at Pupari, 15 km. from Taraiya. There are reports of many similar events.

The Dhanuks of Taraiya, having their past legacy of protest against the exploiters, showed some involvement in the struggle against the zamindar, who was backed up by the colonial regime; they even fought against the British empire in 1940s. The dominant role of the Dhanuk found its fuller expression under the leadership of Buddhi Lal. He was helped in making his closer ties with the Congress leaders by his father, Bhutta Das. Buddhi Lal emerged as an equally effective carrier of the Kabirpanth message and a freedom fighter in 1940s. After his intermediate degree, he had been working as a school teacher in 1930s. His first appointment was at Bangara, a village 5 km. from Taraiya. Village Bangara is populated by the dominant caste of Bhumihar among whom Jang Bahadur Thakur was the most active Congress leader during this period. During his long span as a teacher, Buddhi Lal was appointed at many places but his most successful phase started during his headmastership, particularly at Sahargahat and Sonae, about 10 to 12 Kms. from Taraiya.

Buddhi Lal played a significant role during the Quit India Movement in 1942, in which all the members of Bhutta Das family fully participated. Village Taraiya resounded with slogans like '*Gandhi Baba Ki Jai*'. Some other members of Dhanuk caste were also brought into the movement and they all followed the directions given by Buddhi Lal who had now started taking a lead in political matters. His father, in ill-health, had withdrawn from politics by now, confining himself to the panth activities solely.

Under the leadership of Buddhi Lal, plan to uproot the railway tracks at Pupari and Kamataul was chalked out during the Quit India Movement. These railway stations are 15 and 20 km respectively from Taraiya. Meanwhile, schools were closed by the Congress young volunteers and *Prabhat Feris* (Morning March) were taken out with slogan-shoutings. But the sabotage plan was leaked out by an agent of the Taraiya zamindar, and the disclosure of the plan was followed by such a quick and massive crackdown by the Thana police in the village that all the male members of Bhutta Das and those of the village had to flee away to their distant open-fields to elude the police. Consequently, the plan failed and warrants against all the members of Bhutta Das family were immediately issued but mediation offered by one of the Kabirpanth followers, close to both Bhutta Das and the *daroga* of the thana, Benipatti, saved them. The *daroga* was bribed to withdraw the warrants and he withdrew it.

By the end of the Quit India Movement, Buddhi Lal started withdrawing himself from active political life, but, as his third brother Subodh Das remembered, 'kept in inspiring us in different ways'. The ideas of communism and socialism were first talked about by him. In 1966, it was only he who first openly challenged the Brahmin priest invited in one of the funeral rituals (*Antyeshti Kriya*) of his father, Bhutta Das. Before dwelling on the spread of the Communism and its association with Kabirpanth, I discuss the expansion of the Kabirpanth in nearby villages of the region.

Taraiya is surrounded by villages which are predominantly inhabited by peasant families. All villages adjoining it (mentioned earlier), have numerous Kabirpanth followers and they all seem to have got inspiration from the dynamic personality of late Bhutta Das in the main.

Sakaram, to the north of Taraiya, had the first Kabirpanth group among the lower caste, Tatma, the first family of whom came into contact with Bhutta Das and the first Sahib (Mahant) of Taraiya Math in 1950. This village has almost half of its population comprising of the upper caste Bhumihar, who are landed aristocrats, and all the lower caste labuorers work in their fields. But Tatamas have been working as craftsmen in the village and have been supplying items like baskets and other households goods made of the bamboo sticks to Taraiya also. This occupational pursuit had brought them in contact with Kabir followers and thus, they got drawn and initiated at Taraiya Math.

The Kabirpanth Math at Taraiya was already founded in 1948. Its foundation became possible thanks to an offer from Nathuni Das, a *Gwala* by caste, who had no child and who wished to donate all his landed property of about 7 acres to the Kabirpanth.[8] The immediate reason for his land donation was, according to one contemporary informant, 'Nathuni Das's sense of guilt coming from the death of his only son'. Nathuni Das took his son's death as a divine retribution on him; and to him, donation to the cause of Kabir was a means of redemption from the unknown sin committed by him. With his offer, he approached Bhutta Das who was, during this period, the most influential Kabirpanth disciple in the region.

Siyadhari Das remembered that his father had immediately seized upon the opportunity and assured Nathuni that no hurdle would come in the way of forming a Math. In the words of a Mahant at Taraiya Math, due to the anticipated fear of unwanted interference by the landlord and other opponents, 'Bhutta Das managed to get the registration of the donated land done at Pupari Registry office instead of Banipatti Registry office'. Benipatti has the official land Registry office of Taraiya (See Anx. 32). According to the Mahant, during the entire operation, Bhutta Das kept Jhari Lal in his confidence so that no unnecessary opposition could raise its hand. Only after the completion of the formalities of the entire registration, the matter was thus made public. The Math was put under the control of a trust committee consisting of five members. Bhutta Das and Jhari Lal names were put first, and all the members including the two,were made life members; they were to be succeeded by their eldest sons and thus trust-membership was made hereditary. But the seat of the Mahant of the Math was bestowed on the donor Nathuni.

It was this Math of Taraiya where the first batch from Sakaram got initiated by Nathuni Das where Bhutta Das had high regard. One Tatama informant here told me that 'the first man that attracted our attention was Bhutta Das'. Tatamas of Sakaram are the second largest group in the village and their present number is around 150 out of which only 30 persons were followers. The second group which came under Kabirpanth influence was that of Chamars who were first initiated in 1980. The oldest member among them was Soman Das (62), related to Taraiya through his traditional occupations of supplying household goods made of bamboo sticks to peasant families since 1960s. He cited the names of Shobhit Das, Bechan Das and Nathuni Das, the former two being the main singers among followers of Taraiya, the latter the founder Mahant of Taraiya Math, who used to arouse his consciousness (*chetana*) on his visit to Taraiya. In 1980, 'he could not escape these elders' persuasions; and so along with 12 members of his own family and some *pattidars* (kinsmen) got converted to the panth.

North of Sakaram is village Amanapur which has Bhumihar as the dominant caste, but the numbers of lower castes in the village are not much less than those of Bhumihars. The eldest Kabirpanth follower, Maheshwar Das (80), a Dhobi by caste, turned to Kabirpanth in 1950. Being Dhobi by caste, he used to wash clothes of Nathuni Das as well as some other families of Taraiya. As he remembers, the massive gathering of followers at Taraiya Math on the occasion of Chaitra Ramanavami and the sonorous bhajans sung by Bhutta Das had inescapable effect on them. He got initiated by Nathuni Das and since then his whole family has abandoned Brahmanical rituals, worshipping *gosain* (family deity) in his house and have been burying the dead family members instead of burning. Several other followers of the panth at Amanapur reported that their first contact with Kabirpanth was made through its followers at Taraiya headed by Bhutta Das.

South of Taraiya is Balasa populated entirely by lower castes. There were almost 500 Kabir followers at Balasa. Most of these followers could be initiated in late 1960s when some Kabirpanthis from Taraiya made concerted efforts to convert their own caste fellows. Balasa has Dhanuks as majority caste, many of them claimed that they were inspired and initiated at Taraiya but I was told at Taraiya that two hundred of them were initiated. The uninitiated adherents also do not take non-vegetarian food. Another converted group at Balasa was Musahars who consisted primarily of itinerant labourers. They have been persuaded by eminent Kabirpanthis of Taraiya to convert. In this village, the economic and educational level of the people was very low till the end of the 20th century. Only one family had more than 20 acres of land, that also is now divided with the partition of the joint family. There were only three matriculates in the village and these three belong to Dhanuk caste; matriculation is the highest educational qualification obtained by any of them before the turn of the 21st century.

Baramotara, practically a *tola* (hamlet) of Balasa, is populated by not more than 500 persons and has only two castes, Musahar and Goar. A majority of them is Musaharas, among whom there were numerous followers. Almost 100 members were formally initiated in the panth and they all followed the *adesh* (religious commands) given to them by the guru at Taraiya. Strictly, guru's *adesh* comprises of his commands given to disciples in particular circumatances; for instance, a disciple may seek the guru's *adesh* in case he has continuous strives in the family.

Administratively, village Balasa lies in the Sitamarhi district and its location in another district may have reduced the involvement of Taraiya's Kabirpanthis there. But an explanation for relatively late influence of Kabirpanth in Balasa and Baramotra can also be sought in factors like the low economic and educational standard of their dominant castes. In contrast, the educational standard of the Chamars of Taraiya was better than that of any castes of Balasa and Baramotara; they had five matriculates, one of them is employed as a school teacher. Chamars of Taraiya, primarily a labouring group, have around 50 followers. The strength of Kabirpanth influence among Chamars of Taraiya can also be attributed to the proximity of their hamlet to the Kabirpanth Math and the role of the dominant caste, Dhanuk, at Taraiya. The hamlet inhabited by the Chamars is separated from the Math only by some plots of land in between.

On the eastern side of Taraiya is Pakari, which is dominated by the upper caste Rajputs, among whom

Kabirpanth influence is not seen. In addition to Rajputs, the village is populated by the lower castes, approximately 300 out of the total population of 700. Among the lower castes, Kabirpanth followers are not less than 60, comprising members from Dhanuk, Mallah, Dusadh and Chamars. Among Dhanuks, the first converted family had an old relative in a Dhanuk family of Taraiya; and it was the influence of the latter family that drew them towards the Kabirpanth. Apart from Dhanuk, Kabirpanth influence can be noticed among some Dusadh families who were predominantly illiterates. Chamars had also five Kabir followers who reported their conversion just 30 years ago. Chamars had been the agricultural labour force like Dusadhs, apart from their decadent ancestral occupation of leather works.

To the west of Taraiya is Parari, which had three-fourth of its population inhabited by Goar caste. Like Balasa, the village has extremely poor economic and educational standard. Only one family has around 20 acres of land; the rest of them had very small landholdings. The Kabirpanth influence at Parari was also very thin, only one family among Goars was converted to it by the end of the last century. Only one family among Dhanuks there had Kabirpanth adherents. The entire village had not more than six formally initiated followers. They all reported Taraiya as their source of inspiration, where they were initiated.

The case studies of these villages bring to our attention the crucial role of Taraiya in spreading the panth particularly under the leadership of Bhutta Das. Almost similar had been the case in villages more distant from Taraiya. For instance, village Utara, 6 km. from Taraiya, has a large number of Kabir followers, mostly from lower castes like Dhanuk, Koiri, Dhobi, Dusadh, Chamars, Musahar, Khatabe, Tatama, Tamoli, Halkhor, Dom and Goar. Recently, the most respected Kabirpanthi at Utara was Jagadev Das whose father immigrated from Taraiya almost 140 years ago. The main reason for this migration was the absence of any inheritor in the family of Jagadev Das's father's father-in-low at Utara. Jagadev Das's father too was a kinsman of Bhutta Das.

Jagadev Das asserted that his Kabirpanth background played a favourable role when his father came to settle at Utara, for, some Kabirpanthis among Koiris already living there, extended wholehearted support to his father. Very soon his father took lead in spreading the panth and therefore had to face a lot of hurdles. The whole Kabirpanthi movement had to go underground during the early decades of 20th century. Unlike Taraiya, almost 30% of Utara population comprises of upper castes, mainly Bhumihars, Brahmins and Kayasthas, but the lower castes are more numerous, so it has been difficult for the upper castes to dominate the lower castes always successfully. During the colonial period, Utara, too, had a *kachahari* of zamindar, based at Khirahar who collaborated closely with Bhumihar, Kayasthas and Brahmins–all opposed to the activities of Kabirpanth. Jagadev Das remembered that his father was an *agua* (a Kabirpanth leader chosen sometimes in a particular village to inspire individuals to draw towards Kabirpanth) for a Mahant of Kurthaiya, a sub-branch of the Krishna Karakhi Dharamdasi *shakha*. His father had a large following among lower castes. Having this background, he was appointed as the *Khabas* of the Kachahari in 1925. *Khabas,* in those days, attended to the menial services required by the zamindar and his family while they would stay at the *Kachahari* itself.

According to Jagadev Das, 'the zamindar by such an inhuman measure, could check the uprising of lower castes labourers'. Amidst hostilities of the landlord, Kabirpanth movement had to pass through a precarious phase because his father was constrained by the *khabasi* obligation imposed on him. In this adverse situation, the progress of Kabirpanth was halted for the period. When Jagadev Das himself became an *Agua* in late 1950s, the movement saw its most successful phase and, since then, the number of Kabir followers is said to have reached almost 700 out of the total population of 3000 by the end of the 20th century.

At Utara, Rameshwar Mahto, 58, was initiated into Kabirpanth in 1990, by the Mahant of Garri Math (reported to be the most popular Mahant of the Kabirpanth in that locality till his death in 2004). Mahto was one of the most active Communist leaders of the Madavapur Block. He had narrated to me the most unusual way of punishment given to people by the zamindar of Uttara if one was noticed by him joining Kabir's *panth.*

The punishment was known as *Gai-Ganga*: a person found to have participated in Kabirpanth activities was forced to donate a cow to a Brahmin priest in punishment and had to take a purifying bath in the Ganges later. This punishment generally was awarded by zamindar in collaboration with the Brahmins of the village. This collaboration was frankly admitted by Mukhiyajee, who was the oldest Brahmin at Utara among those I could meet. Mukhiyajee was more reputed for his, as yet, undefeated career of Mukhiya of Utara Panchayat since 1947 till his death in 1999. Shobha Kant Jha, more famous as Mukhiyajee, admitted that his family had been the *Purohit* at the *Kachahri* and hence had required considerable hold over zamindari affairs since the beginning.

The singer's band of Taraiya under Shobit Das commanded deep respect at Utara and they were often invited to celebrations by Kabirpanth followers of this village.

Between Utara and Taraiya there are some other villages too, but mention of the village Bangara is necessary to show the influence of Bhutta Das family. Bangara has been linked to Taraiya in many other ways too. Before foundation of a middle school at Taraiya, only Bangara had a middle school in the region, where Bhuddi Lal and his youngest brother had education upto seventh class. Bangara used to have the polling-booth for Taraiya in pre-and post-independent elections till 1962. Bangara provided a powerful Congress leader during late 1930s in Jang Bahadur Thakur, died in 1999 at the age of 101, who exercised a stronghold in politicals affairs over the leading families of Taraiya.

Bhutta Das and his eldest son Bhuddi Lal were both closely related to him since 1930s. It was with the active support of Jang Bahadur Thakur that Bhutta Das could win a seat in the Anchal Congress Committee. Even Bhuddi Lal's first appointment as a teacher could be facilitated with the help of Jang Bahadur, who himself had never been a Kabir follower. Being Bhumihar by caste, he had to face a bitter contest from his other caste fellows in elections for the Chairmanship of the District Board. Elucidating his point, Jang Bahadur Thakur stated that there used to be many candidates from upper castes, rendering it very difficult for him to depend solely on his own caste members. Further he informed that he fought for this post till 1955 and all through this long period, he got ungrudging support of the family of Bhutta Das who, 'like a genuine Kabir follower was never fanatic about his panth and never brought his religion between me and him.'

On my visit to this village, I found Kabirpanth followers only among the Dusadhs, Kurmi and Dhanuks. 85% of Bangara's population consists of Bhumihars alone; rest of 15% consists of Dhanuks, Kurmi, Dusadhs, and Lohar. Like many other villages, there also the Kabirpanth mainly had followers among lower castes, though some of the Bhumihar families did have respect for Bhutta Das and his eldest son Bhuddi Lal. One of the Kabirpanthis among Kurmis consider Bhuddi Lal as having inspired them during the period when the latter was working as a teacher in the Bangara government school.

After leading the Quit India Movement at Taraiya, Buddhi Lal did not enjoy political activities and 'to keep his academic career free of all stains' he became more deeply engrossed in his job as a teacher, Subodh Das told me. In late 1940s, Bhuddi Lal got himself transferred to other villages but his longest period was his stay at *qsba* Saharghat, as the Headmaster of a government Middle School. At Saharaghat, Bhuddhi Lal's service as a Headmaster made him a popular teacher in the district but, beside his service as a teacher, he did inspire a number of people by acts and behaviour to follow Kabir in the socio-religious field. One of Bhuddhi Lal's closest students at Saharghat, Pulkit Mandal, a Dhanuk by caste, recalled, 'under his constant inspiration, I found himself changed and one day got initiated into Kabirpanth in 1965'. He pointed out: Master Sahib (Bhuddhi Lal) never actively propagated Kabirpanth but through his deeds, he conveyed the message.

Saraghat is a *qasba* about 10 kms. from Taraiya. From here, some Kumahars used to bring their hand-made baked earthen-pots for sale twice a week until these items gradually gave way to the increasingdem and of metallic machine-made pots even in the far-flung rural areas. This village proved to be the most successful place of his career. He was awarded even '*Rajyapal Puraskar*' (Governor's Award) in 1975 by the Bihar Government for his excellent work in the field of education there. My informants from villages Sonae and Saharghat, places where Buddhi Lal had been appointed as a headmaster successively, considered him as the real founder of their middle schools, because it was he alone who could infuse fresh lease of life in the then existing schools of both the places. Both these villages are dominated by a large Brahmin population.

At Saharghat also, Brahmins are outnumbered by the aggregate of the lower castes. Among the lower castes, the number of Kabir followers was, as per a conservative estimate, 150. Some of them were highly influenced by the religiosity of Buddhi Lal and considered him as an ideal for all Kabirpanthis. Bhutta

Das's name was found to be household name among the followers of this village also. Yogi Mandal, who cooked for Buddhi Lal as long as he stayed at Saharghat school, informed me that 'I enjoyed serving him, not because I was given higher payment, but because I enjoyed the closeness of a guru in him.' Feku Jha, a Brahmin and an ex-sarpanch of Sahar Panchayat during 1980s responded that 'I never considered Buddhi Babu as belonging to a low caste rather I found the best of a teacher in him.' Many other Brahmins to whom I met concurred with this view. According to Feku Jha ' Though Buddhi Babu was a Kabirpanthi and had dropped Brahmin and Brahmanical rituals in his family functions, he never showed any personal grudges against my profession of purohit.' Jha was also a popular *tantric* in the locality.

The second half of 1940s witnessed at Taraiya the coming together of Kabirpanth and Communist activists. By this time, the zamindar had won some robust *pahalawans* (wrestlers) to his side and had been using them against any opposing group in the village. But almost all these *'lathaits* '(lathi-wielders) were drawn from the locally dominant Dhanuk castes, a few of them were kinsmen of Bhutta Das also. The fear of zamindar's direct punishment, in case the lathaits' demands were not met, had been their common concerns particularly among weaker sections of the village. On the other hand, the common caste composition of 'lathaits' also provided an unseen advantage for the leading Dhanuk family of Taraiya, which sometimes used their caste's muscle power to exert pressure upon the zamindar. Thereby Bhutta Das's family bolstered its position both in the eyes of the zamindar as well as other castes living in the village.

I was told that despite his patronage to the *lathaits*, the local zamindar could not obtain unswerving loyalties from them. For instance, it was one of these lathaits who had earlier beaten his *diwan* while defecating; it was the same group of lathaits who, in the late 1940s had showed willingness to cooperate with the nascent communist activists in the village. They were ready to sever their ties with the zamindar; for according to one robust lathait of that period, Bisheshvar Das (71), 'we found the zamindar looting our *jati* and *samaj*.' This sort of awareness had begun to change their minds through the socialist propaganda being spread by Buddhi Lal who always claimed to be a 'Gandhian Socialist.' According to the oldest communist leader in the village, Subodh Das, third son of Bhutta Das, 'it was Master Sahib who let us know what communism and socialism are'. Subodh Das has served Vishanapur panchayat as the sarpanch continuously for 25 years. He was once elected for the post of sarpanch unanimously in 1972. He always contested as a communist candidate for post. In 1987 he gave up his candidature in favour of the present sarpanch Surat Das. Both were caste fellows and active Kabirpanthis in the village. Subodh Das breathed his last in Jan 2010 and Surat Das in 2013.

Subodh Das and all other Communists of the village considered Buddhi Lal as the first man who sowed the seeds of communism in the village Taraiya. According to Subodh Das, 'Master Sahib used to discuss how exploitation of raiyats had been systematically carried forward at the local level.' He further pointed out that it was the insight provided by Buddhi Lal that easily brought people under the influence of an outside communist leader, late Bhogendra Jha, one of the earliest founders of the Communist wing in the old Darbhanga district, who won parliamentary seat elections as a CPI candidate from the Madhubani constituency more than once.

A school teacher, Ram Vilas, while assessing the role of Buddhi Lal, remembers that 'Master Sahib's vocal description of the plight of tenants, sharecroppers and *bataidars* led us to realise the commonness of the problems faced by all the sections at Taraiya 'and thus the majority of villagers, cutting across different castes, became united against the common exploiter, the local zamindar. Against this background of a simmering agrarian tension, vociferous appeals were first made by a young communist leader, Bhogendra Jha in 1949. Remembering that period of his career, Bhogendra Jha told me that during late 1940s, he was on a whirlwind tour of the region and, as a result, people from different castes and classes had begun to approach him for redressal of their local as well personal grievances. Vishanapur, the head office of the Panchayat, in his opinion, was in limelight in these days, for extreme exploitation was practiced by the family of 'Chhote Babu (as the then zamindar at qasba Vishanapur was known). Bhogendra Jha had immediately realised the need of mass awakening to shake off the zamindari exploitative machinery . Therefore, he undertook vigorous campaigns there and at Taraiya also, 5 kms. from Vishanapur. Subodh Das, an eyewitness of

Bhogendra Jha's first visit, remembered that he found a young man of 25, full of youthful vigour and fiery speech, speaking to them forcefully about what they had been discussing for the last few years. According to his memory, Bhogendra Jha's arrival was sudden; nobody had earlier heard his name, but 'word and views uttered by Bhogendra Jha were, as it were, heartfelt experience of ours.' A small group of young men soon began to follow his gospel, 'Get united and fight hard.'

Subodh Das and Ram Balam Prasad, a Sibahare by caste, took the lead and started spreading the radical messages left by Bhogendra Jha at the meeting. Subodh found many people dissolving their narrow differences and joining the Communist Party then being organised in a small group. This group started participating in other meetings called by the Communist leaders of the neighouring village. Thus, the first member of communist party in the village was also drawn from the family of Bhutta Das who himself was once a congressman. According to Subodh, his father did not object to his interest in Communism, nor did his eldest brother, Buddhi Lal, but Buddhi Lal himself maintained a distance from the Communists and lent them passive support continuously till 1977.

In his communist campaign, Subodh Das was actively supported by his fourth brother, Shobhit and Ram Balan Prasad, who helped him in penetrating the barrier raised by the Mahajan family, a resourceful anti-communist family. The latter is said to have never supported or voted for the communists, I was told. In the 1950s, some members of this family even tried to keep the entire Sibahare caste members out of the communist fold . The opposition by the Mahajan family was seen by the then communist activists as the opposition from the money-lenders' class, who also were, however, Kabirpanthis by their religious affiliation. At this stage, the entry of communist ideas and leaders introduced an element of conflict in the hitherto amicable relations between co-religionists of Dhanuks and Sibahare castes. The conflict became increasingly intensified in coming years.

By the beginning of 1950s, the zamindar's families of Chhote Babu at Vishanpur, and Mathura Prasad at Tariaya joined together to fight the belligerent communists tooth and nail in the locality. The inter-village united actions on the part of zamindars also compelled communist followers to learn importance of inter-village communist fronts too. The earliest inter-village joint action was precipitated by an event at Pakari, a village adjoining Vishanpur. Bhogendra Jha, the emerging communist leader himself was forced to came to take stock of the event when some *lathaits* of Chhote Babu had taken away all the household goods of a Koiri family leading the communist movement in the region. Even some vegetables planted in the backyard of the victim's house were uprooted by the *lathaits* .

During the same period, Baba Ramchandra is said to have visited Chhote Babu's house. Baba Ramchandra's involvement in the rise of the peasant movements of U.P and other parts of India has been well documented in a number of many recent works. According to Bhogendra Jha,[9] it was Baba Ramchandra who narrated to him the extreme gravity of the event. Baba Ramchandra had carried two pieces of brinjals in his hands plucked from the *bari* (backyard of victim's house), thus thoroughly uprooted. He showed those brinjals to Chhote Babu, and asked for his response to the episode. Chhote Babu is said to have admitted his involvement in the event by keeping silence before Baba. It was this *Koiri* family at Pakari which eventually had produced a prominent communist leader in the Vishanpur panchayat. He was Srilal Mahto, who has been in a very close relationship with the family of Bhutta Das at Taraiya. Srilal also emerged as a constant guide for the communist activists of Taraiya. During the Sarpanchship of Subodh Das, the former was also elected as the Mukhiya of Vishanpur panchayat. Now onwards, both Srilal and Subodh remained friendly as a comrade. Srilal due to his ill health, has decided to withdraw from active politics but kept on guiding the young communist activists of the region till his death in 1997.

The most disturbing event however took place in this locality in the aftermath of the passage of the Zamindari Abolition Act, 1952. The communist leaders of the panchayat had already made Chhote Babu's family their first target. Chhote Babu himself had nonetheless won the seat of an M.L.A. from the Benipatti constituency in 1952 but he could not check the smouldering discontents of the communists. Some of the communist leaders tried to persuade Chhote Babu to part with his land beyond ceiling, but he could not realize the gravity of the situation. To begin with, communists resorted to silent means to take over the disputed surplus land, still they were retaliated by armed lathaits of the zamindar. The gun firings made communists all the more furious and in the following stampede, one of the *pahalwans* employed by Chhote Babu was killed. A few persons from the communists' side were also shot dead by the gunmem in 1968.

At Taraiya itself, as soon as the abolition of the zamindari Act was passed, the zamindar, Mathura Prasad, decided to dispose off all his properties sooner than later. Here his method of closing his zamindari properties remained peaceful because of his tactical approach in the prevailing situation. He left the *Kachahari* land and its buildings for his faithful *Diwan*, sold most of his landed assets at throw-away prices to the leading families of Taraiya; and during the disposal of his properties, kept on maintaining cordial relations with all the prominent figures of the village.

The success of the communist movement in its initial stage is still a living memory amongst half a dozen of villagers, who are in their late 70s and 80s at Taraiya even today. This success against the zamindar helped the communists gain hold over the village community. This was substantiated by the victory of communist candidates in local elections for the Sarpanch and Mukhiya. In most elections, both the posts in the Vishanapur panchayat had been won by communists till the end of the 20th century. Subodh who had won the post of sarpanch twice in the elections, attributed his victory to two factors–first, his candidature as a communist and, second, his Kabirpanth lineage. His experience was that 'none of the Kabirpanthi ever ditched me while contesting for the post of Sarpanch. According to him, Kabirpanthis of the entire panchayat had always treated him as their own candidate, for 'the message delivered by Kabir and communists has more similarities than differences.' Moreover, he himself had found Bhogendra Jha, at the very first meeting, as 'a spokesman of Kabirpanth in late 1940s.

In fact, Bhogendra Jha himself traced back his first lesson of communism 'not from Marx or Engels, rather from his own mother who was a true Kabirpanthi in spirit; and he had always found, during his early political career, Kabirpanth Maths nearby his village, as a centre of solace for his anguished mind. He asserted that 'wherever I moved, I found Kabirpanthis as natural allies of communists; I had no difficulty ever in communicating with the Kabirpanthis.'

The moral boosting of Kabirpanthis of Taraiya by their success at Vishanapur against the Zamindar was followed by their anti-Brahmanical moves in the same period. The lead in this regard, too, was taken by Buddhi Lal who had shown his disregard for the sacredness of Brahmin purohits at the *shradha* (funeral) rituals of his father, Bhutta Das in 1966. Buddhi Lal challenged the *purohit* on account of his incorrect readings of Sanskrit words. This act of Buddhi Lal infuriated the *purohit.* Accidentally this event was followed by a devotional congregation at Kurthaiya Math, where Kabir followers of different villages had proposed a resolution to drop Brahmins and the rituals prescribed by them. But very few present on the occasion except Shobhit dared to accept the resolution. Still, he took a solemn vow that he would carry forward the resolution in his native village at least. Recalling the occasion, Shobit Das told me, that 'because I had not consulted any other members of my family, I was scared about my vow' but when he told his eldest brother about his vow, Buddhi Lal assured Shobit, at least, for his own family's support in this radical step.

Buddhi Lal's reassurance helped Shobit seek others' favour in spreading his resolution throughout the village. He found Ram Balam Prasad most helpful. Even Ram Bilas, a school-teacher, showed his willingness to cooperate. Both Ram Bilas and Ram Balam Prasad had emerged as active leaders of Communists also. Under the leadership of Buddhi Lal, a village level meeting was organized in which the proposal to drop Brahmins was defeated by other castes. Then Buddhi Lal and his other open supporters called a caste-level meeting of all Dhanuks in which a majority agreed to drop Brahmins. Since then almost all the Dhanuks had been following the decision except a single family which showed its unwillingness even in the first meeting. The role of this Dhanuk family has always been controversial, for most of its members are not considered to have a consistent loyalty. They are said to keep their loyalties changing according to the vagaries of the situations.

The earliest instance of clash of interests among Kabirpanth co-religionists had already been noticed when Kabirpanthis of Taraiya began to associate with and participate in the Communist campaigns. Since the beginning of 1950, the Mahajan family and most other Sibahare distanced themselves from the Communists, though some of them are still Kabir followers. The anti-

Brahmanical development added a new point of friction within an already divided *panth*. Now onwards any event occurring at the local or larger level easily got associated with either of the two divided groups. At the political level, thus there came into existence two groups at Taraiya: Communists Kabirpanthis and non-Communist Kabirpanthis. This division was reinforced by the anti-Brahminical stand accepted by a majority of the followers at Taraiya. The non-Communist followers under the Mahajan family supported those who did not agree to the anti-Brahminical stance. Increasing factions within Kabirpanth led to the rise of internal infightings between these groups.

The most glaring event occurred when a particular section of the non-Communist tried to loot crops of some Dhanuk families repeatedly at nights. Dhanuks came forward with a new device to defend themselves. They formed a *Dharam Bakhari* in 1969, implicitly designed to check the high-handedness of Sibahare, who were following the policy of supporting one of the factions involved in loot, as one of the founder members of the *Bakhari* told me. The *Dharam Bakhari* was a large-storing container in which all Dhanuk members were to deposit a fixed amount of grains, to be used when a crisis befell on any of them. Alarmed by these developments, Sibahare, too, formed its own Dharam Bakhari but kept its formation secret. The usefulness of the Bakhari was realized in 1972 when a criminal case against a Sibahare attempting to molest a Dhanuk lady was lodged in court. Most of the expenditure in the case was incurred from the stock of Bakhari formed by Dhanuks. But Dharam Bakhari could not be run for long. By 1976 it started running out of stock. According to Subodh Das, who maintained accounts of the Bakhari, this happened because some members borrowing from the Bakhari did not return their loans.

Such tendency to conflict was exacerbated by 1988 when several court cases and counter-cases were instituted against each other. Some non-Kabirpanth group developed alignments with a dissenting Kabirpanth group who had previously supported the Communist Party. The conflict became quite complicated. Firearms were used. These events, mingled with other elements like the caste-politics of the present Chief Minister of Bihar, Laloo Prasad Yadav, in which a direct appeal was being made to the depressed sections of Hindu castes to rise against the upper castes. The incessant call of caste politics had been powerful enough to erode the long association between Communists and the Kabirpanth followers particularly after Bhogendra Jha could not contest in election before his death in 2000.

Interestingly enough, the methods used in spreading both communism and Kabirpanth in the region have also been similar in some ways. Shobhit Das remembers that he learned to sing bhajans at Kabirpanthi gatherings informally under his own father, Bhutta Das. Even now, bhajans organised in different village are the chief means of spreading the message of Kabirpanth. The same method seems to have been followed by the Communists as well. It had been a major feature of a Communist meeting in the region that singing bands of activists move around playing drums and other instruments marching towards the venue of their pulic meetings. Every village would form its own band party that accompany the mob going to attend meeting organized by the communist leaders. The importance of this similarity can be seen in the words of Shobhit, who had participated in communist campaigns since their inception in 1950s, that 'people saw my dual role of a communist singer and a Kabirpanthi singer, with their eyes wide open in surprise'. In others words, similarity between the modes of their functioning seems to have made Kabirpanthis' minds more receptive to the radical Communist ideas.

This micro-study of Kabirpanth in and around Taraiya in its socio-historical milieu thus shows that its spread was made possible through the leadership of individual disciples like Bhutta Das. Kabirpanth came to village Taraiya almost two hundred years ago. It became strong at Taraiya by the beginning of 20th century. From Taraiya, the panth spread to other villages under the multi-faceted leadership of Bhutta Das who was not only a religious stalwart but also an active congress leader during 1915-30.

Like a traditional intellectual', a term coined by A. Gramsci,[9] Bhutta Das presented the ideology of the Panth in a manner befitting the mental mooring of the lower castes. In Gramscian terminology, "traditional intellectual" refers to that dominant class which, in course of history, establishes a separate and independent dominant social group. David N. Lorenzen[10] also applied this concept of traditional intellectual for such Kabirpanth Sadhus in other parts of India.

A large number from relatively lower castes could be brought into Kabirpanth. Bhutta Das's gradual withdrawal from active politics after 1930, provided opportunities for his sons to show their abilities in the field of politics and religion simultaneously. His eldest son, Buddhi Lal, like Bhutta Das, his father, did not succumb to the temptation of Kabirpanth Maths offering seat of the coveted Mahant to both the father and sons. They showed their disinterest in 'material gains or showy position of Mahants', a strong perception prevailing among a sizeable number of the followers in several parts of India. Buddhi Lal, along with his younger brothers, could shape the movement which entered into a long-time association with the communists which continued till the rise of Lalu Prasad Yadav in 1990s.

Andhre Beteille's assertion seems to be justified in the case of Kabirpanth followers of Taraiya in that 'An individual has a plurality of roles.... In such cases his attitude will be shaped by a delicate balance of specific personal interests'.[11] Responding to changing political, economic and social forces, certain members of Kabirpanth have moved in seemingly promising directions offered to them by the recent political leaders in Bihar. The tendency of increasing infiltration of politics seems to be making Kabirpanth faction-ridden which, in turn, erodes *panth* cohesion slowly but steadily.

References

1. I have consulted R.R.Diwarker (ed.), *Bihar Through Ages*, Orient Longman, Calcutta, 1950; Paul R. Brass, *Language, Religion, and Politics in North India*, Vikas Publishing House, Delhi 1974, and a doctoral thesis of Gulab Jha, *Caste and the Communist Movement in Bihar with Special Reefrence to Madhubani District*, (unpublished thesis), JNU, New Delhi, 1987.

2. I discuss the impact of the Panth and its association with the Communists in the fifth chapter of my book (2008), shift in the economic base of the peasant community, too, is discussed there in details.
3. Because of repeated mention of the names of of Siyadhari Das and his family members, I would like to present their names and relationship with each other. Bhutta Das was the son of Hazari Das, who was the son of the first Kabirpanth follower at Taraiya, Girdhari Das. Bhutta Das had five sons and a daughter. The names of his sons are Buddhi Lal, Siyadhari, Subodh , Shobhit and Sone Lal. By 2017, all of them, except Shobhit Das are dead. (P.S. Shobhit Das also expired on 2018.
4. Kurthaiya village has five Kabirpanth Maths, all relating to the Krishna Karakhi Dharamdas *vachan vanshi* branch. *Pachhiari Patti* Math is one of them, I had conducted field-work in this village, 10-11 July, 1997.
5. *District Censes Handbook, Madhubani*, Pt. XIII. A & B, Government of India Publication, 1981, pp. 74-75.
6. M.N. Srinivas, 'The Dominent Caste in Rampura', *American Anthropologist*, Vol. 61, No.-1, 1959. p. 87. The concept of a dominant caste was introduced by late M.N. Srinivas, the reputed sociologist of India.
7. *Home Political File*, No. 357, 1921. The major part of the file deals with events at Bettiah, but the concluding section reviews the wider political scene.
8. See, Anx. 32, i.

   It is a photocopy of the Registry documents of the Taraiya Kabir Math completed in 1948. The document is originally written in *Kaithi* script. I got it translated into Hindi by late Yogendra Prasad, a retired auditor from the CDA, Patna in 2012 and showing my personal tribute to him, I also attach the Hindi manuscript written in his handwriting. He was the lone son of Buddhi Lal; Yogendra unfortunaltely died of heart attack in 2013.
9. Visit of Baba Ramchandra, originally Shridhar Balwant Jodhpurkar, an organizer of a militant and radical peasant movement in the Uttar Pradesh's countryside, was reported to me by the then M.P. of the Madhubani Parliamnetary Constituency,

late Bhogendra Jha, interviewed, New Delhi, 5 August 1996. According to him, Baba was on a tour of this region where he had heard of serious agrarian tensions. Baba Ramchandra's leading role in the peasant movement can be seen in details in in M.H. Siddiqi, *Agrarian Unrest in North India,1918-1922*, Vikas Publishing, New Delhi, 1978, Kapil Kumar,*Peasants in Revolt: Tenanats,Landlords, and the Raj in Oudh 1886-1922*, Manohar, Delhi,1984, and Gyanendra Pandey, 'Peasant Revolt and Indian Nationalism: The Peasant Movement in Awadh,1919-22', *Subaltern Studies I*, OUP, New Delhi, 1982, pp.143-197.

10. A. Gramsci, *Selections from the Prison Notebooks*, International Publishers, New York, 1971, p. 7.
11. David N. Lorenzen, 'The Kabirpanth and Politics', *Political Science Review*, Jaipur, 1982, 20:3, pp. 263-282.
12. Andre Beteille, *Caste, Class and Power, Changing Pattern of Stratification in a Tanjore Village*, Oxford University Press, 1969, p. 207.

Conclusion

> As their influence spread, among kings and courtly elites as much as peoples, these sects sought ways of institutionalizing themselves, which perforce lessened the radicalization of their messages and led to the construction of hierarchies within themselves. Charismatic leadership gave way to the acceptance of order and the routinization of authority through stricter attention to ritual practices.[1]

Above scholarly observations fit in well with the growing character of the Kabirpanth as it had increasingly institutionalized itself during the last two centuries. Almost all the scholars who have studied this panth, have, unexceptionally, found Kabir's iconoclastic and radical views amiss among the sadhus in particular and laity in general. Instead, a number of rituals have replaced the non-ritualistic radicàlism of Kabir in most of the religious events of the panth. The *Chauka-Pan*, one of the most important rituals of the Dharamdasi *Vansh,* the Dharmdasi *Nirwan*, Jagodasi and to some extent in Kabir-Chaura branches as well , has got further sub-categorization as *Anandi or Khushyali Chauka, Chalawa chauka, Janm Chauka* and *Ekotari Chauka.* These rituals have become a routine affair on most of the ceremonious occasions as performed by the Acharyas of these two branches. At the same time, the growing observance of such rituals have in recent times, has emerged a matter of grave concern for the present Acharya of the Kabir-Chaura branch; namely Vivek Das, who misses no chance to denounce the ritualization and the tradition of hereditary Acharyaship having been followed by the Dharmdasi *Vansh* branch, centred at Damakhera, since its inception.

Within the Kabirpanth, they seem to have developed pretentious layers of hierarchies among themselves as well. The heads of Kabir Chaura, at least since the time of the last two Acharyas, Ganga Sharan Shastri and Vivek Das, have begun to reassert their position as the head of the '*mul-gaddi*' (original seat of Kabir) in the sense that the Math was the earliest abode of Kabir and that it had also emerged as the earliest seat (*gaddi)* of a Mahant after Kabir's death. Hence, all other branches must be subordinate to it. The claim of *mul-gaddi* is however contested by the heads of the Dharamdasi branches, who trace the origin of the Kabirpanth with Dharamdas, who alone, in their view, was anointed and authorized by Kabir himself to initiate the panth. Moreover, they also find not much substance in Kabir-Chaura's claim of being the lone abode of Kabir. According to some Dharamdasi spokespersons, Kabir had spent his life for a reasonable period at several places; such as, Bandhogarh, Chatiya-Barharawa, Dwarka, Jagannathpuri, Kabir Vad and Magahar etc. The Bhagodasi and the Jagodasi Acharyas too consider themselves superior to the Dharamdasis on the ground of their Mahants' adherence to the principle of *brahmcharya*/celibacy, a value not being followed by the latter.

I take liberty in this section to throw some light, based on my own observation, on the prevailing condition of the panth at this juncture of the 21st century. Kabirpanth during modern India, as has been described in the for going chapters, has definitely witnessed both elements of change and continuity like many other bhakti sects (*sampraday*) of the period. Needless to say, it too had to contend with the forces emerging out of the colonial rule that had hegemonic presence throughout the length and breadth of the country. No doubt, British rule came as a mixed baggage for the panth, as, on the one hand, it tended to sharpen its organizational identity, it also released the forces which intensified sectarian rivalry adversely affecting the devotional tenor of the panth, that was presumably extant as its distinctive feature, at least, till the eighteenth century. Further, its horizontal expansion got a strong fillip during this period, to the extent that it not only took on a pan-British India character but also an international character primarily owing to the introduction of the indenture system in between mid-nineteenth and early 20th century.

Simultaneous to its expansion, Kabirpanth came to be sharply divided into its present constituent branches, namely Bhagatahi/ Bhagodasi, Dadupanthi, Dharamdasi *Vansh Gaddi*, Dharamdasi Nirwan/Nad vanshi, Garibdasi, Ghisadasi, Jagodasi/Jagudasi, Kabir-Chaura, Fatuha and Burhanpur *shakhas*, Krishna Karakhi *Vachan-Vanshi*, Paltudasi, Parakhpanthi, Radha-Swami, Ram-Kabir so on and so forth. All of these branches have their Acharya Gaddi or headquarter at different parts of the independent India. While Parakhpanthi has its formal origin during the post-independent India, all others had been in existence since pre-modern period except Radha-Swami Satasang. Among these branches, both Dhanauti and Fatuha branches have lost their past glories, consequent to several instances of murders and counter-murder incidents having taken place at both these Acharya Gaddis. At Burhanpur Acharya Gaddi which had seen its heyday during the long tenure of Acharya Ram Swarup Das, has lost its momentum in the absence of a deserving successor after his death in 1997. Although present day Parakhpanthi sants show Burhanpur Math as one of the main centres of '*Parakhi*' (enlightened) Mahants; their main centre in the present has been the centre which was opened by late Abhilash Das at Allahabad.

In the passing, we must note that presently there has been protracted absence of an Acharya of the Bhagatahi branch since the imprisonment of the former Acharya Guru Prasad Goswami alias Garbhu Goswami on the charge of murder and financial mismanagement in 2006. He is however now out of jail on bail after spending about 6 years, but leading a life of a domineering strongman among Bhagatahi Kabir followers. Presently Shatrughan Goswami has been the head and nominal Acharya, placed at the ruined Dhanauti Math, working under the tight security cover of the Bihar police.

Fatuha branch too has met more or less the same fate. During the last 25 years alone, three of its Acharya

Mahants staying at this Math has been murdered in the ensuing fight for succession on the coveted seat of Acharya. As a result, this Math has also lost its prominence and presently has been struggling for its survival, what to talk of Acharyship. It is said that till 50 years ago, this Math has had 1100 acres of landed property, which, according to a conservative estimate, has now come down to less than 100 acres. At the time of my field work, Brijesh Muni was the Acharya Mahant, but he was also removed by Kishore Kunal, IPS, the then Chairperson of the Bihar State Board of Religious Trust, Patna on the charges of impropriety and misappropriation of fund. Similarly, the landed property of the Dhanauti Math has nosedived from about 2000 acres about a century ago to 50 acres as per the rough estimate of my informants.

Another source of heightened acrimonies between the Dharmdasi and the non-Dharmdasi branches has been the persistent claim of the former that both Jagodas and Surati Gopal, the initiator of the Jagodasi and the Kabir-Chaura branches, had been functionaries/ employees of Dharmdas since the time of his rich business before becoming a close disciple of Kabir. This claim has once again been highlighted in the latest and revised edition of *Kabirpanth ka Udbhav aur Prasar*, (2015) written by Rajendra Prasad, a Ph.D. holder Mahant of an Agra-based Math, UP and Barbariya Ziyaganj, Murshidabad, West Bengal, associated with Damakhera for the last two generations. None of the Acharyas or Mahants of the non-Dharmdasi branches have been comfortable with the depiction of their founder Acharyas in so lowly status by the Dharmdasi ideologues; such as, Rajendra Prasad. They see not even an iota of truth in such 'lowly' depiction, and instead argue that there cannot and had ever been any connection between Dharamdas, Jagodas and Surati Gopal, as Dharamdas was not at all a contemporary of Kabir,whreas Jagodas and Surati Gopal had been immediate disciples of Sadguru Kabir. Both Dharmdasi and non-Dharamdasi groups have forwarded and reformulated *Sabads* and *Sakhis* of Kabir according to their convenience in order to prove their points and counter-points.

Rajendra Prasad has gone a step forward in tracing the antecedents of Jagodas presently and pointed out in his book that Jagodas's parents, Jagardatt and Hanso Bae, originally hailing from Cuttack in Orissa - lived as 'mantri' (a respected functionary) in the mercantile network of Dharamdas. Jagardatt and his wife took initiation from Kabir at the same day when Dharamdas was initiated by Kabir. Jagodas was born after the death of his father and yet he was initiated by Kabir himself. Further, it was Churamani, the successor son of Dharamdas, according to Rajendra Prasad, who had deputed Jagodas as the '*Pujari*' of Puri Kabir Math and later as the Mahant of Cuttack Math in Orissa (pp.127-128). Adding salt to the 'insult' heaped on Jagodas, as the Jagodasi present Acharya, Ram Dayal Das opines, Rajendra Prasad has similar version of story for Surati Gopal. He writes, "Surati Gopal and Sarvanand had been two different personalities in the Kabirpanth.... Sarvanand ji is not the same Surati Gopal....Surati Gopal was a Brahmin who was employed as a 'mantri' in the flourishing multi-millionaire business of Judawan Sahu alias

Dharamdas...While Kabir was initiating Dharmdas as a disciple, on the same day, Surati Gopal also got initiated by Kabir in Bandogarh itself."[2] According to his findings, Surati Gopal's descendents still live in village named Umaria and Barera situated in the Bandhogarh region.

As a counter-attack on the Dharamdasi narratives of Jagodas and Surati Gopal's antecedents, both Ganga Sharan Shastri, formerly an ousted Mahant, and Vivek Das, the present Acharya of Kabir-Chaura, has tried to prove that Dharamdas himself was the *path-bhrashtak*; i.e., the deviant from the path of Kabir, as he had laid the foundation of hereditary guru-ship and invented unnecessary rites and rituals in the name of Kabir and the Kabirpanth, leading to the rise of various types of ill-practices including worship of fictitious and undeserving '*Gurua*' (Gurus) thus blunting the radical and iconoclastic teachings of Kabir. Most of the recently published book/booklets by the Kabir-Chaura has Dharamdas and his successors as the main target and been shown in low esteem. The Jagodasi branch having no substantial publication except Munishwar Nath Munish's booklet, has just been maintaining itself a reasonable distance and publicly refutes the Dharmdasi assertions in public *satsangs*, wherever opportunity warrants. The Bhagodasi branch too keeps a reasonable distance from the Dharamdasi as the latter does not accept Bhagodas as the sole compiler of the *Bijak*, as the Bhagodasi leaders have been asserting all through. Instead, it has been mainly the allegation of the Dharamdasi section that Bhagodas had, in fact, fled away with the manuscript of *Bijak* from Bandogarh where Dharamdas had made a major contribution in the preparation of the *Bijak*. In the circumstance, the relationship between these branches has always been at the lowest ebb, never enabling these Acharya to come face to face on a single platform of the Kabirpanth.

The Dharamdasi branch, in its own history, has nonetheless witnessed at least two splits on this very contentious issue of celibate Mahantship, as has been described in my last (2016) and present book. In all likelihood, non-Dharamdasi branches, too, may have had some roles in these splits of the Dharamdasi branch, as its spokesperson forcefully point out. Despite all these constraints, Dharamdasi branch has however been successful in bringing largest number of followers within its own fold, in which disregard to *brahmacharya* principles, and adherence to the household life are said to have played a great role. Seen in terms of number of followers, the Dharamdasi *Vansh* branch ranks itself at the top of all the branches, largely owing to its adoption of Kabir's doctrines of devotion while leading normal family life.

By the turn of 20th century, Kabirpanth, as we have seen, had already expanded its branches from Jammu & Kashmir to the north-eastern parts of the then British India. As the century progressed, it also began to expand further towards the southern parts of India. Although it could not expand towards the extreme southern parts of India; i.e. Tamil Nadu and Kerala, barring a few cases of migrant followers, it could firmly establish itself in the capital cities of the present-day Telangana and Karnataka. My field-work findings in all these regions make it clear that some leading members of the North Indian Kabirpanth community had played pivotal role in its expansion across all these regions. As the Kabirpanth could not make headway towards the extreme southern parts of India, so has been in the north-eastern parts of India where it could not expand beyond Shillong in Meghalaya. It could also expand upto parts of Karachi of the British India, while almost all the present day metropolis of independent India already had centres of Kabirpanth except Madras (Chennai).

Based on the historical accounts, we can establish that while Kabirpanth continued to expand its geographical horizon in hitherto unpenetrated areas of the British India, its splitting tendency too intensified in the early 20th century. In regions like Panjab, it also had to confront proselytizing acts both of the Sikhs and the Arya Samajis, leading to a decline in the numerical strength of the Kabir followers, as noted in the colonial censuses of the century. Due to continued splits, the headquarters of the Dharmdasi branch once again shifted to Damakhera, situated in Chhattisgarh after 1934 split to Kharsiya, whereas, Kabir-Chaura and Bhagodasi branches found patrons in some royal families of their localities, adding to their material resources.

Growing resources of some of the Bhagatahi, Jagodasi and Kabir-Chaura and Ram-Kabir branches and sub-branches brought in their trail severe ailments for most of these. Many of these tended to take on airs of undeclared independence gradually from the Acharya Gaddi's over-all control. Consequently, most of these resourceful Maths were left with no time and incentives to spread Kabir's message what they typify as '*Jeev Chetaana*', i.e, act of spiritual re-awakening in the line of Kabir's *nirgun* bhakti. It has been one of the most prominent reasons that the Acharya-Gaddis, in general, have got a very few followers on their own. In addition, growing resources also fuelled internal feuds and rifts at intra-branch level. The earliest instance of the shift of Acharya-gaddi from one to another Math had taken place presumably towards the end of the eighteenth century when the Acharyship of the Chatiya-Barharawa Math was overtaken by the Dhanauti Math, Siwan, Bihar, within the Bhagatahi branch. A number of maths earlier associated with the Kabir-Chaura branch have also taken on the semblance of independence; such as, Kabir Bag Kabir Math, Gaya; Sikandarpur Math, Sikandarpur and Bahadurpur Math in Nalanda district, Bihar, and Kabir Math, Daliganj, in Lucknow, Kabir Samadhi, Magahar in Uttar Pradesh particularly during the Acharyaship of Vivek Das, continuing for the last 20 years or so. Major cause of all these splits has been disputes relating to the control, management and share of the resources these Maths have been bestowed with. Almost all the resourceful Maths of Gujarat, called Ram-Kabirs have developed their own religious Trusts to manage their resources and just show token obeisance to their respective Acharyas if at all warranted.

The earliest intra-branch instance of litigations, as we have seen, goes back to the 1850s, during which I have shown that the Mahants of the Dhanauti Math, Bihar had got judgements against some of its sub-branches from the respective English Diwani court. However within the Jagodasi branch, the available earliest revenue court litigation and judgement I could discover dates back to 1903-04, which is related to the Andharatharhi and Bidupur Maths. It has lost its control over a few Kabir Maths in Orissa, nor has it enough time to maintain necessary rapport with the Andhratharhi Math, Madhubani, Bihar, one of the oldest among its sub-branches and Shivpuri Math situated in the suburb of Varanasi. Its sub-branches in Punjab and Delhi have lost almost all reverence for the Acharya Gaddi, so much so that the head of the Kabir Math situated at Paharganj in New Delhi, one of its sub-branches, do not hesitate to assert that the existing Math building no more houses a Kabir Math, primarily because Chandra Bhan Das, the actual Mahant, has been trying his best to convert the building into his own family property through fair or foul means.

A resourceful Math at Neola in Muzaffarnagar district of Uttar Pradesh, which was earlier a sub-branch of the Jagudasi branch and under the supervision of the Paharganj Math's Mahant, is no more in existence. So has been the fate of a number of Maths which is no more in existence. While this book is going to the Press, a Kabir Ashram Bhupatiwala Dharamshala built at Haridwar, Uttarkhand in 1934, has found itself in the vortex of a forceful capture by a rival group. The attempts of forceful capture by the rival group were somehow foiled by the present trustees who, perforce, had to seek intervention of revenue and police officials. Presently the dispute has been brought to the notice of the Uttarakhand High Court in Deharadun and the matter is still sub-judice. Internal rivalry between Mahants of Kabir Samadhi, Magahar and that of Kabir-Chaura, has culminated in the imprisonment of Vichardas Shastri, the Kabir Samadhi Mahant in 2016, for several months, although he is now out of jail on bail.

Earliest Kabir Math in Haridwar, Uttarakhand

The most disquieting incident among Kabirpanthis in India recently took place at Barwala in Hisar district of Haryana where one of the most popular self-proclaimed 'godman', Baba Rampal (67) was put into jail under the charges of arson, sedition and murder by the Haryana Police on 19 November 2014. His earlier clashes with Arya Samajis leading to the murder of a lady activist had also landed him in jail for about 20 months after 2006. He had been out on bail under the charge of murder since 2008 till his present imprisonment. Before 1993, he was a junior engineer in the Haryana government. Rampal is said to have declared himself, after the death of his guru, as incarnate of Kabir and had also challenged a number of Arya Samaji's derogatory remarks about Kabir and Kabirpanth, being propagated by its local activists, in addition to the land disputes with the latter. It is said that much of his landed assets owed to Ramdevanand, his Kabirpanthi Guru, an inhabitant of Bada Paintvaas, district Bhiwani, Haryana, to whom Rampal had succeded in 1995. Rampal had then developed his 'Satlok' Ashram on the sprawling area of about 12 acres at village Karauntha first and later at Barawala in Hisar district. He is still in jail. However his ashram once again appears to be limping back to regain it lost glory. All Kabirpanth leaders nonetheless have not been supporters of Rampal's spiritual claim such as Vivek Das, the Kabir-Chaura Acharya, who had also criticised Rampal's defiance of law leading to his present arrest.

Yet, Kabirpanth did witness the rise of a legendary personality in Dashrath Manjhi, popularly known as 'mountain man' born in a village named Jalour in the present Gaya district of Bihar during the latter part of the 20th century. He belonged to the *Musahar* caste, one of the lowest castes of the Hindu community in Bihar. Although his 73 year old life came to an end in 2007, he is said to have single-handily dug out a wide road across a hillock by his spade and chisel. It had taken him an incredible perseverance of about 22 years to accomplish this task during 1970s and 80s. Quite expectedly as a devout Kabirpanth follower, he had attributed his exemplary achievement to the blessings of Sadguru Kabir, during an informal conversation with me when I had met him in one of the conferences on labouring classes organized by an NGO in New Delhi in 2000. I could not commence conversation with him on desired topics as, by that time, he had lost his normal hearing ability. His legendary deed had however drawn attentions of film makers and a number of documentary, docu-drama and movies have been picturized on his life, some during his life-time itself.

While some legendary figures did introduce dramatic

moments in the Kabirpanth, the formation and closure of its devotional centres too has gone side by side. Why and how did some of the Kabir centres come to close, requires intensive case studies before making appropriate statement about these; for instance, Kabir ashrams of Kaundapara in Cuttack district, Orissa; of Mubarakpur near Derabassi in Punjab, Balwa near Magahar in Uttar Pradesh, Nawala near Muzaffarnagar in Uttar Pradesh and many others of Narayandasi Dharmdasi branches in Madhya Pradesh and Chhattisgarh. At the same time, new maths have also been coming into existence, but these might not be in large number. In the Punjab, Himachal and Jammu regions, particularly a number of old Kabir ashrams are said to have disappeared, while several Kabir Mandirs have been opened by both Dhanak and Megh/Bhagat Kabirpanthis in almost all the districts of Punjab, Haryana and Jammu regions, if we take into account the Garibdasi centres within it.

To cite a few cases, in Jallundhar, Punjab, a Kabir temple was built over an area of about 1050 sq. yard in Bhargav Nagar area in 1988. The successful opening of this centre however owes considerably to one Amarnath who had already formed an association for the Bhagat/ Megh Kabirpanthis, called All India Satguru Kabir Sabha in 1958. Originally he hailed from Sudehchak near Sialkot of undivided India. But he had to leave his native village near Sialkot forming part of Pakistan and resettle in Bhargav rehabilitation camp of Jallundhar in the bloody aftermath of partition after 15 August 1947. He was however blessed with a long life and died at the age of 92 in 2001. Moreover, his wife had continued to spread

Kabir's teachings in and around Jallundhar till her death in 2012. Towards the end of the 20th century, the most significant centre named Kabir Bhawan was opened at Madangir, New Delhi by Acharya Vivek Das, Kabir Chaura, Benaras. At Taksal, and some villages around Mandi in Himachal Pradesh, they had built a number of Kabir Mandirs during 1980s. Some Kabirpanthis of Chandigarh has also opened a Kabir centre at Bahlana in Chandigarh in 2015, while one of their Kabir Ashrams at Burail in the same city built in 1960 has been misappropriated by the Shaivites; however the ashram building is still intact, yet not in control of the local Kabirpanthis. (See Anx. 33, i, ii).

In Chhattisgarh region, among the recently opened centres, Shri Kabir Brahmcharini Ashram, at Potiyadihi is worth mentioning. This Ashram is situated in qasba Potiyadihi. It was constructed in 1993 with the donations of the villagers and the collective support of the Allahabad Parakhpanthi branch. Since the foundation day till date, this ashram is run by the sister Sushila. In this ashram, only females (sisters) can stay and they can do research studies. Presently there are 40 sisters (females) living in this ashram. This ashram is the largest ashram of this region (area wise and number wise) which is administered by the Allahabad branch. The annual conference, Gurupurnima, Kabir's birth-day as well as that of Abhilash Das have been the main celebrations of this Ashram. The residents of the nearby villages participate and contribute in these celebrations. Normally male members are not allowed to stay in this ashram, it being an ashram exclusively meant for women.

In the area of Ajmer and Pushkar of Rajasthan,

around 40-50 years ago, very few people were associated with this panth and almost all of them belonged to the lower caste groups. However conversion of Hari Singh Rathore brought about significant change in its constituency. Hari Singh was converted to Kabirpanth under the influence of Grindhmuni in 1975.

The prominent characteristic of these new Kabir centres in Punjab, Haryana, Himachal and Jammu has been the formation of temples in the name of Kabir, whereas, in other parts of India, they have been naming most of such centres as *ashrams*, *sthans* or Maths.

The foregoing descriptions suggest that colonial discourses on Kabirpanth had been multifarious. In fact, all the scholars of the period seem to have followed varying perspectives while describing the sect of Kabirpanth Marco della Tomba, who provides the earliest reliable evidence for the Kabirpanth, has left behind details of the Kabirpanth including several other sects of North India for the period during which he had very few written and reliable sources to verify. In fact his writings relied more on the prevailing traditions about the concerned Hindu sects, which potentially appeared promising to him from the point of view of conversion. We also need to underline the fact that his observations of these Hindu sects might have been influenced by the dwindling fate of the missionaries, which in coming days, in turn, was to be decided by the consolidation of the British colonial rule in India. To Buchanan, however, an objective description of the panth, as he himself observed, was to take precedence in his work, as he was conducting the survey on behalf of the imperial government of the Bengal province, which was hard pressed to have knowledge of the native land and people of the region. However, Wilson as a worthy successor of William Jones and Colebrooke, the Orientalists, touched upon the subject in a scholarly manner and thus also referred to a number of indigenous written and oral materials in his descriptions of the sect. Later the census operations which were fully controlled and executed by the colonial administrators stringently considered the panth in terms of its relative political strength.

Many scholars may demur on my inclusion of Radha-Swami Satsang as an extension of the erstwhile Kabirpanth, but to me, the former, in all likelihood was at its early phase founded by those educated admirers of Kabir, who had distanced themselves from the increasingly ritualizing Kabirpanth after the mid-nineteenth century onwards. Mark Juergensmeyer, a celebrated scholar on the Radhaswami history and tradition, has in no uncertain terms, highlighted the elevated position Kabir has occupied in the worldview of the sect:

> Although few of these mythological details survive as such within Radha Soami teachings, the grand role there Kabir plays within Radha Soami thought and its view of history is indisputable; one of the Radha Soami masters, for instance, claimed to have recognized Benares on seeing it for the first time, because he had been there as Kabir in the previous birth...

(The master here in reference is Anand Swarup, who was founder of the Dayalbagh chapter of the Radhaswami

Satsang, Agra,Uttar Pradesh).

To the scholars and leading members of the Kabirpanth, these branches have got distinct connotations, but for the lay followers, most of these branches are either unheard or insignificant, for obvious reasons: first and foremost, none of these deny Kabir as their Sadguru or the ultimate Guru; secondly, almost all of these except Ghisadasi, Radaha-Swami and Dadupanthi, introduce themselves among lay followers merely as a Kabirpanthi, not by the name of the respective branch. At the most, the concerned heads try to persuade the novices to pay their obeisance by visiting the *Acharya Guru* at the respective headquarters of the branch, if possible. The readers may however note that I have not dwelt knowingly on the extraneous differences maintained among all these branches, as one can find details on this aspect in my earliest book (2008). Moreover, the existing differences do not seem to have played a cognizable role in the expansion or on the unmitigated continuance of the panth, which has been the overriding theme of the book. However I must underscore the fact that the internal feuds among many of these branches may have had limiting outcome on the panth's total impact on the socio-religious texture of the society in general.

Apart from the two case studies described in the last chapters, one conducted by me and another under the direction of Morris Opler in between 1954-56, we have a very livid and detailed description of an institutionalized Kabirpanth Math by Fanishwarnath 'Renu' in one of his most famous Hindi novels '*Maila Anchal*', written in 1954. I have already described, in brief, the details on leading Kabirpanthis we can have from the Diary of Ramdhari Singh 'Dinkar' during the early part of the 20th century, in my first study on Kabirpanth published in 2008. Indian film industry has already produced a serials of docu-drama based on this celebrated literary work in which a Kabirpanth Math has been shown as a crucial factor in the village life of Mariganj, situated in then Purnia district, Bihar. During my M.Phil. course (1991-1993), I had had occasions to conduct field studies among several Kabirpanthis of this district, but I was then not aware of the Kabir Math situated at Mariganj. Although Renu himself was born in a neighbouring village, he chose to weave the story of the novel around a village which had a Kabir math. Whether novelist choice of Mariganj was accidental or deliberate remains anybody's guess, yet the finer details which he puts forward before the readers, compels us to believe that he was rather interested in developing the plot of the story in and around a village having a Kabir Math.

I, in the following, present Renu's depiction of the Kabirpanth as the real specimen of the present day condition of Kabir Maths in general. His penetrating eyes could not escape the bitter realities obtaining at a resourceful Kabir Math having 900 *bighas* of landed assets before the abolition of zamindari system in Bihar. It is noteworthy that there had been a number of Kabir Maths, which were more resourceful than this one in other parts of India.

As the plot of the novel has been woven around the period falling between 1930s and 1948, the year Mahatma Gandhi was killed; naturally the condition and events relating to Kabir Math also coincided with the above period. The novel acquires historicity in that it unravels the multi-faceted life of a Kabir Math among many other village issues, by citing back and forth the *Guru-Gaddi*, the background of Lachhmi, the *Kotharin* (the store-keeper), Ramdas, the *Bhandari* (the organizer of communal feast) and the Sadhus visiting and staying there. Ramdas is said to have been serving there for almost 15 years, and had been a master *Khanjari* player. He had left his native village Belahi for good in order to spend his remaining life with Mahant Sewadas, who gradually had deputed him as the *Bhandari* of the Math. He was also a lone disciple of the Mahant Sewadas whose death caused vacancy for the Mahant *gaddi*. Although he had become blind, yet was a very popular Mahant of the Math. Lachhmi was the only other person who was living at the Math, and had allegedly been catering to the sexual advances of Sewadas. The Mahant was not just blind but also an addict of *ganja*. Ramdas, however succeeds to the seat of Mahant also, after overcoming a formidable opposition from a rival candidate associated with another Math at Dupari of then Muzaffarpur district in Bihar.

While describing the selection of a new Mahant, the novelist describes the then prevailing rules being followed, the rules which still hold good in this sphere among the resourceful Kabir Maths. He points out that all the prominent persons and followers of the Math were to be invited on the occasion of the selection of a Mahant. Meriganj Math being a resourceful Math required the consent and presence of Acharya Mahant who would finally declare the name of Mahant and bestow the symbolic *Chadar-tika* on the latter. However, the Acharya was supposed to arrive at a consensus on the suitable candidature for the seat of Mahant, who would practically be the one to whom the dying Mahant would have declared or willed for. Yet Acharya's choice of candidate carried much weight, he being the head of all the associated sub-branches. In this particular case, Acharya was already pre-determined to take advantage of the precarious condition of a Math whose Mahant was a blind man and not a very far-sighted person. He had not left a written will nor had declared his successor in clear terms as he had met a sudden death. The Acharya from Kashi Math had, before reaching Meriganj had made up his mind to install Larsingh Das, an outsider Kabirpanth follower, as the Mahant of this Math at any rate, feigning that Larsingh would always remain a puppet in the Acharya's hands.

However, Renu points out that the villagers' concern for the Math in general and the tactful role of the intelligent but infamous Lachchmi foiled all the manoeuvres of the Acharya and Larsingh Das. She had already won over the hearts of Baldev, a Gandhian Kabirpanthi as well as Kalicharan, a radical socialist leader in the village. Baldev was the one with whom she later started leading a conjugal life informally, once she separated herself from the Meriganj Math, due to the abortive sexual assault on her by Ramdas, the successor Mahant. Earlier, Ramdas, as an illiterate *Bhandari*, had strong support of Lachhami. She was a central figure in the everyday activities of the Math since the time of Sewadas, who had developed physical relationship with her since her childhood. The rumour had gained currency that his blindness owes largely to his illicit relation with her, who always showed her unwillingness for such relation between the Mahant and a Kothaharin, a functionary of the Math. However, her beauty and infatuation of Mahant with Lachhmi had been an additional topic of common parlance in the village. Ramdas had been a lascivious witness of her relation with Sewadas.

On the day of the selection of Mahant, Kalicharan stood up against the decision of the Acharya. He pinpointed the fact before the assembly that entire villagers knew Ramdas, the *Bhandari,* and that he had been the lone disciple dedicated to Sewadas. He reiterated that several villagers had donated their land pieces to the cause of the Math, implying that they would not allow a lumpen figure such as Larsingh Das, the nominee of the Acharya, to take over the *gaddi*. His objections had support of a number of leftist comrades then active in the village, apart from the tacit support of Gandhians led by Baldev. The dispute took on violent turn as one of the *Naga* sadhu among the thirty member team of the *Acharya*, ignited the fury of the young leftist brigands, and was, hence, physically assaulted black and blue. In the ensuing melee, Larsingh too fled away to save his skin. Left with no other choice, the Acharya had to succumb to the pressure of the young radicals and thus he put his stamp on the choice of Ramdas as the successor Mahant of the Meriganj Math. It was an unexpected victory for Lachchhmi who had specially invited daunting Kalicharan anticipating the prejudiced mindset of the Acharya and his team members.

Yet Lachchhmi's joy remain short-lived as once again she began to be harassed and lasciviously assaulted by

Ramdas, who could elevate to the seat of Mahant primarily by dint of her unswerving consent and support. Failed in his attempts of sexual assault, Ramdas, frustratingly, decided to employ another young woman from Meriganj itself as his *Dasi* (care-taker) at the Math, an action which proved to be the last straw for Lachhmi who left the Math for good and started leading a new conjugal life with Baldev, the Gandhian, who had till then taken the vow of *brahmcharya* as many of Gandhi's followers had avowed in those days. Lachhmi had developed soft corner for Baldev since the time of Sewadas, who, too, had immense respect for Baldev as a strict Gandhian and vegetarian. Although she could switch over to her conjugal life smoothly, having a buttress of about 30 *bighas* of land allocated to her in lieu of her devoted service to Math as well as former Mahant, Sewadas.

As a participant observer, I have also heard amongst the enlightened section of Kabirpanthis the feeling of grave concern about the near absence of a centralized or unified body of the Kabirpanth, more so from those who are pursuing path of Kabir abroad. Some Sikh Kabirpanthis have been of the view that there must be a common *rahat maryada* for all the Kabirpanthis irrespective of their branch of affiliation on the similar line of the Sikhs which are determined by the SGPC. To the Kabirpanthis of Canadà, the UK and the USA, the three countries where I could visit and interview many of them, the need of a single platform establishing their common identity was articulated more forcefully. I had to face an awkward situation in a Kabir temple of Surrey, Vancouver, in 2012, where a middle aged NRI lady born in a qasba of Punjab, raised her voice against my inadvertent non-reference of Dr.Bhimrao Ambedkar as the real Kabirpanthi of the 20th century, in my short lecture on Kabir and the Kabirpanth. I could pacify her only by tendering my apology during post-lecture dinner. In the circumstance, what I personally feel, the necessity of the unity and solidarity among Kabirpanthis across the world, may be the need of the hour, yet we must not forget that historically the Kabirpanth as such has emerged as a confederation, and hence it has been hard for it to grow as a homogenous well-knit entity under an umbrella organization.

References

1. Rosalind O' Hanlon & David Washbrook, *Religious Cultures in Early Modern India, New Perspectives*, Routledge, New Delhi, 2011, pp. 2-3.
2. Rajendra Prasad, *Kabirpanth Ka Udbhav Evam Prasar*, (Hindi), (118-119).
3. Marc Juergensmeyer, *Radhasoami Reality: The Logic of a Modern Faith*, Princeton University Press, Princeton, 1995, p. 27.
4. Fanishwar Nath 'Renu', *Mainla Aanchal*, Hindi, Rajkamal Prakashan, 2010 (1954).

Annex-1

Judgment papers discovered from Dhanauti Math,Bihar

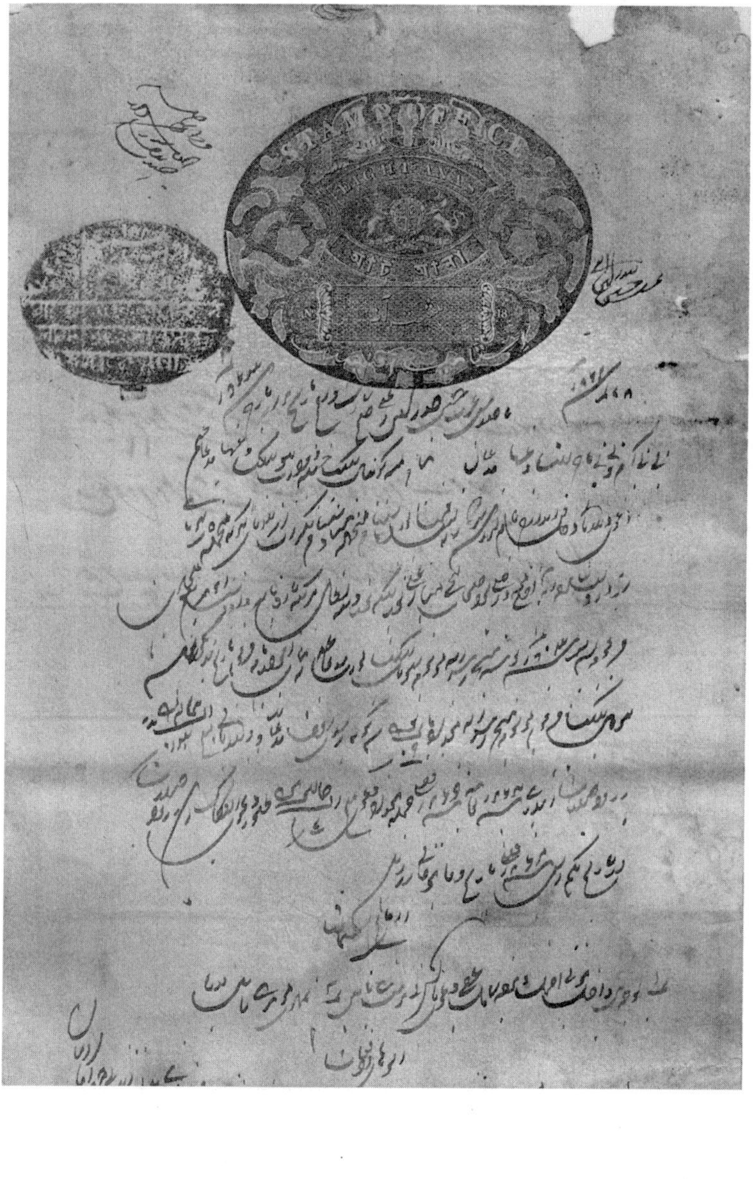

Annex-1 (i)

Annex-1 (ii)

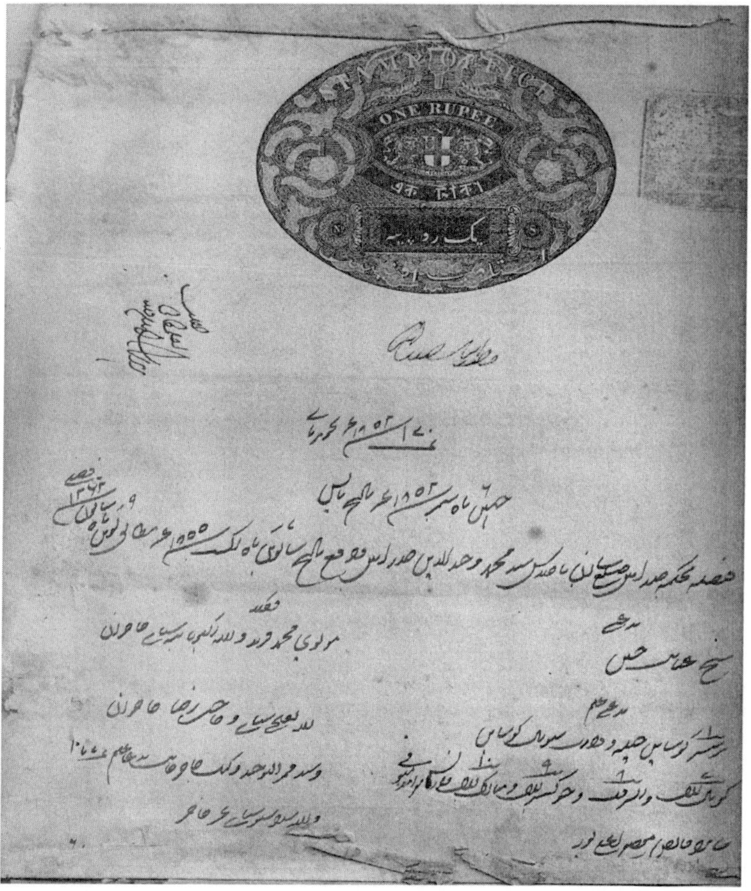

Annex-1 (iii)

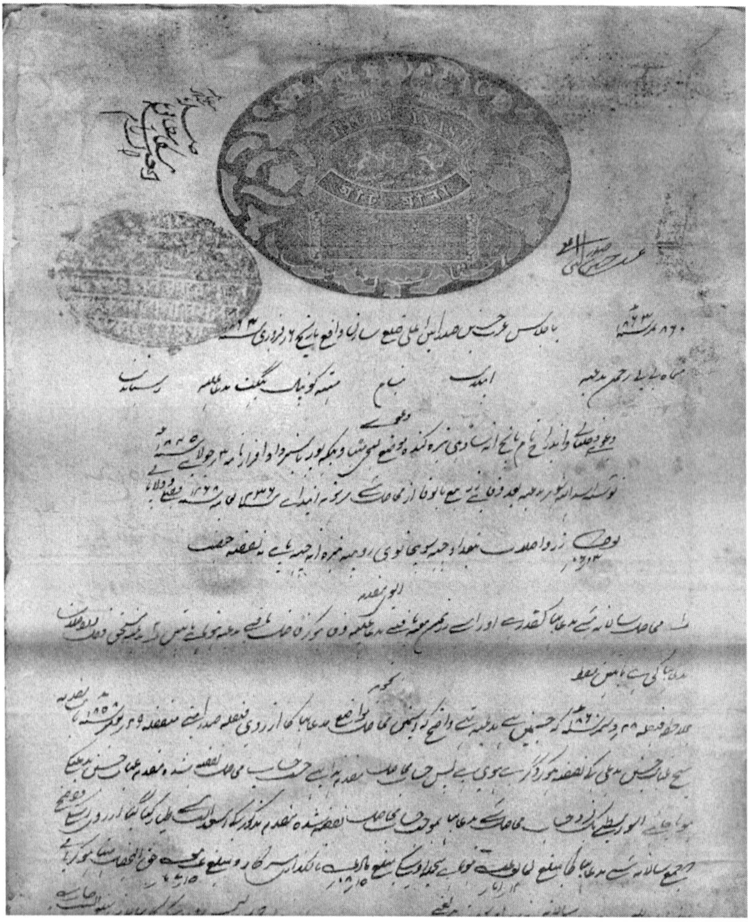

Annex-1 (iv)

Annex-2

Front cover page of the published manuscript, Nadia, Chhattisgarh

Annex-2 (i)

Back page

साक्षात कबीर के प्रतिमूर्ति प्रबुद्ध सद्गुरु :–

कबीर नादवंश हुजुर मुक्तामनी सद्गुरु श्री सेवा साहेब असाधारण प्रतीमा के धनी है। अपने युग में महाशुर इन्द्रीयाजीत संघर्श जीवन में कबीर केसरी थे, जिसे देख काम वासना धन पदादी मद के नशा में हाथी के समान प्रतीद्वंन्दी चीहार करते हुवे भगने के लिये दरवाजा भी प्राप्त नहीं कर पाये। सद्गुरु ज्ञानी कबीर के अंतरआत्मा थे, वे जीनको देखकर बहुत से विरक्त संतों को मार्गदर्शन प्राप्त हुवा। जो विषय भोग वादी बने हुवे पर भी गुरु कडी हार आचार्य हजुर कहलानेवाले के कटघेरा तोड़कर आज वे संत जन स्वतंत्र सद्गुरु कबीर के मानवी ज्ञान प्रचार प्रसार कर रहे है। कबीर पंथ भारतीय नमक्षेत्र में नाद वंश आचार्य सद्गुरु श्री सेवा साहेब आपका बेमीसाल अमर इतिहास है। सद्गुरु कबीर समान, आपके पावन पद कमल साधकों का।

:- भजन -:

नाद उदधि, अथाह अति, गुरु ज्ञान अगम अपार रे।
करीये अर्पण मन वचन नत, कभी न बहे भव धार रे ।।टेक।।
नाम वह सत्यनाम गुरु का, पतित पावन नाम है।।
हृदय से सुमिरन करे कोई, पावै वह निज धाम है।।
ज्ञान यान में बैठे गुरु के, होयगा भव से पार रे ।।१।।
सर्व कामना रहित होकर, गुरु शरण जो जायेगा।।
मंगल मूरत, दिव्य सूरत, निज में दर्शन पायेगा।।
काल भी कुछ कर सके न, आपन सर संभार रे ।।२।।
ज्ञानी गुरु कबीर ने "सेवा" को, जब से ली शरण।।
टूट गई यम बेड़ियां, अरु छुट गया है जन्म मरण।।
देह रहे तक, ज्ञान बोध, विराग निश्चय धार रे ।।३।।

विनम्रता

Annex-3

Bahadurpur Math, Bihar

Appendix-4

Sikandarpur Math, Bihar

Annex-4 (i)

Samadhi room, Sikandarpur Math

Annex-5

Kabir Badi Math, Mumbai

Annex-6

Entry gate of the Paharganj Math, New Delhi

Annex-7

Obituary Published in Hindi newspaper

सत्यनाम्

बड़े दुःख के साथ सूचित करना पड़ रहा है कि श्री श्री १०८ श्री **महन्त मनोहर दास जी** (नावला निवासी) का स्वर्गवा[illegible] तारीख १४ जनवरी १९७८ को पहाड़ गंज, नई दिल्ली में हो [illegible]या।

[illegible]न की पुण्य स्मृति में श्रंद्धाजली समारोह एवं भण्डारा, सोमवार, तारीख ३० जनवरी १९७८ को प्रातः ११-३० बजे से सायं ३ बजे तक ५५२७ शोरा कोठी, पहाड़ गंज नई दिल्ली-५५ [illegible] रखा गया है।

अतः आप सब महन्तो, संतों एवं सेवक जनों से आग्रह है [illegible]क इस अवसर पर पधार कर उनकी आत्मा की शान्ति के [illegible]लये "सद् गुरू कबीर" साहब से प्रार्थना करें।

आपकी उपस्थिति प्रार्थनीय है।

दर्शनाभिलाषी :—	विनीत :
चन्द्रभान दास,	देवकी नन्दन दास
सुबेदार सिंह	रामनाथ शर्मा

तथा सेवक जन

स्वर्गीय श्री श्री १०८ श्री महन्त मनोहर दास जी

Annex-7 (i)

Will paper of Mahant Manohar Das

मैं के महन्त मनोहर दास चेला महन्त गोपाल दास निवासी 5527, शोरा कोठी, पहाड़गंज, नई देहली ।

जो कि जिन्दगी का कुछ भरोसा नहीं है इसलिये हर मनुष्य का फर्ज लाजिमी है कि इन्तजाम अपनी जिन्दगी में ऐसा कर जावे कि जिससे बाद में झगड़ा पैदा नहीं ; क्योंकि मेरी आयु लगभग 74 साल हो गई है । रफ्तारे जमाने को देखते हुए मुझको भी अपनी जिन्दगी का कुछ भरोसा नहीं - नहीं मालूम कि किस वक्त शरीर पूरा हो जायें । इस वक्त होश और हवास मेरे बिल्कुल दुरुस्त हैं और तमाम जिसम मेरा सही काम देता है । आंखों से अपनी देख सकता हूं । पैरों से अपने चल फिर सकता हूं, कानों से बखूबी सुन सकता हूं, जबान अपनी से बखूबी बोल सकता हूं, अच्छाई बुराई को पहचान सकता हूं और अपने नफे नुकसान को समझ सकता हूं । गर्जे कि दिमाग मेरा सही काम देता है मेरे पास अजीज चन्दर भान दास चेला खुद आयु लगभग 13 वर्ष निवासी 5527, शोरा कोठी पहाड़गंज, नई देहली, बचपन से रहता है और मैंने अपना चेला रोबरू भेक कबीर पंथी कर लिया है और उसकी तालीम और परवरिश में अपने खर्चे से बर्दाश्त कर रहा हूं और चेला मौसूफ मेरी खिदमत गुजारी दिल जान से बतौर चेले के कर रहा है जिससे मैं निहायत खुश हूं । और मुझको संपत्ति (जायदाद) मुफस्सिले चेला अपने गुरु महन्त गोपाल दास जी से पहुंची है । और गुरु का देहान्त हो चुका है । और मैं जायदाद मुफस्सिले जैल पर बहैसियत मालिकाना काबिज और दखील हूं । और इसमें इसमें कोई शख्स सहीम व शरीक उजरदार दावेदार व हिस्सेदार हकदार नहीं है । मैं अकेला मालिक कामिल हूं । चुनांचि मैं मुकिर बहाला सेहत बदन व सबाते अकेला व ब दुरुस्ती होश व हवास, बिला दाब व जबर दीगरे बखुशी खुद यह वसीयत ब हक चन्दर भान दास साधू कबीर पंथी चेला खुद साकिन शोरा कोठी पहाड़गंज न0 5527, न्यू देहली के हस्ब जैल करता हूं।-

Annex-7 (ii)

- 3 -

[illegible] दावा करेगा तो उसका [illegible] बहते [illegible] व हाकिमाने [illegible] बहते मोहल्ला कतई नाजायज और झूठा होगा ।

लिहाजा यह वसीयतनामा तहरीर कर दिया कि सनद रहे और [illegible] जरूरत काम आवें ।

[illegible]

1- [illegible] जायदाद नं0 5524 से 5531 इलाका नं0 15 रकबा तकरीबन 700 मुरब्बा गज वाक्या [illegible] कोठी पहाड़गंज, नई देहली ।

2- तीन किता दुकानात नं0 4569 से 4571 इलाका नं0 15 [illegible] मेन बाजार पहाड़गंज, न्यू देहली ।

3- आराजी [illegible] तकरीबन [illegible] बीघे [illegible] मौजा [illegible] तहसील [illegible] जिला मुजफ्फर नगर यू0 पी0

4- आराजी [illegible] तकरीबन साढ़े ग्यारह बीघे [illegible] व आराजी व [illegible] व [illegible] व [illegible] व बागीचा वगैरह [illegible] मौजा [illegible] तहसील [illegible] जिला मुजफ्फर नगर ।

5- [illegible] गद्दी मौजा [illegible] तहसील हाजीपुर जिला मुजफ्फर पुर (बिहार) [illegible] गद्दी और उसके मुताल्लिक

तहरीर तारीख 15 दिसम्बर 1959 [illegible]

रामाचरण - [illegible] दिल्ली

लाइसेन्स नं0 15

[illegible]

Baratooti Mandi, Paharganj, New Delhi

[illegible]

Annex-7 (iii)

[illegible]

नं० १ —

मुज़फ्फर नगर ता० ८-११-६८ को आना यहां [illegible] (अभिमा [illegible]) [illegible] से खेड़ी की ज़मीन का [illegible] [illegible] नहीं मिला। यहां से दिल्ली ८२ कि० मी० गाज़ियाबाद को ६२ कि० मी० है और मेरठ ५३ कि० मी० और खतौली [illegible] दिल्ली ६० कि० मी० मेरठ से [illegible] ३२ मील है। दिल्ली से खतौली रेलभाड़ा ता० १५-११-[illegible] को १-४० पैसे है। (राम किशोर त्यागी खतौली में)

मुज़फ्फर नगर के राजनैतिक व्यक्ति दो हैं [illegible] वीरेन्द्र [illegible] और राजेन्द्र त्यागी निम्न हैं।

[illegible] गुड़गांव के [illegible] जो कॉंग्रेसी [illegible] है। [illegible] गंज मुहल्ला [illegible] शोरा कोठी।

मकान नं० ५५२६ लेडी हार्डिंग सराय के पास बसन्त [illegible] (गुड़गांव रोड)

[illegible]

नं० २ —

खतौली। पत नावले के [illegible] है।

नावले की रजिस्ट्री भी [illegible] है। नावले मठ की प्रणाली निम्न है १ हर्जी दास जी संस्थापक २ शिष्य माधव दास जी ३ गंगा दास जी, ४ गोविन्द दास जी ५ प्रेम दास जी ६ गोपाल दास जी ७ [illegible] हर दास जी वर्तमान हैं।

नावले के बाग खाता नं० ११० खेसरा नं० १ ३८ कुल [illegible] चकबन्दी से ११।।३ [illegible] केहै। कच्चे [illegible] ३५। लगान ६३-६२ पैसे प्रथम [illegible] शेष [illegible] लड़ने से छूटेंगे। १० गुणा जमा करके [illegible]

सन् [illegible] १३६४-१३६६ [illegible] है तीन दुकानें हैं --- दुकानों का नं० ४ [illegible] दिल्ली मकान का नं० ५५२६ और [illegible] इसमें [illegible]

नावले [illegible] गोस्वामी [illegible] [illegible] द्वारा [illegible] ता० ३०-१०-६८ ई०

[illegible] ता० ६-१०-६८ से ता० १६-१०-६८ तक [illegible] और [illegible] १०-६८ से ता० २४-१०-६८ तक दिल्ली [illegible] ता० २५-१०-६८ से ता० १५-११-६८ तक नावले और [illegible] ता० १६-११-६८ को दिल्ली आया।

Annex-8

Samadhi, Daligang Math , Lucknow

Annex-8 (i)

Judgement paper obtaineed from Lucknow Math

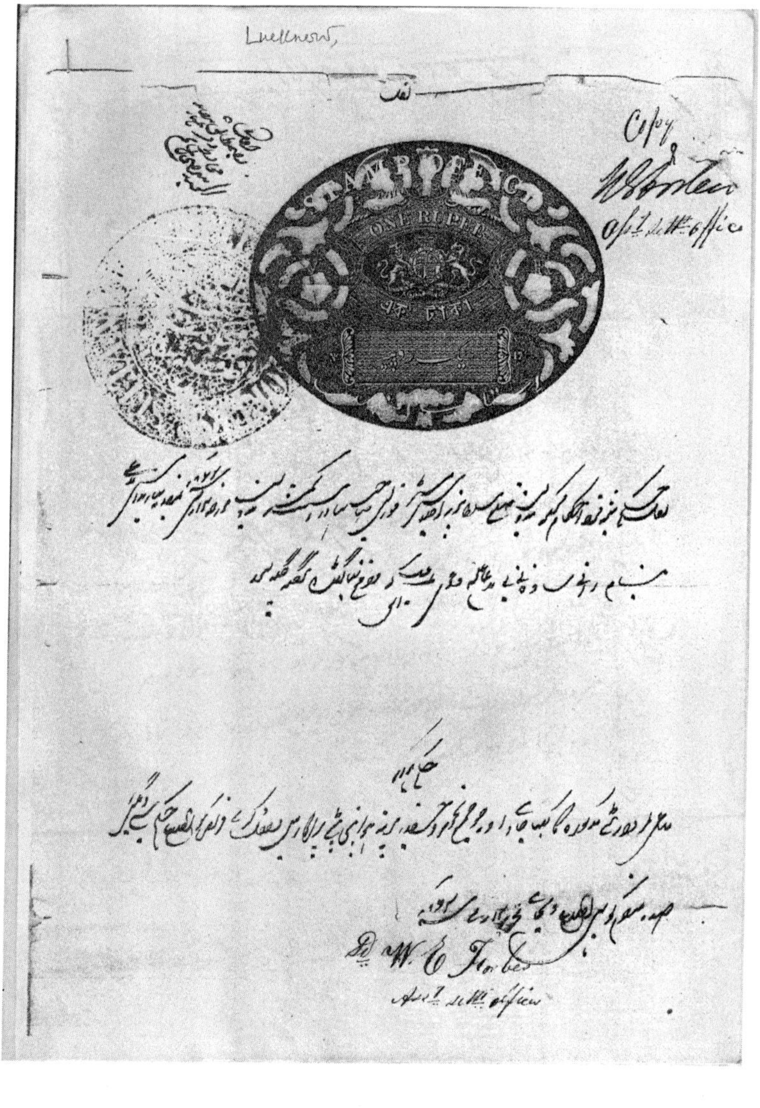

Annex-8 (ii)

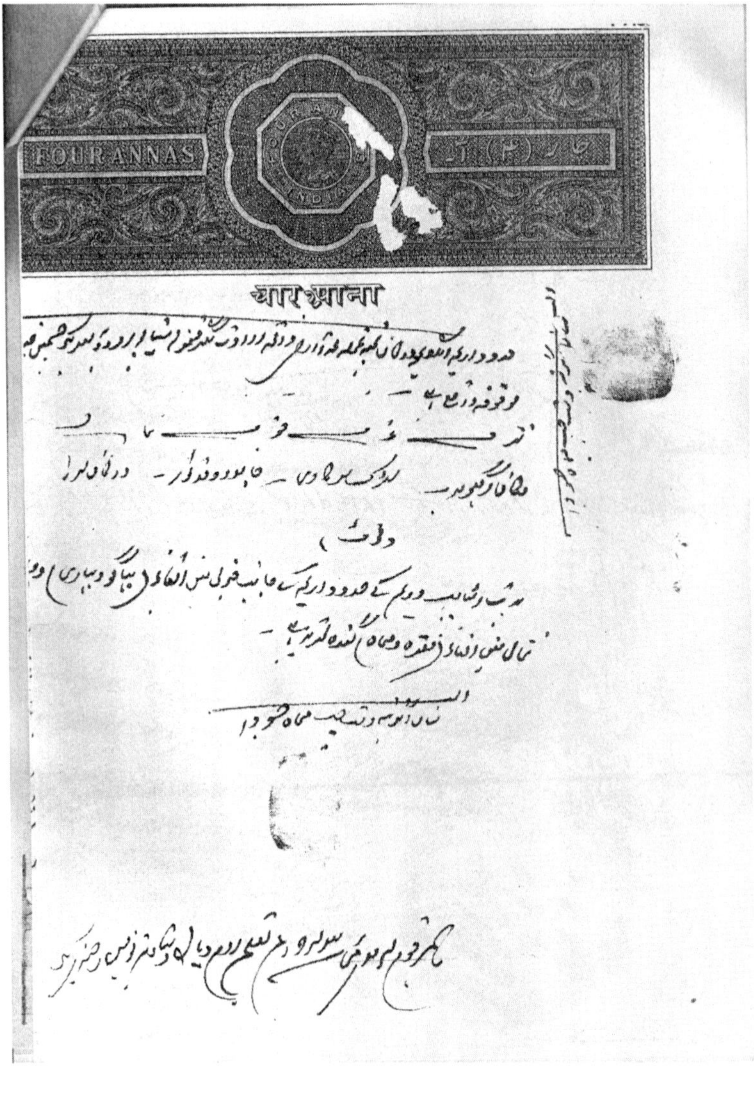

FOUR ANNAS

चार आना

Annex-8 (iii)

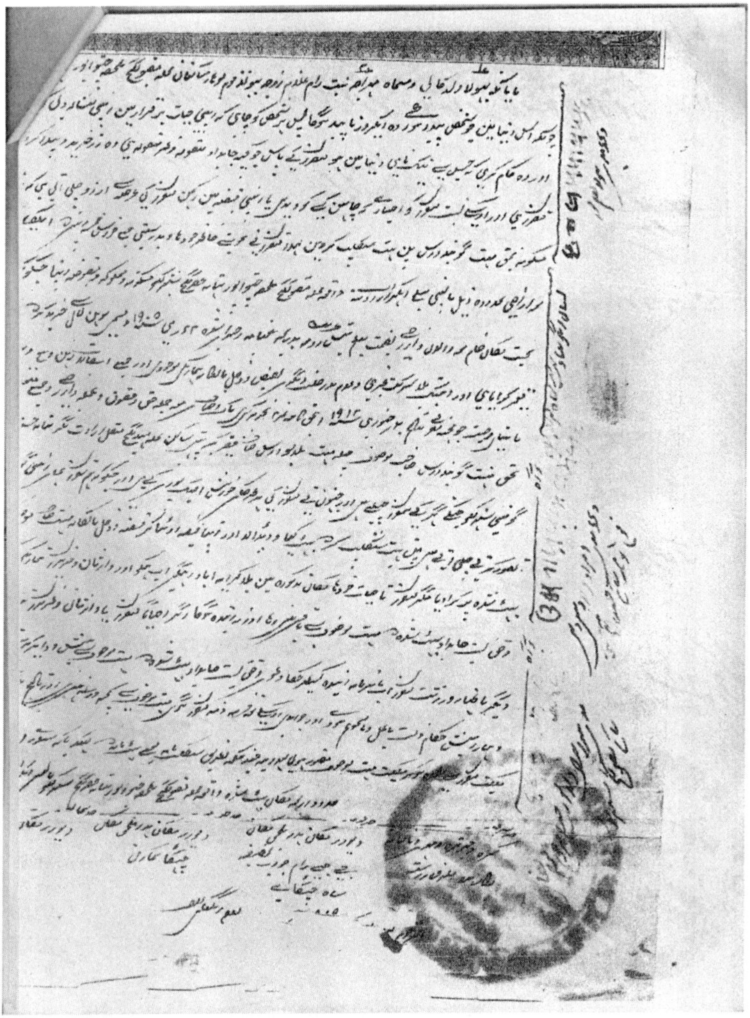

Annex-8 (iv)

Splendid gate of Daliganj Math Lucknow

Annex-9

First page of judgement papers, Saharnpur Math

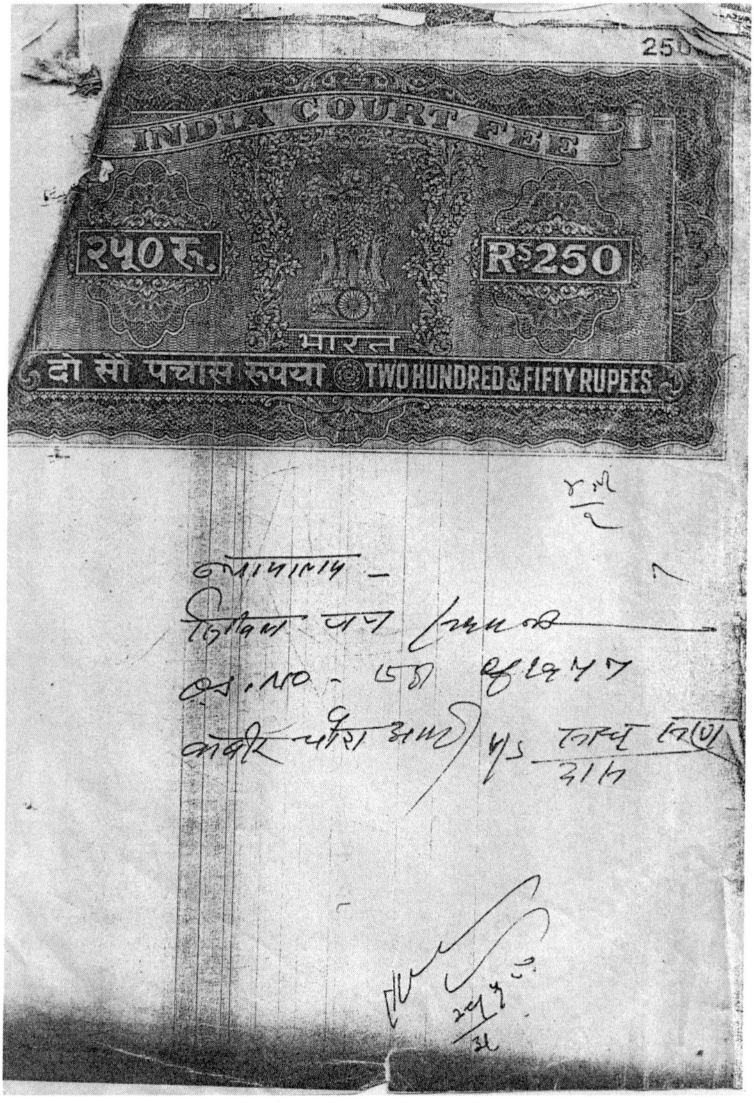
250
INDIA COURT FEE
२५०रु.
R^{s}250
भारत
दो सौ पचास रुपया TWO HUNDRED & FIFTY RUPEES

Annex-9 (i)

Kabir chaura Math Saharanpur, U.P.

Annex-10

Burhanpur Kabir Math, M.P.

Annex-10 (i)

Annex-11

Jamnagar Kabir Ashram, Gujrat

Annex-11 (i)

Inner Temple, Jamnagar Math

Annex-11 (ii)

Group of Mahants, Jamnagar, Gujrat

Annex-11 A

Radhaswami temple under construction, Agra

Annex-12

A photo of Lavleen Das

Annex-12 (i)

The latest Kabir Math formed,Gorubathan,West Bengal

Annex-12 (ii)

Oldest Kabir Math, Guahati, Assam

Annex-12 (iii)

Kabir Math Lingmoo, Sikkim

Annex-12 (iv)

Samdong khese kabir Math,Sikkim

Annex-12 (v)

Cover page of the book

Annex-13

Photo-copy of the diary written by Gyan Das,Bengaluru

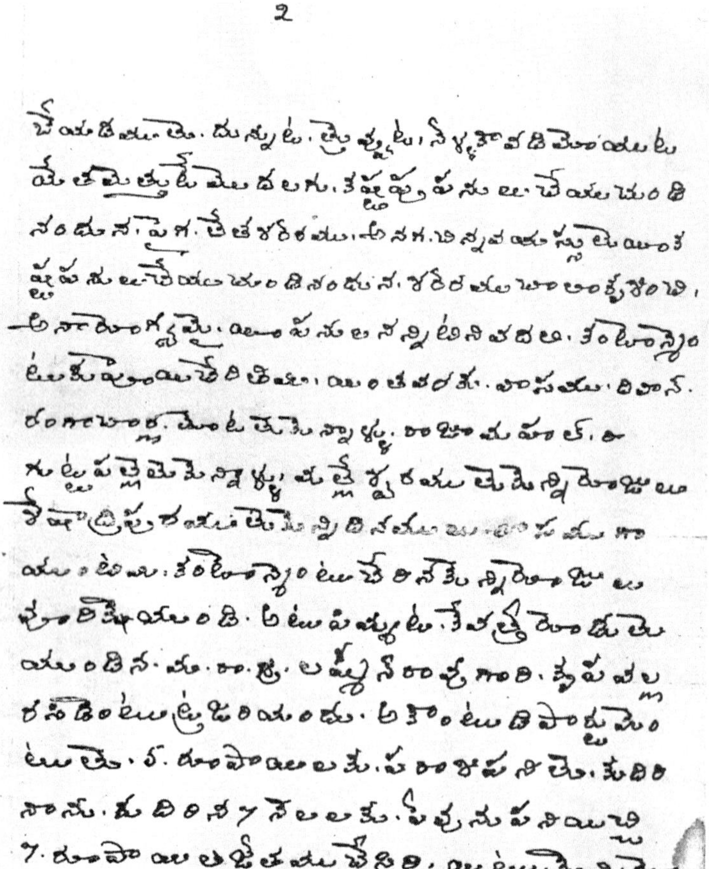

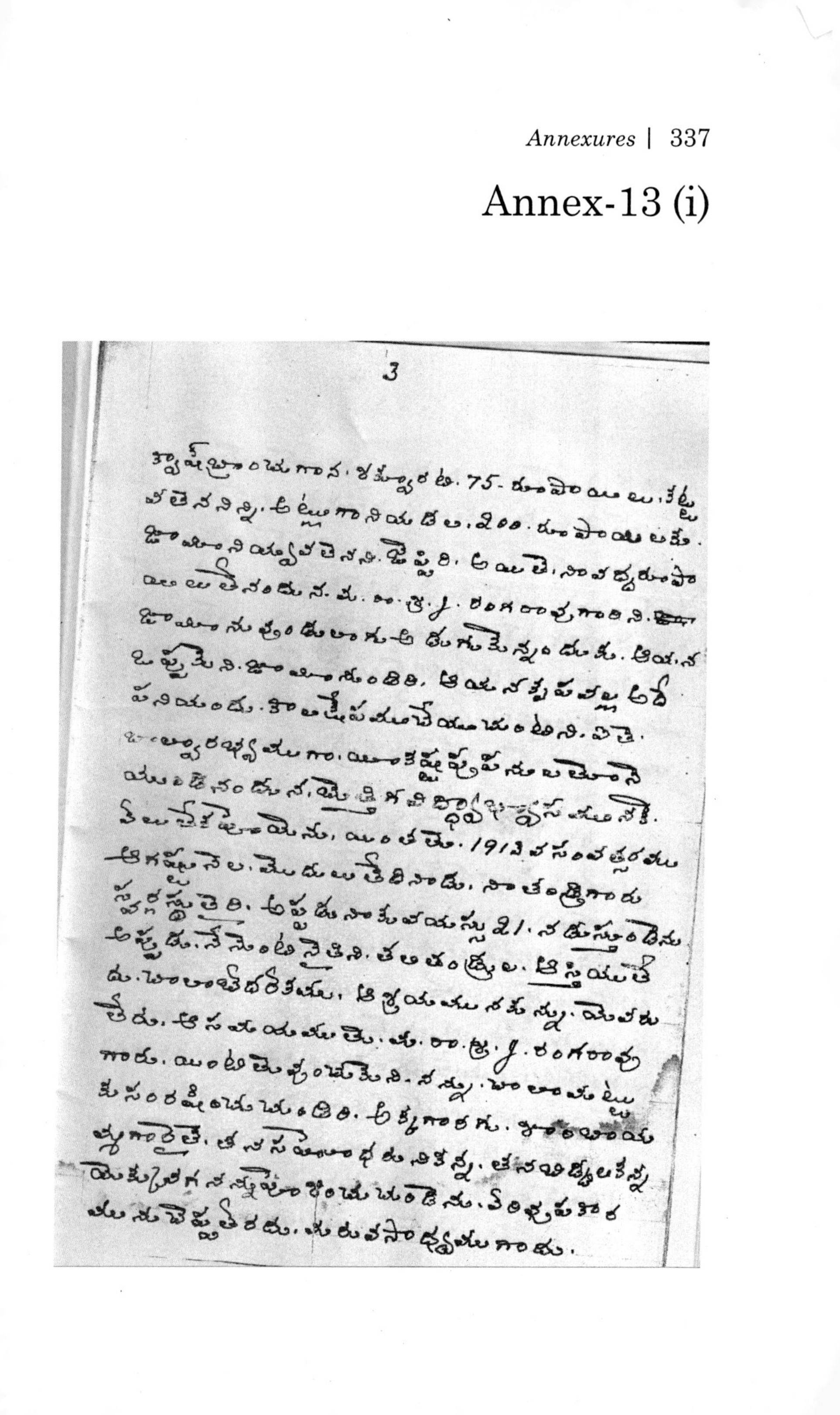

Annex-13 (i)

3

[illegible]

Annex-14

An inscription written on Samadhi cover, Hyderabad

Annex-15

An inscription on marble cover of Samadhi, Hyderabad

Annex-15 (i)

A view of the Giri's Kabir ashram, Hyderabad

Annex-16

First page of the Gyan Das's Diary

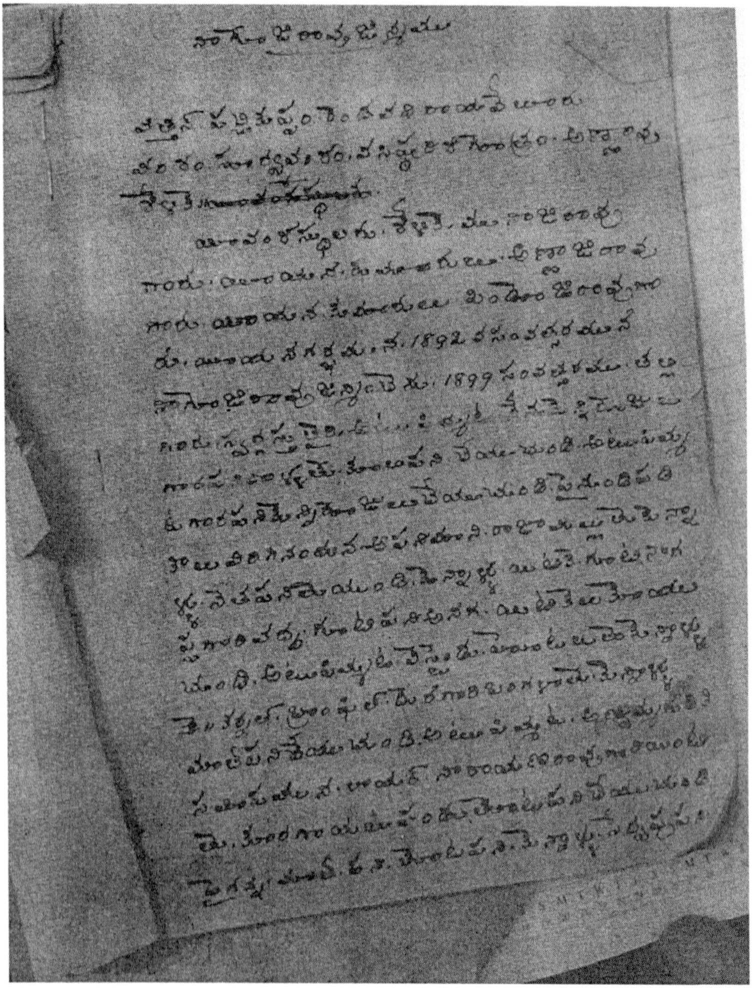

Annex-16 (i)

The earliest Kabir math in Bengaluru,Karnataka

Annex-17

Bhagatahi Kabir Math, Samastipur, Bihar

Annex-18

A board hanging at the entry gate of the Math, HYD

Annex-18 (i)

Late Mahant Kishan Das, Hyderabad

Annex-19

A copy of the land registry paper, Kharsiya Nirwan Math

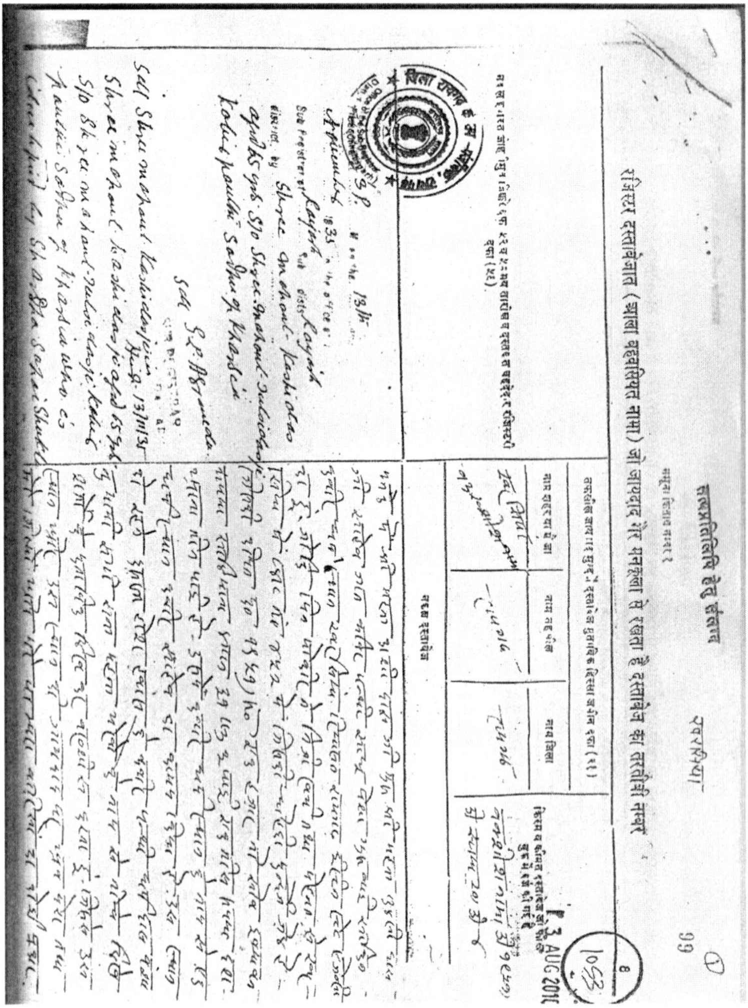

Annex-19 (i)

Last page of the registry paper

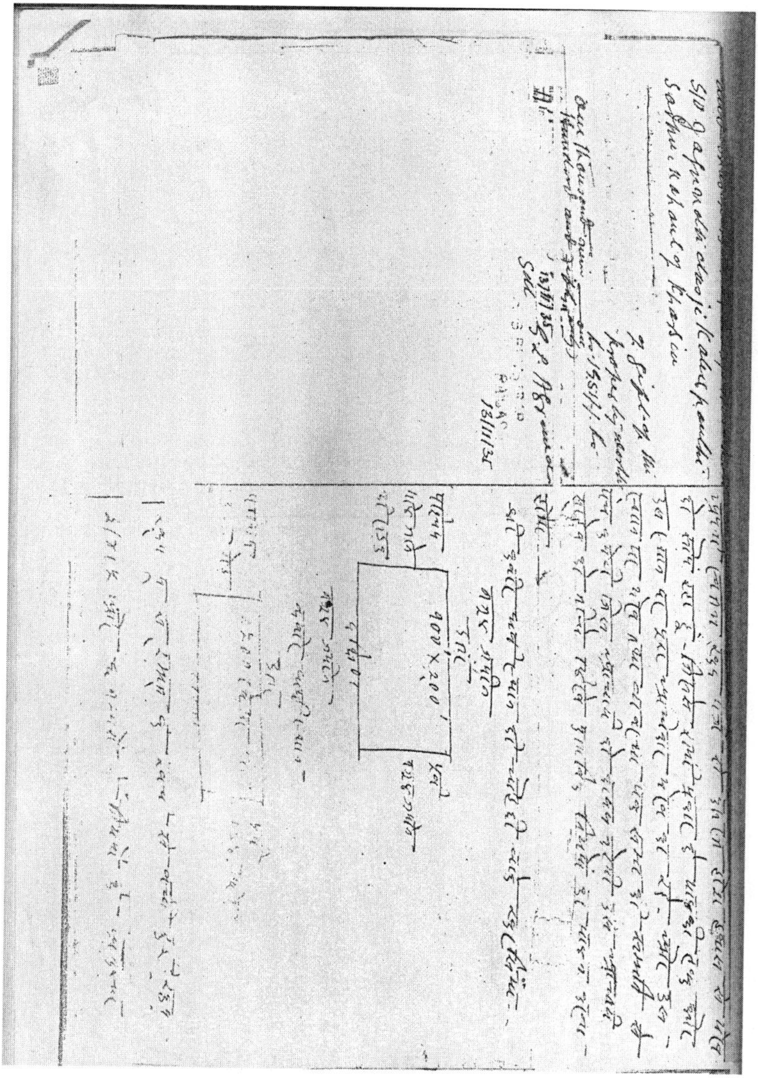

Annex-19 (ii)

Formation of the Kharsiya Math as reported in 1936

स्वसंवेद (मासिक पत्रिका) वर्ष-1 संख्या-1, 1936
सियाबाग, बड़ोदा (गुजरात)
संचालक = महंत श्री बालकदास साहेब.
संपादक = पं० मोतीदास जी साहेब.

पंथ समाचार । २३

गये हैं । एक 'वचनवंश' और दूसरा 'नादवंश' । वचन वंश तो श्रीधर्मदासजी साहेब के पुत्र श्रीचूरामणि नाम साहेब, जो कबीर पंथ के प्रथम आचार्य और आदि पंथ-प्रवर्तक थे, को तथा उनके वंशजों को कहते हैं और नादवंश समस्त कबीरपंथी भेष को कहा गया है ।

लगभग चारसौ वर्ष तक कबीर पंथ का आचार्यपद पं. श्री वचनवंश गुरुओं के अधिकार में रहा । और संवत् १९८४ के पौष सुदि २ को वचन वंश के अन्तिम आचार्य पं. श्री १०८ श्री दयानाम साहेब सत्यलोकवासी बने । समस्त नाद वंश (भेष) ने ग्रंथों को देखकर निर्णय किया कि जैसा सद्गुरु का आदेश था वैसा ही हुआ है और अब से कबीर पंथ का आचार्य पद वचनवंश से हटकर नादवंश के पास आया है । इस लिए समस्त भेष की संमति से संवत् १९९० के माघ सुदि ७ सोमवार ता. २७-१-१९३४ को जिला दरभंगा के अन्तर्गत रोशडा स्थान के वय एवं ज्ञान-वृद्ध १०८ महंत श्री काशीदासजी साहेब को भेष समस्त ने पसंद करके नादवंश के प्रथम आचार्य के रूप में कबीरपंथ के चौदहवें श्रीमान् आचार्य—शिरोमणि १०८ पं श्री ग्रन्थमणिनाम साहेब के स्थान पर प्रतिष्ठित किये । और तब से योगमत का आरंभ हो गया है । अब से समस्त भेष मिलकर पंथ का कार्य चलावेगा ।

नादवंश के प्रथम आचार्यस्थान की, दामाखेडा (कबीर धर्म नगर) जिला रायपुर सी पी. से हटाकर बी. एन. डबल्यू रेल्वे के स्टेशन खरसिया जिला बिलासपुर सी. पी. में 'श्री कबीर धर्म स्थान' के नाम से स्थापना की गई है। इस धर्मस्थान की स्थापना में सत्यलोक वासी श्रीयुत रा. बाजीराव कांटे साहेब, ग्वालियर का आगे हाथ था । उन्हींकी कर्तव्य-परायणता से यह धर्मस्थान कायम हो सका है । उन्हींकी तथा समस्त भेष की विशेष अभिलाषा थी कि यह धर्मस्थान भेष समस्त के नाम से बख्खीशनामा के रूप में रजिष्टर किया जाय ताकि भविष्य में कोई भी आचार्य अपने एकाधिकार के कारण इसको नष्ट-भ्रष्ट न कर सकें । पंथ के समस्त महंत संत तथा सती सेवक भाई और बहिनों को यह जानकर खुशी होगी कि सद्गुरु की असीम दया से सब विघ्न-बाधायें अब हट गई हैं और पं श्री ने गत ता. १३-१?-१९३५ को समस्त कबीर धर्मदासवंशानुयायिओं के नाम से श्रीकबीर धर्म स्थान-खरसिया का बख्खीश नामा लिखकर रजिष्टरी कर दिया है । इसके लिए गुजरात-काठियावाड के महंत साहेबों का समस्त भेष बहुत उपकृत है । उन्होंकी कार्य-तत्परता और धर्म-परायणता के ही कारण यह सुयोग पंथ को उपलब्ध हुआ है । रजिष्टरी के लिये काठियावाड पंच के प्रतिनिधि रूप जामनगर के श्रीमान् महंतश्री शांतिदासजी साहेब तथा गुजरात-पंच के प्रतिनिधि रूप अमदावाद-खाडिया के महंत श्रीरतनदासजी साहेब, पंथ भूषण श्रीमान् महंतश्री विचारदासजी साहेब शास्त्री को लेकर ता. ८-?१-३५ को खरसिया गये थे । और वहां पर जाकर उपर्युक्त तारीख को पं. श्री से श्रीकबीर धर्मस्थान की भेष समस्त के नाम से रजिष्टरी करवा ली है । पं. श्री ने भी इस प्रकार भेष को गौरव प्रदान कर

Annex-20

Kabir Nirwan Math ,Kharasiya, Chhattisgarh

Annex-21

A Ram Kabir Mandir, Limbdi,Gujarat

Annex-21 (i)

Inner view of the temple, Limbdi,Gujarat

Annex-22

Sadhvi Gyananand on the cover page of her quarterly Hindi magazine

Annex-22 (i)

Kabir Math,Giridih, Jharkhand

Annex-22 (ii)

Part of Giridih Math

Annex-23

Part of Giridih Math

Annex-24

Sardar Gurdit Singh(Panjabi Maharaj), Amritsar,Panjab

Annex-25

First page of the Will executed by late Ramswarup Das,Burhanpur, Madhya Pradesh

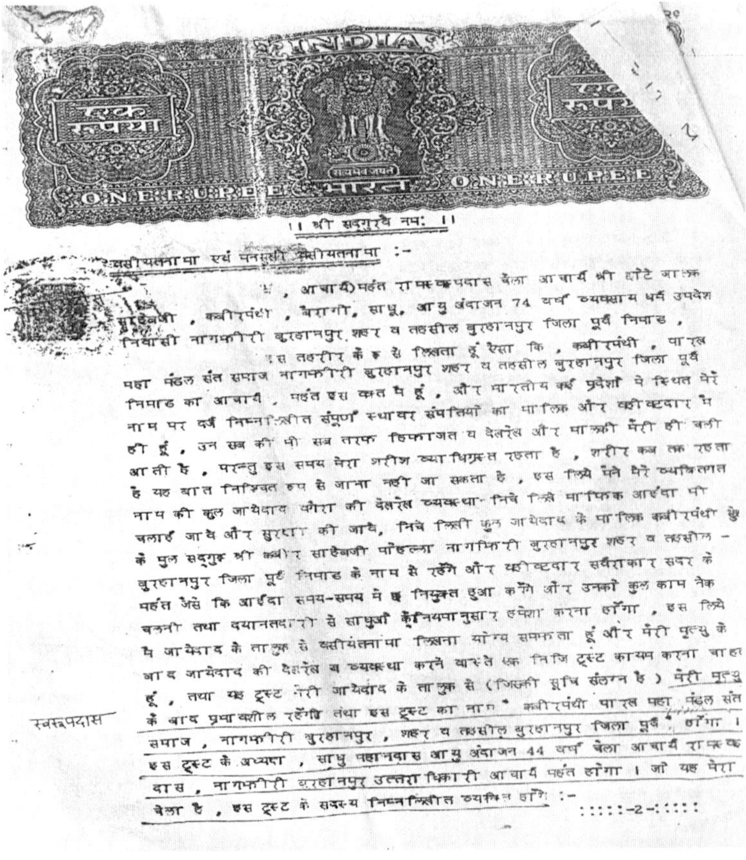

।। श्री सद्गुरवे नमः ।।

वसीयतनामा एवं मनसुखी वसीयतनामा :-

मैं, आचार्य महंत रामस्वरूपदास चेला आचार्य श्री छोटे जानकीदास वल्द गुरु देवजी, कबीरपंथी, बैरागी, साधु, आयु अंदाजन 74 वर्ष व्यवसाय धर्म उपदेश निवासी नागझीरी बुरहानपुर शहर व तहसील बुरहानपुर जिला पूर्व निमाड,

इस तहरीर के रु से लिखता हूं ऐसा कि, कबीरपंथी, पारख महा मंडल संत समाज नागझीरी बुरहानपुर शहर व तहसील बुरहानपुर जिला पूर्व निमाड का आचार्य, महंत इस वक्त मैं हूं, और भारतीय कई प्रदेशों में स्थित मेरे नाम पर दर्ज निम्नलिखित संपूर्ण स्थावर संपत्तियों का मालिक और कब्जेदार मैं ही हूं, उन सब की भी सब तरफ हिफाजत व देखरेख और मालकी मेरी ही चली आती है, परन्तु इस समय मेरा शरीर व्याधिग्रस्त रहता है, शरीर कब तक रहता है यह बात निश्चित रूप से जाना नहीं जा सकता है, इस लिये मैंने मेरे व्यक्तिगत नाम की कुल जायदाद वगैरा की देखरेख व्यवस्था निचे लिखे माफिक आइंदा भी चलाई जावे और सुरक्षा की जावे, निचे लिखी कुल जायदाद के मालिक कबीरपंथी के मुल सद्गुरु श्री कबीर साहेबजी मोहल्ला नागझीरी बुरहानपुर शहर व तहसील - बुरहानपुर जिला पूर्व निमाड के नाम से रहेंगे और कब्जेदार सर्वराकार सदर के महंत जैसे कि आइंदा समय-समय में नियुक्त हुआ करेंगे और उनको कुल काम नेक चलनी तथा दयानतदारी से साधुओं के नियमानुसार हमेशा करना होगा, इस लिये मैं जायदाद के ताल्लुक से वसीयतनामा लिखना योग्य समझता हूं और मेरी मृत्यु के बाद जायदाद की देखरेख व व्यवस्था करने वास्ते एक निजि ट्रस्ट कायम करना चाहता हूं, तथा यह ट्रस्ट मेरी जायदाद के ताल्लुक से (जिसकी सूचि संलग्न है) मेरी मृत्यु के बाद प्रभावशील रहेगा तथा इस ट्रस्ट का नाम " कबीरपंथी पारख महा मंडल संत समाज, नागझीरी बुरहानपुर, शहर व तहसील बुरहानपुर जिला पूर्व " होगा। इस ट्रस्ट के अध्यक्ष, साधु महानदास आयु अंदाजन 44 वर्ष चेला आचार्य रामस्वरूपदास, नागझीरी बुरहानपुर उत्तराधिकारी आचार्य महंत होगा। जो यह मेरा चेला है, इस ट्रस्ट के सदस्य निम्नलिखित व्यक्ति होंगे :-

स्वरूपदास

:::::-2-:::::

Annex-25 (i)

Last page of the Will

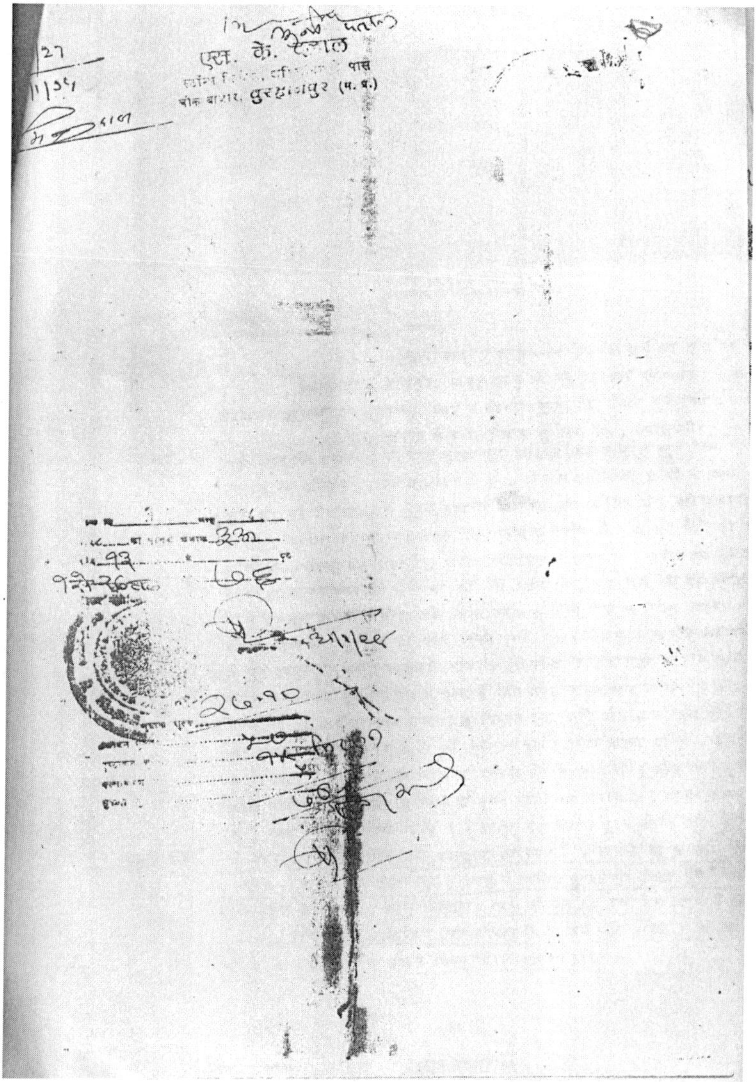

Annex-26

Kabir Mandir, Kanpur, Uttar Pradesh

Annex-26 (i)

Sanctun Sanctorum, Kabir Mandir, Kanpur

Annex-27

Kabir Ashram, Limbdi, Gujrat

Annex-28

Life sketch of late Abhilash Das, founder Parakhi math, Allahabad, Uttar Pradesh

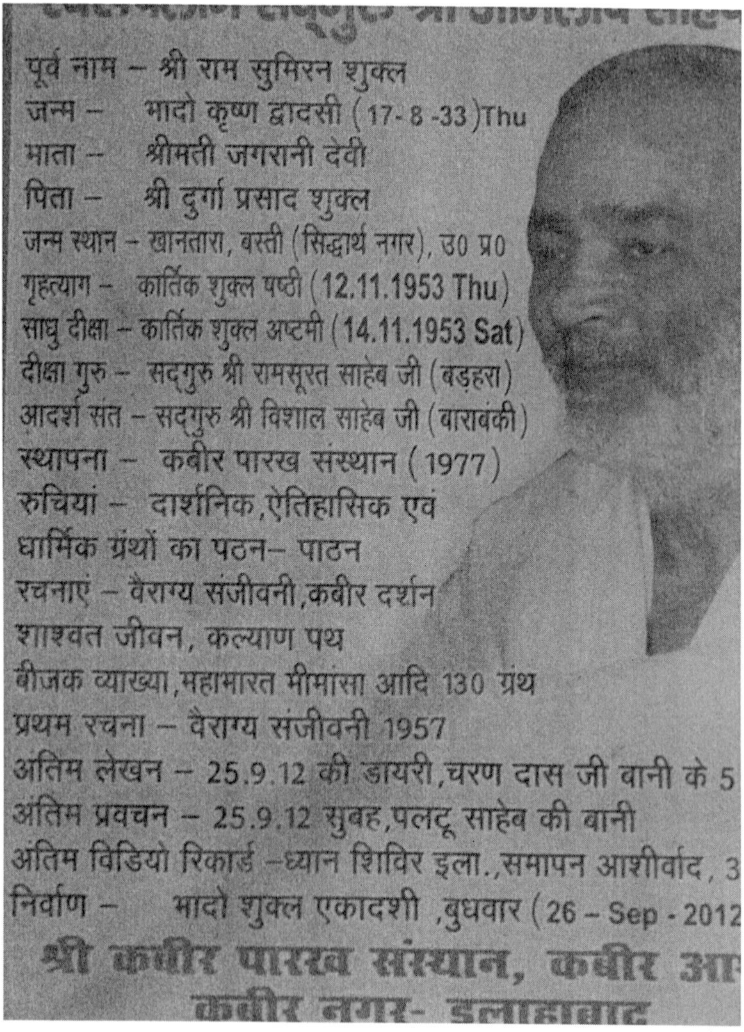

पूर्व नाम – श्री राम सुमिरन शुक्ल
जन्म – भादो कृष्ण द्वादसी (17-8-33)Thu
माता – श्रीमती जगरानी देवी
पिता – श्री दुर्गा प्रसाद शुक्ल
जन्म स्थान – खानतारा, बस्ती (सिद्धार्थ नगर), उ0 प्र0
गृहत्याग – कार्तिक शुक्ल षष्ठी (12.11.1953 Thu)
साधु दीक्षा – कार्तिक शुक्ल अष्टमी (14.11.1953 Sat)
दीक्षा गुरु – सद्गुरु श्री रामसूरत साहेब जी (बड़हरा)
आदर्श संत – सद्गुरु श्री विशाल साहेब जी (बाराबंकी)
स्थापना – कबीर पारख संस्थान (1977)
रुचियां – दार्शनिक,ऐतिहासिक एवं
धार्मिक ग्रंथों का पठन– पाठन
रचनाएं – वैराग्य संजीवनी,कबीर दर्शन
शाश्वत जीवन, कल्याण पथ
बीजक व्याख्या,महाभारत मीमांसा आदि 130 ग्रंथ
प्रथम रचना – वैराग्य संजीवनी 1957
अंतिम लेखन – 25.9.12 की डायरी,चरण दास जी बानी के 5
अंतिम प्रवचन – 25.9.12 सुबह,पलटू साहेब की बानी
अंतिम विडियो रिकार्ड –ध्यान शिविर इला.,समापन आशीर्वाद, 3
निर्वाण – भादो शुक्ल एकादशी ,बुधवार (26 – Sep - 2012
श्री कबीर पारख संस्थान, कबीर आ
कबीर नगर- इलाहाबाद

Annex-28 (i)

A research centre opened by Abhilash Das, Pritam Nagar, Allahabad

Annex-28 (ii)

Inner view of the Parakhi ashram, Pritam Nagar, Allahabad

Annex-29

Dilapidated structures at Kabir Math, Basaha, Lucknow, Uttar Pradesh

Annex-29 (i)

List of sub- branches, Kabir Math, Basaha, Lucknow

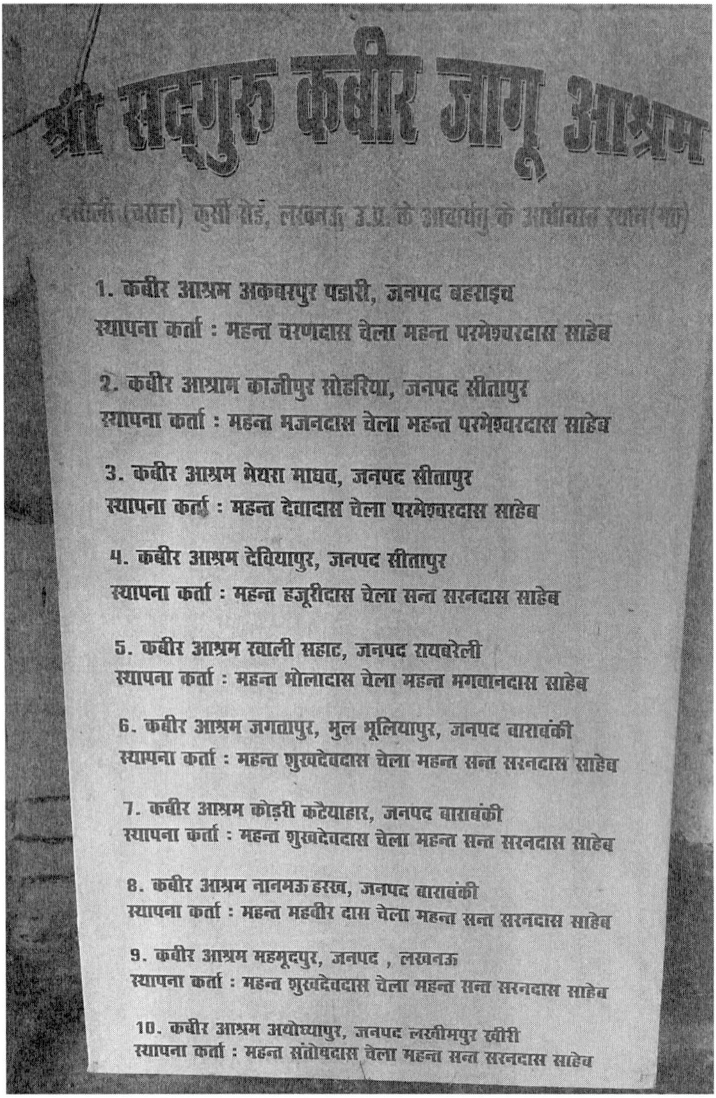

Annex-29 (ii)

Front view of the Acharya Gaddi, Jagodasi branch, Bidupur, and its Acharya Ram Dayal Das (below)

(iii)

Annex-30

The Innigration Pass of Jagessar Das's parents, British Guyana

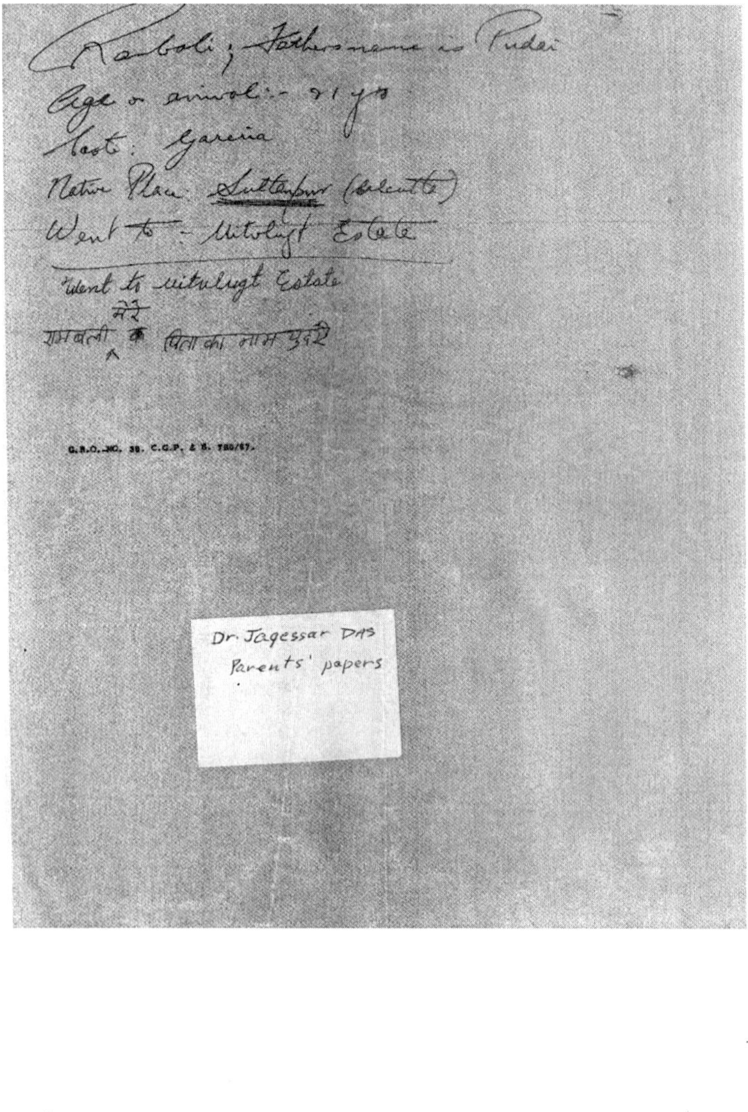

Rambali; Fathers name is Pudai
Age on arrival:- 21 yrs
Caste: Gareria
Native Place: Sultanpur (Calcutta)
~~Went to - Uitvlugt Estate~~
Went to Uitvlugt Estate
रामबली मेरे के पिता का नाम पुदई

G.R.O. No. 38. C.G.P. & S. 780/67.

Dr. Jagessar DAS
Parents' papers

Annex-30 (i)

Exemption certificate from Indenture labour of parents

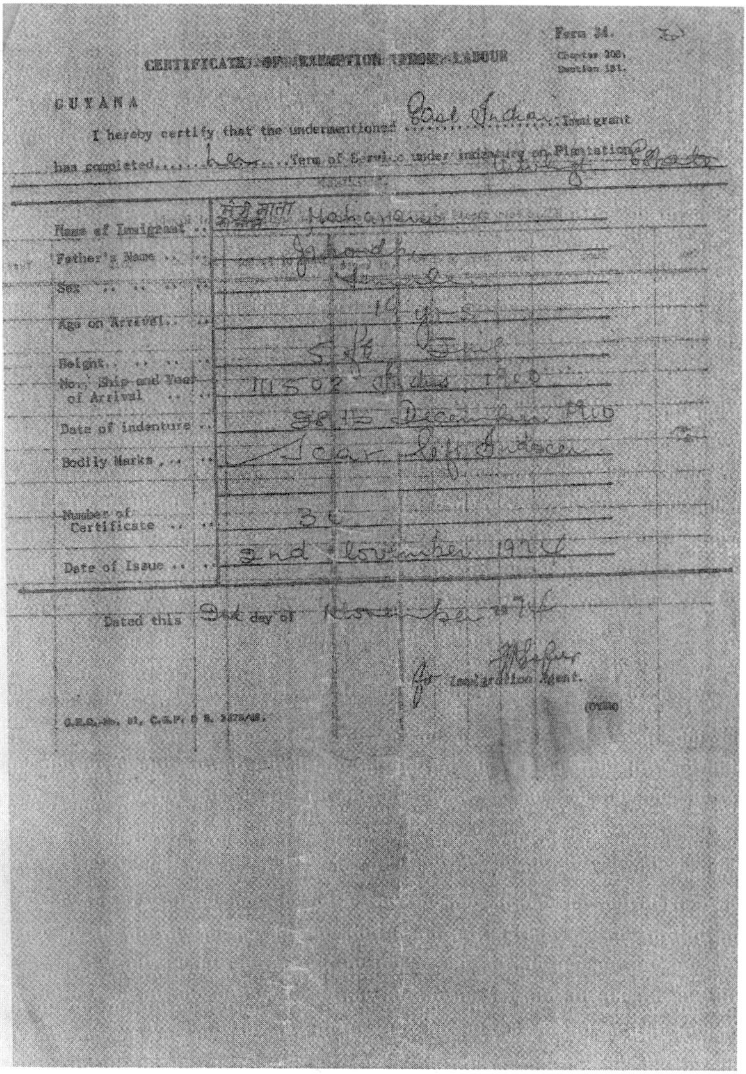

Form 34.

Chapter 206,
Section 131.

CERTIFICATE OF EXEMPTION FROM LABOUR

GUYANA

I hereby certify that the undermentioned East Indian Immigrant has completed her Term of Service under indenture on Plantation

Name of Immigrant ..	
Father's Name ..	
Sex	
Age on Arrival ..	14 yrs
Height	5 ft Five
No., Ship and Year of Arrival ..	11502
Date of indenture ..	
Bodily Marks ..	Scar
Number of Certificate ..	36
Date of Issue ..	2nd November

Dated this day of

for Immigration Agent.

G.E.G., No. 81, C.G.P. S R. 2878/48.

Annex-30 (ii)

Exemption certificate of Dr. Jagessar's in-laws

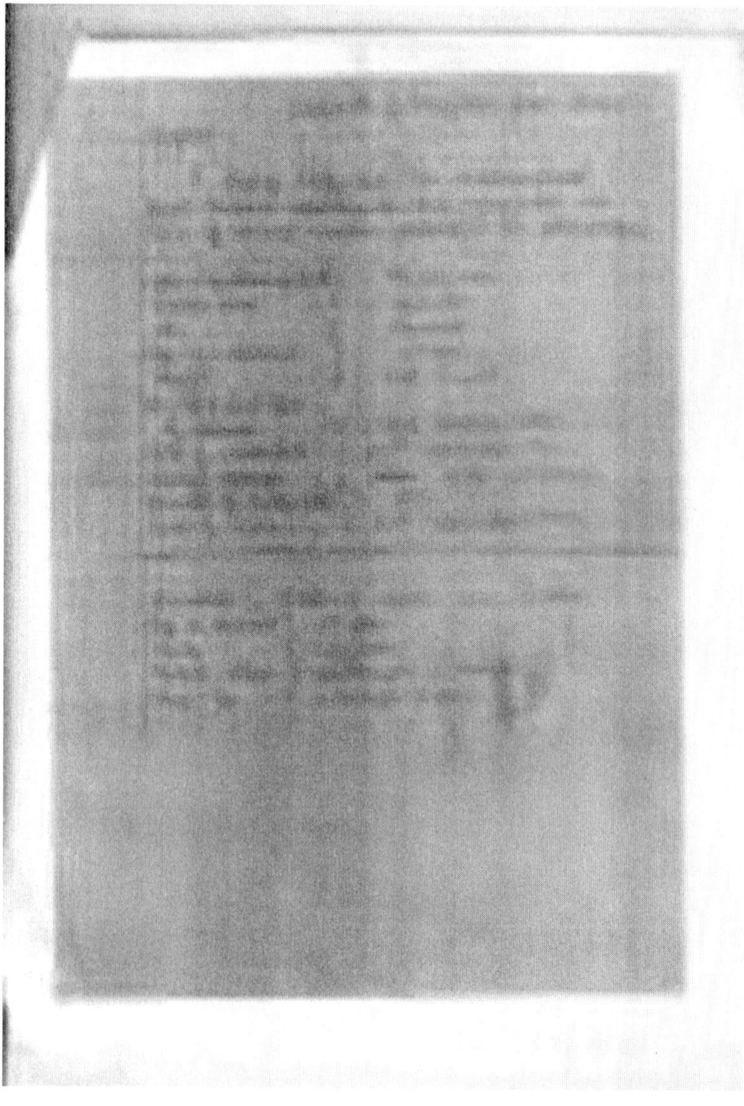

Annex-30 (iii)

A Kabir Centre,Surrey,Vancouver, Canada; founded by the local Kabir devotees

Annex-30 (iv)

Dr.Jagessar Das, a retired medical practitioner and prolific scholar

Mahant Juggesar Das, his wife, Toronto, Canada

Annex-31

Research wing opened at the Ram Kabir temple, Los Angeles,USA

Annex-31 (i)

Sanctum sanctorum, Ram Kabir temple, Los Angeles

Annex-32

Land Registry paper of the Taraiya Math, written in Kaithi language

Annex-32 (i)

Last page of the Registry

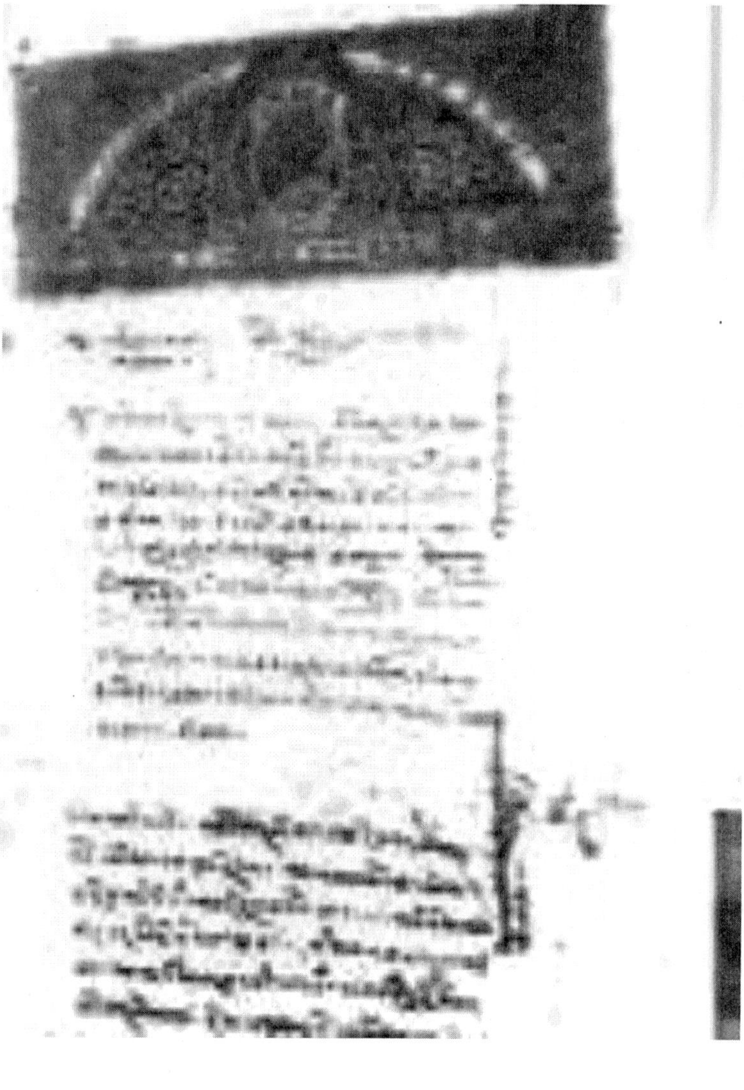

Annex-33

Kabir Math under Shaivites control, Burail, Chandigarh

Annex-33 (i)

Kabirpanthis with the google girl Jahnavi,who is also born in a Kabirpanth family, Chandigarh

Annex-33 (ii)

A group of Kabirpanthis, Punjab

Bibliography

Primary Sources

Anurag Sagar, (ed.), Yugalanand Bihari, (Hindi), Vanketshwar Press, 1914.

Bavan Kasani Ka Janjira, (Hindi), Tirhut Mandalacharaya Satmalpur Publication, Baroda, 1925.

Bhagvat Puran, Vol., 4, Gita Press, Gorakhpur, 1971.

Bijak, Kabir Printing Press, Baroda, 1938.

Buchanan Francis, *History, Antiquities, Topography and Statistics of Eastern India*, (ed. by M. Martin), Vol. IV, Cosmos Publication, Delhi, 1976 (1838).

Census of British India, 1872, 1881, 1891, 1901, 1911, 1921, 1931.

Fani, Muhsin, 'Dabistan-e-Mazahib,' 1843, (trans from Persian by D. Shea and A.Troyer), The Dabistan or School of Manners, Paris, 1665?

Fazl, Abul. *Ain-e-Akbari,*(trans. by H.S. Jarrett), Vol. II, Asiatic Society of Bengal, Baptist Mission Press, Calcutta, 1891.

Guru Pranalis, preserved at the following Maths: Bagicha math, Bidupur Math, Mahadeo Math, Satmalpur Math, Turki Math, manuscript, n.d, Kabir-Chaura Math, Benaras, Chatiya-Baraharwa Math, Damakheda Dharmdasi Math, Kharsiya Math, Vadodara Math, Surat Math, Ahmedabad Math, Aurangabad Math (Maharashtara), Nagpur Math, Kabir-Chaura, Puri Math etc.

Haqa, Abdul, Akhbar-ul-Akhyar, Ahmadi Press, Delhi, 1853.

Hunter, W.W. *Statistical Acccount of Bengal*, Vols. XIII and XXV, Concept Publication, Delhi, 1976 (1877).

Imperial Gazetteers of India, Vol. X, Clarendon Press, Oxford, 1908.

Imperial Gazetteers of India, Provincial Series, Bengal, Usha Publications, New Delhi, 1984 (1909).

Kabir Krishan-Gita, Venkateshwar Press, Bombay, 1952.

Kabir Sagar, (ed.), Yugalanand Bihari, Hindi, Vol. VII, Venkateshwar Press, Bombay, 1953.

Lists of related Maths preserved at the following Maths: Bidupur Math, Mahadeo Math, Satmalpur Math, Turki Math, manuscript, n.d.

O'Malley, L.S.S. *Bengal District Gazetteers,* Darbhanga, Government Secretariat Press, Calcutta, 1907.

Nabhadas, *Shribhaktmal,*Tekumar Press, Lucknow, 1969.

Panji Panth Prakash, Manuscript, n.d.

Panji Panth Prakash, Sunder Press , Muzaffarpur , 1944.

Parmanand, Kabir-Mansur, (trans in Hindi by Madavacharya), Lakshmi Venkateshwar Press, Bombay, 1984(?)

Persian documents called *sanads* or *Parvana* procured from Sunni Waqf Board, Lucknow, Uttar Pradesh.

Sanads preserved at the following Maths: Banni Math, Beri Math, Chatiya-Baraharwa Math, Lucknow Math and Satmalpur Math. apart from revenue documents procured from the Sunni Waqf Board, Lucknow, Uttar Pradesh.

Tavernier, Jean Baptiste. *Travels in India,* Vol. I-II, Forgotten Books, 2015 (1889).

Tomba, Marco della, *Marco della Tomba in Hindustan,* (trans. and ed. by David N. Lorenzen), Yoda Press, 2010.

Wilson, H.H., *Religious sects of the Hindus,* (ed. Ernst R. Rost), Indological Book House, Varanasi, 1972 (1862).

Secondary Sources

Aggrawal, Purushottam. *Akath Kahani Prem Ki, Kabir Ki Kavita aur Unka Samay*, (Hindi), Rajkamal Prakashan, New Delhi, 2009.

Anantdas, 'Kabir Parichai', In R.K.Verma, *Kabir Ek Anushilan*, (Hindi), Sahitya Bhawan, Allahabad,1983.

Askari, S.H., 'A Fifteenth Century Shuttari Sufi Saint of North Bihar', *JBRS*, Vol. XXXVII, Bihar Research Society, Patna, March-June 1951, pp. 66-82.

Babb, Lawrence A., *The Divine Hierarchy, Popular Hinduism in Central India*, Columbia University Press, New York, 1975.

The Satnamis: Political Involvement of a Religious Movement' in J. Michael Mahar (ed.), *The Untouchables in Contemporary India*, The University of Arizona Press, Arizona, 1972, pp. 143-151.

Baird, Robert D. (ed.), *Religion in Modern India*, Manohar, New Delhi, 1981.

Bali, Arun P. 'Organization of Virasaiva Movement: An Analysis in the sect-church Framework', in M.S.A. Rao (ed.), *Social Movement in India, Studies in Peasant, Backward Classes, Sectarian, Tribal and Women's Movements*, Manohar, New Delhi, 1979, pp. 233-268.

Barthwal, P.D. *The Nirgun School of Hindi Poetry, An Exposition of Medievel Indian Santa Mysticism*. Indian Book Shop, Benares, 1936.

Bayly, C.A. *Rulers, Townsmen and Bazar: North Indian Society in the Age of Expansion 1770-1870*, Cambridge University Press, Cambridge, 1977.

Bayly, C. A. 'The Pre-history of Communalism? Religious Conflict in India, 1700-1860,' *Modern Asian Studies*, 19(2), 1985, pp. 177-203.

Bellah, R.N. 'Religious Revolution', *American Sociological Review*, 29, No. 3, June 1964. p. 358-74.

Bhandarkar, R.G. *Vaishnavism, Shaivism and Minor Religious Systems*, Indological Book House, Varansi, 1965 (1913).

Bhattacharaya, J.N. *Hindu Castes and Sect: An Exposition of the Origin of the Hindu Caste System and the Bearing of the*

Sects Towards Each Other and Towards Other Religious Systems, Editions Indian, Calcutta, 1968 (1886).

Bhatt, K.K. *Kabir Parampara (Gujarat Ke Sandarbh Mein)*, Hindi, Abhinav Bharti, Allahabad, 1975.

Bose, Pramatha Nath. *A History of Hindu Civilization During British Rule; Social-Religious Condition, Social Condition, Industrial Condition*, Asian Publication Services, New Delhi, 1975 (1894).

Brass, Paul R. *Language, Religion and Politics in North India*, Vikas, Delhi, 1975.

Brahmaleenmuni, *Sadguru Sri Kabir Charitam*, Sanskrit, Brahmaleenmuni, Baroda,1960.

Briggs, G.W. *Gorakhnath and Kanphatta Yogis*, Motilal Banarasidas, Delhi, 1978 (1938).

Callewaert, Winnand. *The Hagiographies of Anantdas: The Bhakti Poets of North India*, Curzon Press, Surrey, 2000.

Chandra, Satish. *Historiography, Religion and State in Medieval India*, Har Anand Publications, New Delhi, 1996.

Chandra, Satish. *State, Society and Culture in Medieval India*, OUP, New Delhi, 2012.

Chaturvedi, Parashuram. *Uttari Bharat Ki Sant Paramapara*, Hindi, Bharati Bhandar, Allahabad, 1972 (1959).

Chaudhary, Radhakrishna. *History of Bihar*, Motilal Banarasidas, Patna, 1958.

Chaudhary, Radhakrishna. *Mithila in the Age of Vidyapati (C.1330-1525 A.D.) : A Study in Cultural History*, Chaukhambha Orientailia, Varanasi, 1976.

Cobden-Ramsay, LEB. *Bengal District Gazetteers, Feudatory States of Orissa*, Concept Publishing House, Delhi, 1910.

Cohn, Bernard S. *An Anthropologist Among the Historians and Other Essays*, OUP, Delhi, 1994 (1987).

Crooke, William. *Tribes and Castes of the North-West Frontier Provinces and Oudh*, Office of the Superintendent of Govt. Printing, Calcutta, 1896.

Crooke, William. *Popular Religion and Folklore of Northern India*, Munshiram Manoharlal, Delhi, 1968 (1896).

Cunningham, J.D. *History of the Sikhs, From the Origin of the Nation to the Battles of the Sutlej*, Rupa Publications, New Delhi, 2002 (1849).

Das Abhilash, *Kabir Darshan*, (Hindi), Parakh Prakashak Kabir Sansthan, Allahabad , 1982.

Das, Mahesh. *Nad Vansh Ka Sankshipt Itihas*, (Hindi), Nadiya Math, Nagpur, 1996.

Dasgupta, S.B. *Obscure Religious Cults as Background to Bengali Literature*, Firma K.L. Mukhopadhyay, Calcutta,1962.

Das, Raghav. *Raghav Das Krit Bhaktmal*, (Hindi), Rajasthan Oriental Research Institute, Jodhpur, 1965.

Das, Shyamsundar. (ed.), *Kabir Granthavali*, Vani Prakashan, New Delhi, 2014, (1928).

Das Vivek (ed.). *Kabir Sahab*, Hindi, Kabirvani Prakashan, Varanasi, 1972.

Datta, K.K. *India's Social Life and Economic Condition In the 18th century, 1703-1813*, Manohar, New Delhi,1969.

Datta, K. K. and Jha, J. S. (eds.). *Comprehensive History of Bihar*, Vol. II., KP. Jaysawal Institute, Patna, 1976.

Dhanagare, D. and John, J. "Nine Thesis on Social Movements : A Critique", *EPW*, 1988, 33 (21), May, 25, pp.1089-1092.

Dharwarkar, Vinay. *Kabir, The Weaver's Songs*, Penguin Books, London, 2003.

Dheer, Dhananjay, *Dr. Ambedkar: Life and Mission*, Popular Prakashan, Mumbai, 1990 (1954).

Dinkar', Ramdhari Singh, *Dinkar Ki Dayari*, (Hindi), Udyanchal Prakashan, Patna, 1973.

Dirks, Nicolas B. 'The Original Caste: Power History and Hierarchy in South Asia', in Mckim Marriott (ed.), *India through Hindu Categories*, Sage Publications , New Delhi, 1990, pp. 59-77.

Diwakar, R.R. *Bihar Through Ages*, Government Press, Patna, 1959.

Dube, Saurabh. 'Myths, Symbol and Community: Satnampanth of Chhattisgarh' in Pratha Chhatterjee and Gyanendra Pandey (eds.), *Subalterm Studies, Writings on South Asian History and Society*, Vol. VII, OUP, Delhi 1992, pp. 121-158.

Dube, Saurabh. *Caste and Sect in Village Life, Satnamis of Chhattisgarh* ***1900-1950***, Indian Institute of Advance Studies, Shimla, 1993.

Dube, Saurabh. *Untouchable Pasts: Religion, Identity, Power Among a Central Indian Community, 1780-1950*, State University of New York Press, Albany, 1998.

Durkheim, Emile. *Elementary Forms of Religious Life*, (tr. by Joseph Ward Swain), Reprint, Macmillan, New York, 1952 (1915).

Dvivedi, Hazari Prasad. *Kabir*, (Hindi), Rajkamal, New Delhi, 1971.

Dvivedi, Kedarnath. *Kabir Aur Kabirpanth*, (Hindi), Sahitya Sammelan, Allahabad, 1965.

Dwyer, W. J. *Bhakti in Kabir*, Associated Book Agency, Patna, 1981.

Eliade, Mircea. *The Quest: History of Meaning of Religion*, Chicago University Press, Chicago, 1965.

Eliade, Mircea. (ed.), *The Encyclopedia of Religion*, Vols, X, XII, XIV, Macmillan and Free Press, New York, 1987.

Farquhar, J.N. *Modern Religious Movements in India*, Munshiram Manoharlal, New Delhi, 1977 (1914).

Fuchs, Stephen. *Rebellions Prophets: A Study of Massianic Movements in Indian Religions*, Asia Publishing House, Bombay, 1965.

Gokhale, P.V. (ed.) *Bhagavad Gita* , Vol. 4, Oriental Book Agency, Pune, 1950.

Grierson, George A. (ed.), *Linguistic Survey of India*, Vol. 1 . Pt. I, Motilal Banarasidas, Delhi, 1967.

Gross, Robert Lewis. *The Sadhus of India: A Study of Hindu Asceticism*, Rawat Publications, New Delhi, 1992.

Gupta, K. C. *Sri Garib Das, Haryana's Saints of Humanity*, Impex India, Delhi, 1976.

Gusfield, Joseph R. *Protest, Reform and Revolt: A Reader in Social Movements*, John Wiles and Sons, New York, 1970.

Habib, Irfan. 'The Historical Background of the Popular Monotheistic Movements of the 15th-17th Centuries' in Bindeshwar Prasad, (ed.), *Ideas in History*, Asia Publishing House, Bombay, 1969, pp. 6-13.

Habib, Irfan. (ed.), *Religion in Indian History*, Tulika, Delhi, 2001.

Harneite-Sievers, Axel. (ed.), *A Place in the World, New Local Historiographies from Africa and South-Asia*, Brill Leiden, Boston, 2002

Heimsath, Charles. *Indian Nationalism and Hindu Social Reforms*, Princeton University Press, Princeton, 1964.

Hess, Linda and Singh, Shukdev. *The Bijak of Kabir*, Motilal Banarasidas, New Delhi, 1986.

Horstmann, Monika. (ed.), *Images of Kabir*, Manohar, New Delhi, 2002.

Jha, Chetakar. 'Caste and Religion in Indian Polities', in Romesh Thapar (ed.), *Tribe, Caste and Religion in India*, Macmillan, Delhi 1977, pp. 139-144.

Jha, Shobhakant. *Maharshi Kabir Aur Champaran,* Hindi, Bhagtahi Panth, Bettiah, 2003.

Jha, Subhadra. *The Formation of the Maithili Language*, Munshiram Manoharlal, New Delhi, 1985.

Jones, Kenneth W. *Arya Dharm: Hindu Consciousness in 19th Century Punjab*, University of California Press, Berkeley, 1976.

Jones, Kenneth W. 'Social Change and Religious Movements in Nineteenth Century Punjab', in M.S.A. Rao (ed.), *Social Movements in India Studies in Peasant, Backward Classes, Sectarian, Tribal and Women's Movements,* Manohar Publications, New Delhi, 1979, pp. 217-232.

Jones, Kenneth W. *Socio-Religious Movements in the British India*, Cambridge University Press, Cambridge, 1994.

Juergensmeyer, Mark. *Religion As a Social Vision, The Movement Against Untouchability in 20th Century Punjab*, University of California Press, Berkeley, 1982.

Juergensmeyer, Mark. *Religious Rebels in the Punjab, The Ad Dharm Challenge to Caste,* Navayana, New Delhi, 2009 (1982).

Kabir Bijak. (ed.), Yugalanand Bihari, Venkateshwar Press, Bombay, 1906.

Keay, F.E. *Kabir and His Followers*, Association Press, Calcutta, 1931.

Khandelwal, R.L. 'Kabirpanth and its Social Contents' in S.P. (ed.), *Social Contents of Indian Religious Reform Movements in the Nineteenth Twentieth Centuries,* Institute of Historical Studies , Calcutta, 1978, pp. 75-83.

Kumar, Raj. *Ambedkar and His Writings, A Look for the New Generation*, Kalpaz Publications, Delhi, 2008.

Lamb, Ramdas, *Rapt in the Name: The Ramnamis, Ramnam, and Untouchable Religion in Central India,* Suny Press, Albany, 2002.

Lingen, Jan, *Marwar Jodhpur State, History and Coinage*, Jaipur, 2012.

Lokhande, G.S. *Bhimrao Ramji : A Study in Social Democracy*, G.S., Sterling Publications, New Delhi, 1977.

Lorenzen, David N. 'The Kabirpanth: Heretics to Hindus' in Lorenzen (ed.), *Religious Change and Cultural Domination*, EI Colegio de Maxico, Maxico, 1981, pp.

Lorenzen, David N. 'The Kabir Panth and Politics', *Political Science Review*, 20:3, Jaipur, 1982, pp. 263-282.

Lorenzen, David N., 'The Kabir-Panth and Social Protest, Karine Schomer and McLeod (eds.), *The Sants, Studies in a Devotional Tradition of India,* Motilal Banarasidas, Delhi, 1987, pp.182-303.

Lorenzen, David N. 'Traditions of Non-Caste Hinduism : The Kabirpanth', *Contributions to Indian Sociology*, 21:264-83, 1987.

Lorenzen, David N. *Kabir Legends and Ananta-Das's Kabir Parichai*, Sri Satguru Publications, Delhi, 1992.

Lorenzen, David N. (ed.), *Religious Movements in South Asia* 600-1800, Oxford University Press, N. Delhi, 2004.

Lorenzen, David N., *Who Invented Hinduism? Essays on Religion in India*, Yoda Press, New Delhi, 2006.

Madhava, *Virbhanudayakavyam,* (ed.), (trans. by K.K. Lele and A. S. Upadhyay), Rewa Darbar, Rewa, 1938.

Mahipati, *Bhaktvijay,* Marathi, (trans by Justin E. Abbot and Narhar R. Godbole, *Stories of Indian Saints,* 2 Vols., Motilal Banarasidas, Delhi, 1982.

Malinowaski, Bronislaw. *Magic, Science and Religion and Other Essays*, Doubleday and Company, Garden City, 1948.

McLEOD, W.H. *Guru Nanak and Sikh Religion*, OUP, Delhi, 1986.

McLEOD, W.H. and Schomer, Karine. (eds.), *The Sants, Studies in a Devotional Tradition of India,* Motilal Banarasidas, Delhi 1987.

McLEOD, W.H. *Essays in Sikh History, Tradition and Society,* OUP, New Delhi, 2007.

Malik, S.C. (ed.), *Dissent, Protest and Reform in Indian Civilization,* Indian Institute of Advanced Study, Shimla, 1977.

Mohammada, Malika. *Foundations of the Composite Culture in India,* Aakar Books, New Delhi, 2007.

Muir, J. *Original Sanskrit Text,* Pt. I. Oriental Publisher, Delhi, 1972.

Munish, Munishwar Ray. *Kabirpanth ki Jagu-Shakha,* Hindi, Kabir Math Jago Shakha , Bidupur, 1977.

Nabhadas, *Sribhaktmal,* (Hindi), Tejkumar, Lucknow,1969.

Oberoi, Harjot S. *The Construction of Religious Boundaries, Culture Identity and Diversity in the Sikh Tradition* , OUP, Delhi, 1994.

Oddie, G.A. *Social Protest in India. British Protestant Missionaries and Social Reforms* 1850-1900, Manohar, Delhi, 1979.

O'Hanlon, Rosalind and Washbrook, David., (eds.), *Religious Cultures in Early Modern India, New Perspectives*, Routledge, London, 2011.

Pandey, A.B. *History of the First Afghan Empire in India*, Bookland, Delhi, 1956.

Parmanand, *Kabir Mansur*, Lakshmi Venkateshwar Press, Bombay, 1942 (1880).

Parpola, Asko and Hansen, Bent Smiḍt. (eds.) *South Asian Religion and Society*, D.K. Agencies, New Delhi, 1986.

Pettazzoni, Raffaele. *Essays on the History of Religions* (trans. H.J. Rose), E.J. Brill, Leiden, 1954.

Pettazzoni, Raffaele. 'The Formation of Monotheism' in William A. Lezza and Evon Z. Vogt (eds.), *Readers in Comparative Religion : An Anthropological Approach*, Row Peterson and Company, Evanston 1958, pp. 40-46.

Pinch, William R. *Peasants and Monks in British India*, University of California Press, Berkeley, 1996.

Prasad, Rajendra. *Kabirpanth Ka Udbhav Avam Prasar*, (Hindi), Dharmdas Vanshgaddi Pratinidhi Sabha, Damakheda, 1981.

Prasad, Rajendra. *Ashirvad Shatabadi Granth,* (Hindi), Dharmdas Vanshavali Pratinidhi Sabha, Damakheda, 2004.

Pratt, Mary Louise. 'Fieldwork in Common Places', in James Clifford and George E. Marcus (eds.), *Writing Culture,* OUP, Delhi, 1900. Pp. 105-117.

Premaram, *Madhyakalin Rajasthan Mein Dharmik Andolan*, (Hindi), Rajasthani Granthagar, Jodhpur, 1977.

Raghuvanshi, V.P.S. *Indian Society in the Eighteenth Century*, Associate Publication, New Delhi, 1966.

Ranjan, Purnendu. 'Kabirpanth and Politics in Mithila', In Ashish Ghosh (ed.), *Dalits and Peasants: The Emerging Caste-class Dynamics*, Gyan Sagar Publication, Delhi,1999.

Ranjan, Purnendu. 'Historical Evidences for the Study of Kabirpanth', In *Proceedings of the Indian History Congress*, New Delhi, pp.1042-1065, 2007.

Ranjan, Purnendu. *History of Kabirpanth, A Regional Process*, Anamika Publishers, New Delhi, 2008.

Ranjan, Purnendu. 'Kabirpanth in the Colonial Discourse', In *Proceedings of the Indian History Congress*, Kolkata, 2008, pp. 781-789.

Ranjan, Purnendu. 'Reconstruction of the History of Kabirpanth, a Devotional Sect Active in the North and Central India', In *Proceedings of the Indian History Congress*, Delhi, 2012, pp. 551-569.

Ranjan, Purnendu. 'Expansion of the Kabirpanth in the Northern India', In Academia, Vol. II, June 2013-July 2014, Darbhanga, pp.122-132.

Ranjan, Purnendu. 'Kabirpanth in the Medieval Punjab', In *CIJHAR*, Vol. IV, Panna, January-March, 2015, No. 16, pp. 32-33.

Ranjan, Purnendu. 'Diaspora of the Kabirpanthis in the Carribean Countries', In *CIJHAR*, Vol. V, Panna, April-June 2016, No. 18, pp. 57-61.

Ranjan,Purnendu, 'Secondary Sources for the Study of Kabirpanth', In *EIIRJ*, Vol. V, April 2016, pp.16-23.

Ranjan, Purnendu, 'A Case Study of the Expansion of Kabirpanth in Taraiya', In *AMIER*, Aug 2017

Ranjan,Purnendu, 'Kabir and Kabirpanth during Sixteenth Century', In *EIIJR*, Vol. Sept., 2017, pp.???

Renou, Louis. (ed.), *Hinduism*, Prentis-Hall International, London, 1961.

'Renu', Fanishwar Nath. *Maila Anchal*, Hindi, Rajkamal, Delhi, 2016.

Rizvi, S.A.A. *A History of Sufism in India*, 2 Vols., Munshiram Manoharlal, Delhi, 1978.

Rudolph, Loyd L. and Rudolph S.H. *The Modernity and Tradition: Political Development in India*, Chicago University Press, Chicago, 1967.

Russell, Robert V. and Hiralal, Bahadur. *The Tribes and Castes of the Central Provinces of India,* Vol., I, Anthroppological Publication, Osterhot, 1969 (1916).

Sadarangani, Neeti. M. *Bhakti Poetry in Medieval India: Its Inception, Cultural Encounter and Impact,* Sarup and Sons, 2004, p. 81.

Sarkar, Benoy Kumar. *The Folk Element in Hindu Culture , A Contribution to Socio-Religious Studies in Hindu Folk Institutions,* Oriental Books Corporation, Delhi, 1972 (1917).

Sarkar, Jadunath. *Fall of Mughal Empire,* Vol. I, Orient Longman, Bombay, 1971.

Sarkar, Sumit. Modern India (1985-1947), Macmillan, N. Delhi,1992 (1983).

Sarkar, Sumit. *Writing Social History,* Oxford University Press, Delhi,1998.

Sen, Kshiti Mohan. *Medieval Mysticism of India,* Oriental Books, 1974 (1929)

Shah, Ahmed. *The Bijak of Kabir,* Ahmad Shah, Hamirpur, 1917.

Shahabuddin, Mohammad. *History of Kabirpanth,* Unpublished Thesis, Department of History, Aligarh Muslim University, 1975.

Shakir, Moin. (ed.), *Religion and Politics in India,* Meenakshi, Meerut, 1981.

Sharma, Krishna. *Bhakti and the Bhakti Movement, A New Perspective,* Munnishiram Manoharlal, New Delhi, 1987.

Sharma, Krishna. *Bhakti and the Bhakti Movement, A New Perspective,* Munshiram Manoharlal, New Delhi, 1987.

Sharma, Sarnamsingh. *Kabir: Yyaktitv, Krititv evam Siddhant,* Sahitya Sammelan, Jaipur, 1969.

Sharma, Satish, K. *Reform Protest and Social Transformation,* Ashish Publishing House, New Delhi, 1987.

Sharma, Vasumati. *Rajasthan Ka Sant Sahitya,* (Hindi), Rajasthan Prachyavidya Pratisthan, Jodhpur, 2002.

Shastri, Heranand. *The Baghel Dynasty of Rewa,* Archaeological Survey of India, No. 21, Govt. of India, Calcutta,1925.

Shastri, Gangasharan. *Kabir Jeevancharitra*, Kabirvani Prakashan, Varanasi, 1976.

Sidhpeeth Kabir-Chaura, (eds. Krishna Kalki and Ram Murari), Kabirvani Prakashan, Varanasi, 2007.

Singer, Milton. *When a Great Tradition Modernizes, An Anthropological Approach to Indian Civilization*, Praeger Publishers, New York, 1972.

Singh, Mohan. *Kabir: His Biography, Kabir and the Bhagti Movement*, Vol. I, Atma Ram and Sons, Lahore,1934.

Singh, Shukhdev. *Kabir Bijak*, Hindi, Allahabad,1972.

Singh, Shukhdev. *Sant Kabir aur Bhagatahi Panth*, Hindi, Vishwavidyalaya Prakashan, Varanasi, 1998.

Smith, D.E. *South Asian Politics and Religion*, Princeton University Press, Princeton, 1963.

Srinivas, M. N. *Social Change in Modern India*, Orient Longman, New Delhi, 1972.

Srivastav, A.L. *The Mughal Empire*, Shivlal Aggrawal, Agra,1964.

Thakural, Uma. 'The Avatar Doctrine in the Kabirpanth', in David N. Lorenzen (ed.), *Religion in North India, Community Identity and Political Action*, State University of New York Press, Albany, 1995, pp. 221-229.

Thakural, Uma. *Kabirpanth: Sahitya, Darshan, Evam Sadhana*, (Hindi), Book Centre, New Delhi, 1998.

Thapar, Romila. 'Origin, Myth and the Early Indian Historical Tradition', in Debi Prasad Chttopadhyaya (ed.), *History and Society: Essays in Honour of Prof. Nihar Ranjan Ray*, K.P. Bagchi, Culcutta, 1978, pp. 271-291.

Tiwari, Parasnath. *Kabir Granthawali*, (Hindi), Sahitya Bhawan, Allahabad, 1961.

Trump, Ernest, *Adi Granth,The Holy Scripture of the Sikhs*, Allen & Co., London,1877.

Toynbee, Arnold. *An Historian's Approach to Religion*, OUP, London, 1956.

Upadhyay, Ayodhya Singh, *Kabir Vachanavali*, Nagari Pracharni

Sabha, Varanasi, 1946.

Vanshi Baldev.(ed.), *Kabir ek Punarmulyankan*, (Hindi), Aadhar Prakashan, Panchkula, 2012.

Vansina Jan, *Oral Tradition: A Study in Historical Methodological*, Aldine Publishing Company, Chicago 1965.

Varma, Dhirendra., *Hindi Sahitya Kosh*, (Hindi) Gyanmandal Ltd., Varanasi, 1986 (1963).

Vaudeville, Charlotte. *Kabir*, Vol. I, OUP, Oxford, 1974.

Vaudeville, Charlotte. *A Weaver Named Kabir*, OUP, Delhi ,1993.

Verma, Ram Kumar. *Kabir Ka Rahasyavad*, (Hindi), Sahitya Bhawan Ltd., Allahabad, 1969 (1944).

Verma, Ram Kumar. *Hindi Sahitya ka Alochanatmak Itihas*, Hindi, Ramnarayan Lal Beni Madhav, Allahabad, 1971(1964).

Verma, Ram Kumar. *Sant Kabir*, Sahitya Bhawan Ltd., Allahabad,1966.

Voigt, Johnnes H. *Max Muller: The Man and His Ideas*, Firma K.L. Mukhopadyaya, Calcutta, 1967.

Westcott, G. H. *Kabir and the Kabirpanth*, Sushil Gupta, Calcutta, 1907.

Wilkins, W. J. *Hindu Mythology (Vedic and Puranic)*, Delhi Book Store, Delhi, 1972.

Wilkinson, Paul. *Social Movements*, Pall Mall, London,1971.

Williams, Monier. *Religious Thought and Life in India: Vedic, Brahmanism and Hinduism*, Reprint and Oriental Books, New Delhi, 1974 (1883).

Wilson, Bryan R. *Religious Sects: A Sociological Study*, Weidenfield and Nicolson, London, 1970.

Yinger, J. Milton. *The Scientific Study of Religion*, Macmillan, New York, 1970.

Zadra, Dario. 'Symbolic time' In Mireca Eliade (ed.), *Encyclopedia of Religion*, Vol. XIV, Macmillan and Free Press, New York, 1987, pp.193-198.

Index